SAVAGE ATTACK

"You don't want to go in there," the man blocking the bedroom doorway said.

"I'm a doctor," Lowry said, pushing his way past. "I think I can handle it."

A woman was lying on the bed, arms at her sides and a towel wrapped like a turban around her head. Clothes and papers were strewn about the room, and on the floor beside the bed were two knives, one of them bent and bloodstained.

Lowry leaned over the woman and saw that a third knife protruded from her skull near the right temple. Her pulse and respiration were weak and irregular. The doctor lifted the soggy towel from the woman's face to see her head discolored, misshapen and drenched in blood. Her eyes were swollen shut so hard he was unable to check her pupils. The knife was embedded two inches into her cranium, but it seemed almost to dangle, as if mired in pudding. It withdrew with such ease that Lowry estimated the skull had been thoroughly shattered.

Who in God's name could have done this? Lowry wondered, stepping back to let the paramedics take the dying woman away.

DAMAGED GOODS

Jim Henderson

PINNACLE BOOKS
KENSINGTON PUBLISHING CORP.
http://www.pinnaclebooks.com

PINNACLE BOOKS are published by

Kensington Publishing Corp.
850 Third Avenue
New York, NY 10022

First Pinnacle Printing: September, 2000
10 9 8 7 6 5 4 3 2 1

Printed in the United States of America

For Rick and Greg—
my sons, my best friends

Author's note, with acknowledgments

When I first approached the story of Patricia Willoughby's murder, I anticipated many of the elements that would weave their way into the telling. Certainly, it would be the story of a lust- and greed-driven crime of barbarous measure, a crime with many victims, a crime that gouged deep wounds into a murdered woman's family and her community. It would be the story of a long and tedious investigation across national borders.

But the story also possessed a subtext as compelling as the crime itself. It is no exaggeration to say that the killer's undoing had its roots in a long-ago, faraway place called Promontory, Utah, and a hardscrabble farm where a young girl's iron will was fashioned by hard work, hardship and tragedy.

In time, Thera Huish would become the matriarch of a star-crossed clan—four sons and a daughter—that carried in its blood the grit of her own birth and childhood. She lost a husband to a plane crash, a son to alcoholism and kidney failure, and a daughter to a fiendish murder plot. She never lost the will that had seen her through each setback.

Without the generous assistance of Thera Huish, her husband Sterling, and her sons, Val, Bob and Nick, this book would have been impossible. They shared memories and emotions, both pleasant and painful, which were invaluable to this effort.

Invaluable also was the assistance of Kay Lines and Debbie Schwartz, investigators for the Arizona Attorney General's office, and Gilbert police detective Joe Ruet, who was a sergeant at the time of these events and has since been promoted to lieutenant. They not only shared memories, but investigative reports, court documents, photographs and transcripts of their interviews conducted during the course of their investigation.

All of the scenes and dialog in this book were reconstructed from my interviews with the Huish family, friends and neighbors of the victim, investigators and the documents they provided, and the sixteen volumes of trial transcripts. Where participants of specific conversations could not, or would not, be interviewed, I relied on accounts they had given to members of the Huish family or to the authorities.

I am indebted also to others who made this book possible. To my agent, Janet Manus, for her forbearance of my erratic temperament; to my editors at Kensington Publications, Paul Dinas and Karen Haas, for their tolerance of my tardiness, mental lapses and general cantankerousness. My gratitude to them is greater than they will ever know.

Finally, I owe more than thanks to my friend Carlton Stowers, a two-time Edgar Award winner and, in my opinion, the reigning master of the true crime genre. The time he allotted to coaching and consoling me during the year this book was being assembled was sufficient to qualify him for a royalty interest.

Everyone who assisted me must share credit for any strengths this book possesses. I, alone, am responsible for its shortcomings.

Commit a crime and the earth is made of glass. Commit a crime, and it seems as if a coat of snow fell on the ground, such as reveals in the woods the tracks of every partridge and fox and squirrel and mole.

—Emerson

Everybody is a potential murderer.

—Clarence Darrow

PART ONE
The Murder

Chapter One

February 23, 1991

Sirens scraped against the still night like a glass cutter. In all their visits to Puerto Penasco, the Lowrys had never heard sirens here. Now they drew closer, screaming up the dirt road from the gatehouse, mechanical wails and squeals that were as intrusive and abrasive as a drill bit, finally dying with a mournful sigh behind the bleached stucco beach house.

Harold Lowry hurried outside, turned to circle toward the rear of the bungalow and stepped into the arc of flashing red lights of an ambulance. The paramedics had already gone inside the neighboring house and a large man, perhaps fifty years old, muscular and darkly tanned, with a thin mustache and salt and pepper hair, stood near the doorway. As Lowry approached, the man thrust out his arm to block the entrance.

"You don't want to go in there," the man said. "It's too awful."

"I'm a doctor," Lowry said, pushing his way past. "I think I can handle it."

Angling across the front room, Lowry turned down a short hallway and into a bedroom, where a woman was supine on the bed, arms at her sides and a towel wrapped like a turban around her head. Clothes and papers were strewn about the room, and on the floor beside the bed were two knives, one of them bent and bloodstained.

The paramedics huddled around the woman and seemed paralyzed by something uglier than they were trained to deal with. They muttered to each other in Spanish, which Lowry understood a little, just enough to detect that they were out of their depths with the injuries they were observing.

At the bedside, the doctor leaned over the woman and saw that a knife was protruding from her skull near the right temple. Checking her pulse and respiration, he found both were weak and irregular. Her breathing stopped and restarted and stopped again, a pattern suggestive of severe brain injury. Lifting the soggy towel from the woman's face, he saw a tumescent blob, a head discolored and misshapen and drenched with blood. Her eyes were swollen shut, shut so hard that he was unable to examine her pupils.

What in God's name could have done this? the doctor wondered. The knife was embedded two inches into her cranium but it seemed almost to dangle, as if mired in a mound of pudding. When he reached to remove it, it withdrew with such ease that Lowry estimated that the skull had been thoroughly shattered, enough so that the blade probably entered the brain with no skeletal resistance.

Speaking in broken Spanish and hand gestures, he asked the Red Cross medics for IV equipment and a plastic tube, which he inserted into the woman's throat to allow air to reach her lungs. There was little more he could do here. He helped the medics lift her onto a stretcher and watched as they carried her through the house.

* * *

Following her husband outside, Leigh Lowry saw three children walking toward the beach from the house where the ambulance was parked. The oldest, a girl, appeared to be about sixteen or seventeen. With her were another girl, perhaps ten, and a boy a few years younger.

She followed and caught up with them. "What happened?" she asked the older girl.

"Our mother was attacked," the girl said, almost matter-of-factly. She had brown hair and dainty features on a face that was remarkably stolid, a face that did not suggest that serious harm had been done.

"Oh, I'm sorry," Leigh Lowry said. "Do you want to come to my house . . . have something to drink?"

"Okay," the girl said.

They followed her back across the beach and past the ambulance. Leigh looked for her husband and, not seeing him, assumed he had gone inside to check on the mother of the three children.

After giving the children soft drinks, she went back outside to rejoin her husband. When he came out of the house, his arms and clothing stained by the woman's blood, she knew instantly that something more ghastly than a simple attack had occurred. She stood beside her husband as the ambulance raced away, trailing a plume of dust that arose from its tires and mingled with the deepening twilight.

The man who had tried to block the doctor's entrance to the house was also watching the ambulance disappear. From his demeanor, Lowry might have figured him for a disinterested spectator, another neighbor summoned by the sirens. There were no formal introductions, but Lowry soon learned this was the husband of the woman whose blood was coagulating on the bed inside the beach house.

"You should go with your wife," the doctor told him.

The man looked confused.

"We'll watch your kids if you want to leave them here," Leigh said.

Declining the offer largely by ignoring it, the man began a hurried explanation of what had happened. He had taken the children to a museum at about four o'clock, he said, and afterward they had driven down the beach to where a dead whale had been tossed ashore. His oldest daughter was preparing for her driver's test, so he had let her drive the van around the back roads on the way back.

As he rambled on, the Lowrys wondered why he was lingering here, why he was not on his way to the hospital. His eyes were glazed and bloodshot and his speech was vaguely slurred. He may have been suffering some form of shock, but Lowry believed that, more than likely, he was intoxicated.

They had returned to the house about six o'clock, the man said, and the two younger children, excited by the museum and the sight of the beached whale, had rushed inside to share stories of their excursion with their mother.

"They found her like that," he said. Then, as casually as if he were asking for the time, the man said, "What do you think her chances are . . . of surviving this?"

She may already be dead, Lowry thought. *If that knife even nicked the meningeal artery, it was a miracle that she had lived more than a few minutes. Why is he hanging around here?* "I don't know," he said. "She's in bad shape. That's the worst trauma to the head I've ever seen."

Still, the man, as blasé and phlegmatic as a junkie with a fresh load of smack in his veins, dawdled and gazed absently at the ground. Leigh Lowry wanted to push him toward his van. Instead, she reiterated her previous offer. "We'll be happy to watch your kids," she said. "You should go check on your wife."

Several more minutes passed before the man gathered his children and drove off toward the gatehouse and the highway to Puerto Penasco. For a few minutes, the Lowrys stood beside the house where the attack had taken place. The doctor described to his wife what he had seen inside and the ferocious damage to the woman's head. "She looked like she was beaten by a very large boxer," he said. "I don't see how she can survive it."

Darkness finally settled over the beach and the winds that blew in from the Sea of Cortez had abated. They turned and started back toward their own house when they saw the van again. It had not been gone more than a couple of minutes and had not had time to reach the hospital. Now, it was following a police car back up the dirt road, back toward the scene of the attack. For another fifteen minutes, the driver talked with the policeman before finally heading back toward town and the hospital where doctors were working over his critically battered wife.

Up and down the beach, the news crackled like electricity. Puerto Penasco, or Rocky Point as it is known to most Anglos, was a quiet and comfortable sanctuary, a family retreat with warm waters and secluded coves and inlets, miles of dunes to explore on all-terrain vehicles, and abundant fish and shrimp, fresh off the boats, for evening cookouts. The nightlife was about as exciting as watching the tide go out, but few came to Rocky Point to raise hell. They came for the stillness and languor, and they rarely were disappointed. Fishing boats chugged unhurriedly in and out of the small port, and at twilight the pelicans fed and bathed on the rocky coastline beneath the seawall. Each evening, the Baja made its nightly appearance eighteen miles across the Gulf of California. Invisible during the harsh light of midday, the barren finger of land seemed to rise out of the water as the sun set behind it, appearing first as a wisp of haze, then a translucent mirage, and finally, just before darkness, a fully formed pencil line separating the sea and the sky—an optical phenomenon that was part of the magic of this place, part of the surrealism that enchanted the thousands of gringos who claimed Rocky Point as their personal playground.

Now, for the Lowrys and the others who dwelled on the

beach that Saturday night, the diamond starlight had been dulled and the warm air was foul, like the breath of something evil, something dreadful that had broken the spell of this place and stripped them of their defenses.

News of the events at Las Conchas reached the Motel Senorial long before the man and three children arrived and requested a room. Antonio Silva, the manager, knew who they were and knew a little of the horror they had experienced that night, which accounted for his astonishment that none displayed a distress level above that of fleeing a leaking roof. *They act perfectly normal, like any other tourists checking in for a weekend on the beach,* he thought. There were no tears from the children. They laughed and teased with each other and with their father.

The next day, they were in and out of the lobby, buying soft drinks and snacks and romping on the motel grounds and posing for souvenir snapshots at the front entrance. *Americans are hard-hearted,* Silva thought. *Not like Latinos. Not at all like Latinos.*

Chapter Two

For Thera Huish, it had been a hopeful but restive weekend. At a family gathering on Thursday night, her daughter had confided that she wasn't especially eager for this trip. Trish didn't like Mexico. She didn't speak the language, and the poverty and squalor that seemed to be almost everywhere depressed her. All Rocky Point had to offer was seawater and sunshine and, with her fair complexion, she could take either in limited doses.

"Oh, relax and have fun," Thera told her. "You have some busy weeks ahead and you could use a few days of rest."

What she secretly hoped was that this trip would help mend the rift that she had seen widening in her daughter's marriage. Though they had never discussed it in detail, Thera knew that the problems between Trish and Dan were serious enough to send them to a marriage counselor and that their children had begun to exhibit some of the classic symptoms—anger, irritation, sullenness—of a troubled household. Sterling had noticed it too and they discussed it with each other, but rarely with their daughter.

That Thursday night at Trish's house, though, surrounded by her daughter and two of her sons and two of her daughters-in-law, her spirits were lifted. Bob and Arlene had come from California to spend a few days. Nick and Cara, who lived only a few miles away in Mesa, were there with their children. There was no special reason for the family assembly other than to see Trish and Dan off to Mexico, but the evening took on a special texture for Thera, something like the glow of Thanksgiving or the buoyancy of Christmas, the whiff of a sensed renewal.

Dan was even more gregarious than usual. He hugged each of his in-laws, told jokes, promised to get tickets for everyone when baseball spring training opened. He took Bob and Arlene for a ride in a 1954 Ford pickup—the legacy of his father—he planned to restore.

At first, Thera resented his gushing display of charm. She had seen flashes of his belligerence toward Trish and that had caused her own relationship with him to deteriorate. Watching him kneeling beside Arlene's chair, regaling her with yet another funny story, she found herself thinking, *You've been a 24-karat jerk lately. Why are you so glowing and solicitous of everybody now?*

At the end of the evening, as they were preparing to leave, Dan had another surprise for Thera. He put his arms around her and the gesture seemed heartfelt. "You're so wonderful," he said. "Life is so wonderful."

For an instant, she felt a pang of regret that she had judged him so harshly. Dan Willoughby had been a member of the family for fifteen years and from all appearances had been a loving and attentive husband and father until the last year or so. Maybe his problems with Trish were nothing more than passing consequences of a midlife crisis. Being out of work for eight months and dependent upon a wife's income is enough to ravage any man's self-esteem. How could she know all the personal demons that tormented him? Maybe he had whipped a few of them and this trip would be the turning point, the curve that would take all of them back to where they had once been.

They had been happy and close. Dan wasn't just Trish's husband, he was a son to Thera and Sterling and a brother to Trish's four brothers. He had even adopted their faith—The Church of Jesus Christ of Latter-day Saints—not just in deference to his wife, it seemed, but with a genuine missionary zeal. He took on a variety of Mormon Church responsibilities that required a considerable concession of his time. For a church member needing money or a friend needing a loan, Dan was quick to reach into his own pocket. He helped Bob get a job in the air freight business, accompanied Nick to World Series baseball games, bought bicycles for neighborhood kids, bank-rolled Trish as she struggled to get a toehold in the sales and marketing business she had formed with Thera.

The last year had been difficult, Thera thought, but maybe her son-in-law was close to coming out of that dank tunnel of middle-age angst he had been sucked into. Tonight could have been a new start.

Everyone was in a good mood on the drive home. Especially Bob and Arlene. Because they lived in California, they had been spared the steady unpleasantness Thera and Sterling had seen in their daughter's marriage. But even they made note of Dan's unusual exuberance

"Ol' Dan was really wound up tonight, wasn't he?" Bob said.

"Yeah," Arlene agreed. "I've never had that much fun with him."

She kept looking at the empty seat beside her and thinking that her daughter should have been there. Trish loved to hear her father sing with the Phabulous Phoenicians, and Thera had bought the tickets for the Saturday night event weeks earlier, before she knew the dates Dan had selected for his family's Mexico vacation.

"I'd much rather stay here," Trish had told her on Thursday night. "I hate to miss Papa's concert."

The Phoenicians, a large men's choral group—150 members or more—was sometimes called a barbershop choir and mostly sang music from a bygone era, but Trish was fond of it and marveled at the intricate harmonies that could be wrung from so many voices. She had recently taken a personal interest in singing, and when she could find time from the demands of their growing business, availed herself of the personal services of a voice teacher.

Thera had trouble keeping her mind on the concert. Occasionally, she exchanged glances with Bob and Arlene or Nick and Cara and forced a smile or a nod or a whispered comment, but the empty seat gnawed at her like a murky premonition. She checked her watch frequently as the night seemed to lengthen, and she was relieved when the show was over.

When they returned home, it was well past midnight, but Thera hurried to check her answering service. No messages.

Thera and Sterling dressed for church. They planned to drive Bob and Arlene to the airport, attend services and then stop somewhere for lunch. Bob was outside placing a suitcase in the car and Arlene was in the bedroom, still packing, when the phone rang at nine thirty.

Phone calls were not unusual at this weekend hour. *Probably the bishop,* Thera thought. The Mormon Church is highly participatory and the bishop could be calling with a special request for that day's services. She picked up the receiver and a band tightened around her chest.

"I have a collect call from Mexico," the operator said. "Will you accept it?"

Something has happened to one of the children, she thought. "Yes, I'll accept it," she said, expecting to hear Trish's voice on the line.

"Is Sterling there?" Dan asked.

She knew something was wrong, but not with the children. If that were the case, Trish would have called. "Yes, he's here," she said.

"I need to talk to both of you," Dan said.

Suddenly her mouth was as dry as an arroyo in August. She yelled for Sterling and he came into the bedroom. "It's Danny," she said, pressing the button that would switch the call to the phone's speaker. "He's right here, Danny." she said.

"There's no easy way to say this," Dan began. "There's been trouble here in Mexico."

Sensing what his next words would be, Thera clenched her fists and fought back the urge to scream.

"There was a robbery last night and Trish is dead," Dan said.

Hearing her mother-in-law cry out, Arlene left her packing and went into the hall.

"It was terrible what they did to her," Dan said. "The children went in and found their mother, but they didn't see anything, Thera, honest. Her head was wrapped in a towel and the room was pretty dark. I ran right down to the Red Cross station for help, but she was too far gone. It was best that she died, Thera. She could never have been normal after what they did to her."

Arlene approached their bedroom and saw her in-laws sitting by their phone, sobbing. She could hear a voice droning out of the speaker but could not make out the words. She ran outside to where her husband was loading the car.

"You'd better come in," she said. "Something has happened and your parents are crying."

Bob was confused by the scene he found upon entering the bedroom. He heard Dan on the speaker phone, calmly talking about three Indians in a black truck and how someone had seen them go into the house. A burglary? Thera's face was buried in her hands and Sterling was leaning across the bed. The voice on the phone was a dispassionate monotone muttering gibberish about Indians, yet his parents were in anguish. Bob stood silently while his brain tried to sort out the incongruous input it was processing.

Sterling sat up and leaned toward the phone. "Danny, why didn't you call us last night?"

"I tried to, Sterling, but I couldn't get a call through. You know how the Mexican phone system is. I moved the kids out of the beach house and took them to a motel. We don't have a phone in our room, so I had to have the desk clerk try to place calls."

Bob was beginning to figure out that something had happened to Trish, but he wasn't certain until his father looked up at him and said, "She's dead."

Nick was working in the yard when Cara came to the door.

"Your mom's on the phone," she said, "and she doesn't sound happy."

That by itself didn't cause him great concern. His mother was an intense and driven woman who could get worked up over small things, who could be impatient when plans went awry or unexpected details had to be dealt with. She had made a life and a modest fortune out of order and persistence and determination, and it wouldn't take much more than a flat tire to irritate her.

He picked up the portable phone and said, "Hi Mom."

"Your dad and I are on the phone," his mother said. The terseness in her voice told him this was no small thing. "Is Cara on the phone with you?"

"No."

"You need to get her on the phone. We have something to tell you."

Christ, Nick thought. *Are they getting a divorce or something?*

He gestured to his wife, who picked up the extension and said, "I'm here."

"There's been an incident down in Mexico," Thera said. "Trish has been murdered."

Before Nick could speak, he heard his wife scream, "No, no, no" and then throw the phone to the floor.

"How did it happen?" he asked his mother.

"We don't know all the details. You'd better get over here right away."

While he showered, Cara helped dress the children, who were frantic and confused.

It was only a three-mile drive to his parents' house, but it seemed to take forever. Nick felt as though he were cruising in slow motion between two rows of tall trees. He could see nothing on either side, just the hood of the car and a narrow ribbon of pavement. He felt as though he had stepped outside of reality, through a portal into someone else's nightmare. *Trish can't be dead. This isn't happening.*

For some reason, he kept thinking of the food fight. Last Thanksgiving, he and his sister had stood at the kitchen sink cleaning dishes after the family meal. One playfully splashed the other with a little water—who remembers who starts such foolishness?—and the battle quickly escalated to weapons of leftovers and didn't end until the kitchen was awash in whipped cream.

He hardly knew his sister until he was an adult. She was eleven years older than he and had left home when he was seven. For several years she had been largely estranged from her family, for reasons Nick didn't fully comprehend, and he was nineteen before they really knew each other. But, for the past eleven years, they had been as close as a brother and sister could be. They loved each other, but teased each other mercilessly. He reveled in telling "dumb blonde jokes" in her presence and she playfully treated him like a pesky and spoiled kid brother. He chided her driving—lost in thought, she would terrify him by blowing through stop signs—and she feigned resentment that at holiday dinners their mother always baked more of his favorite pies. Suddenly, he remembered the pie. That's what started the food fight.

Trish can't be dead, he told himself.

Thera's eyes were swollen and red but she seemed eerily calm as she related to him the few details that she knew. There was an edge to her voice that Nick knew well, and it told him now that something besides grief was twisting its way around her.

Dan called again late in the morning and everyone gathered by the speaker phone.

"What happened, Dan?" Nick asked him.

He told the same story—his trip to the museum with the children, Trish staying behind to rest, the three Indians in a dark pickup truck, a man seen going into the house, Trish's missing jewelry. But this time he added a new detail, a new horror he had not mentioned earlier.

"It was awful, Nick," he said. "They cut her from her pelvis to her neck."

After he hung up, Thera told the others, "I want you all to take notes when he calls. The story keeps changing."

It wasn't the story itself that chewed at Thera, it was the way he told it: a pat, rehearsed recitation that had the cold, rote inflection of an alibi. "Remember, I told you we were gone about two hours," he would say, as if to embed the highlights into their minds. "Remember, I told you about the Indians that were seen . . ."

Val arrived from California at mid-afternoon and found his family in a frantic state. They knew little and felt that they could do little, and the sitting and waiting was wearing on everyone. Val was the eldest of Thera's children, eleven months older than Trish, and his steady, assured manner had a calming effect on the others.

After briefing him on the latest word they had received, Thera stood with her arms folded and said, "I want Trish home. I want them all home."

His mother was not a woman to wear fear or doubt on her sleeve, but Val knew that beneath the iron clink in her voice there was the soft pith of helplessness.

He had already decided what needed to be done immediately.

"Somebody has to go to Rocky Point and bring those kids home," he said. Dan might have to stay, to be questioned by the police or to make the legal arrangements to get Trish's body out of Mexico, but there was no reason for the children to remain there.

Thera wondered how they were coping. Hayden, her adopted grandson, was only six and Thera, her namesake granddaughter, was ten, but they had been the first to discover their dying mother. Now they were stuck in a strange place in circumstances they could not possibly comprehend. And what of Marsha? She was seventeen, and her life had been deeply troubled before Dan and Trish had adopted her four years before and given her a structured, tender home. Now, another horror had intruded into her world.

Dan called again later in the afternoon.

"We'd like to come down there and get the children," Thera told him.

"No, no, you just stay there," he insisted. "I'll take care of everything here."

She was incredulous. "Danny, those children need to be at home. There's no reason for them to stay there," she said.

"I've got everything under control," he said. "Just let me handle it. You'd just be in the way. There's a lot going on right now and I speak the language, so I'll take care of it."

After hanging up, Thera sat alone for a while trying to sort everything out. Her daughter had died at seven thirty the night before and she was not notified until nine thirty this morning. Now, six hours later, she knew only the skimpy details her son-in-law chose to share. He was determined to keep the family at arm's length from everything—even from his children.

Of her four sons, Nick was probably the most like her—impatient, tenacious, perhaps a little cynical—and he seemed to sense what she was thinking.

Taking her aside, into the home office from which she and Trish ran their business, he said, "Mom, something's not right. Do you think Dan's involved?"

It was precisely what she thought, but hearing it expressed in words caused her to shudder. "Be quiet about that," she said.

"Well, something's screwy. I think Dan's hiding something."

"Just keep it to yourself," she said. "You and I are the only ones who believe it."

Chapter Three

Like many western states, Arizona is tolerant of speed. The posted limit on most interstate highways is seventy-five, and nearly everyone tests the leniency of the state troopers. Even on the broad, six-lane thoroughfares of Phoenix and its suburbs, obeying the speed laws can get you shouted off the street by type A drivers who assume you are either a tourist, a bluehair or a cowardly dweeb.

That considered, Nick and Val still were pushing the envelope. In Trish's Mercury Marquis, which she and Dan had swapped for Nick's van for the weekend, they shot through Phoenix at eighty miles an hour or more and rolled out Interstate 10 into a blinding sunset that was beginning to turn the sky into the familiar canvas tinged with streaks of orange and blue and lavender. At times exceeding one hundred miles an hour, they sailed across flat, featureless desert and squinted as they searched for the exit to Highway 85.

Shortly before six o'clock that Sunday afternoon, the family had made the decision that Nick and Val would go to Mexico and bring Trish's children home. If Dan objected, they would deal with that when they got there. But they would have to race the clock because the border crossing at Lukeville closed at midnight. It could take more than two hours to reach the border, an hour to get to Rocky Point and another hour to get back to Lukeville. That would leave them no more than an hour, probably a lot less, on the ground. An hour to pry the children from their father.

Twenty-five miles west of Phoenix, they found the exit and turned south toward the Gila River. Approaching Ajo, the landscape began to change from monotonous and austere sand and scrub land to a rich tapestry of jagged ridges, wildflowers and stately saguaro cacti. Here, the Mojave, Sonoran and Chihuahuan deserts gently overlap, seeding the ancient seabed with an astonishing variety of plant and animal life, all hardy survivors in an environment with little water and less pity. Deadly Gila monsters and scorpions share the turf with ill-tempered javelinas, bighorn sheep, pronghorn antelope and carrion-eating birds.

This was alien and foreboding real estate to the two brothers bound for Puerto Penasco. Pockets of population were few and far apart and somewhere north of Why (no one seems to know why the town was so named) the Merc's alternator light came on.

"Dammit," Nick muttered.

"Don't worry," Val said. At forty-three, he was twelve years older than his brother, cooler headed and more philosophical about the turns of fate. "There's bound to be a mechanic in Why."

Sure, anywhere there's a highway, there's a mechanic. Racing down Highway 85 with the alternator warning taunting them from the dashboard, they practically held their breath until a faint bubble of light flickered in the distance above the creosotes and ocotillos.

They discovered with sickening disappointment that Why was just an intersection of two outback byways on the western fringe of the Papago reservation—a gas station and convenience store, a grocery and an RV camp. No mechanic. No auto parts store. No hope of help at eight o'clock on a Sunday night. They had to decide whether to turn back and try to get the car repaired in Ajo or Gila Bend the next morning, or ignore the warning light and plunge into Mexico.

They stood for a moment in the pale light of the gas station and looked down the long, dark road toward Mexico. Valuable time had been lost, but the decision to push on was not one to be made casually. From here, the drive would intrude upon uninviting acreage. At night, the desert can be at its most beautiful—the shy, pearl-white blossoms of the saguaro show themselves only after sundown—but also at its most treacherous. The things that crawl and forage and stalk, the snakes and bobcats and gray wolves, spend their days hiding from the blistering sun, but emerge hungry and energetic under the blackened sky.

Except for the alternator light, all the Merc's vital signs were normal and the engine was running perfectly. Though their expertise was at the level of shade-tree mechanics, both men knew that the computer brains of these accursed vehicles malfunction, misread data and emit false signals.

"It may not be anything," Val said, summoning as much optimism as his liver would surrender.

Nick agreed. "We're not going back," he said.

On the edge of their nerves, they pulled back onto the highway and headed into the Organ Pipe Cactus National Monument, an immense federal preserve where the planet seems to tilt and send the highway uncurling down its far side, a toboggan chute into nothingness. Stark, barren mountains, driven up from the desert's volcanic bowels by the forces of creation, hold hidden canyons and sheer bluffs and some of the hemisphere's strangest vegetation, not the least of which is the one for which the preserve was named. It grows nowhere but in a narrow range of southwestern Arizona and Sonora, Mexico, clinging to the torrid slopes in clusters of perhaps twenty or more prickly columns thrusting upward nearly twenty-five feet, speckled at certain times of the year with lavender-white blooms. Like much of the desert flora, the organ pipe cactus can be both elegant and grim, as though its majesty long since had been scarred by the brawl for survival in an inhospitable habitat, buffeted by the elements and forced to compete with other species for space and moisture.

Val and Nick were oblivious to the curious foliage and the razor-spine mountains that scrolled past the car windows. While they encountered no traffic, they knew the highway was rife with hazards—animals frequently crossed or congregated in the middle of the road—but Val kept the Merc cranked at nearly full throttle and they arrived in Lukeville just after nine o'clock.

Because of the limited access to the Sonoran coast, the free zone designation and the steady stream of repeat visitors, Lukeville-Sonoyta may be the border's most amiable crossing. On the American side, there is little but a general store, a gas station and a U.S. Customs office. Sonoyta, on the other side of the fence, is larger, but hardly a place where tourists linger. Except for a few small eateries, curio shops and hotels, it is but a dusty, sun-baked sojourn on the road to Rocky Point. Without the clamor of heavy commerce that clogs larger border crossings, this one is languid and neighborly.

"We heard about that," one of the guards said after the two brothers explained about the murder and the urgency to get their sister's children out of Mexico that evening. If the border closed before they returned, they would have to spend the night in Sonoyta, a prospect they did not relish.

"We'll be here when you get back," a guard said, promising to keep the crossing open late if necessary.

Approaching Rocky Point, they passed a small landing strip and a stone-enclosed baseball field that sat beside a triangular park. Farther along, the highway became a strip of markets and taverns and side streets that branched off at forty-five-degree angles toward railroad tracks that followed the coastline where it curled south beneath the town. To someone accustomed to the orderly grid of the Phoenix environs, the small Mexican town was a hopeless jumble of twists and turns, and they became lost.

Stopping once to ask directions, they finally found the two-story, pink brick Motel Senorial where Dan had taken the children. They got his room number from a bewildered night clerk, ascended the stairs and knocked on the door. Someone inside yelled, "Come in."

Stepping into the room, the two brothers were brought up short by what they saw. Dan was sitting on a bed, talking on the phone. They heard him say, "I'll have to call you back," before he hung up and pushed the phone under the bed. Nick rummaged through his memory for something Dan had said earlier in the day. *There is no phone in our room.*

The children were sprawled on the beds watching television amid an array of empty potato chip bags and other snack food containers and soda cans. Clothes were strewn everywhere. *A picnic,* Nick thought. *It's like a freakin' picnic. Their mother has just been killed and they are dry-eyed and having fun. What is wrong here?* The children, absorbed in the television, barely acknowledged their uncles.

Willoughby stood up, but didn't approach his brothers-in-law. He clearly resented their presence.

Val said, "We're really sorry, Danny. We feel really bad. How are you feeling?"

"Oh, I'm doin' fine," he said. "It's a terrible thing."

He began to repeat the story he had been telling them by phone since morning, and Val interrupted him.

"We can talk about that when you get back home," he said. For an instant, he caught a flicker of fear in Dan's eyes.

"I don't know if the Mexican police believe my story," Dan said. "They might even arrest me."

All the more reason to get the children out of here, Val thought. He looked at his watch. They would have to be on the road in fifteen minutes if they were going to reach Lukeville by midnight.

"They're doing an autopsy—"

"Dan," Val stopped him, "we don't have a lot of time to talk right now. We've got to get the kids across the border."

"Fine," Dan shot back, the resentment returning to his voice. "Go ahead and take the girls."

"We've got to take them all," Val said.

"No, no, no. I want Hayden to stay with me. He wants to stay with his dad."

Six-year-old Hayden was lying on the bed with no interest in the conversation.

"Dan, this is stupid," Val said. "Let us take him home."

"No, I want him to stay."

They stared at each other for an instant. This was no time for a confrontation, Val decided. "Okay, let's go," he said to the two girls.

Dan had little else to say as they crammed Thera and Marsha's clothes into bags, hurried out to the car and loaded the trunk.

"I'll call in the morning," Dan said as the Merc roared to life.

Leaving the parking lot, Nick looked back at his brother-in-law, who turned quickly and headed toward his room. *He's keeping Hayden here for a reason,* he thought. *Hayden is his shield against the cops.* In the presence of his two nieces, and remembering his mother's admonition against expressing his suspicion of Dan, he kept the thought to himself. Besides, Val had been noncommittal. If he felt it was possible that Dan had a hand in Trish's murder, he masked that belief carefully. Nick would let Val sort out his feeling in his own time, with no pressure from him.

As soon as they pulled out of Rocky Point and into the tunnel that was bored into the charcoal night by the headlights' high beams, the brothers breathed easier. The alternator light had not come on.

Thera curled up in the backseat and fell asleep. Marsha leaned forward, the glow from the dashboard lights softly illuminating her young face, and talked with her uncles. She was completely relaxed, Nick noticed, as she gave them yet another account of the previous night, an account far more complete than the one they had received from Dan.

"I didn't want to go to that museum," she said, "but Dad said we all had to go. Mom was tired and he said she needed some time alone so she could rest."

"Was she asleep when you left?" Nick asked her.

"I guess. We all went out and got in the van, but Dad said he had to go back and get his passport."

The two brothers looked at each other. Dan had said nothing about going back into the house. And why would he return for a passport, which certainly wasn't required in Rocky Point?

"So we waited for a long time and I got bored," Marsha continued. "I was going to go back inside and get a Granola bar, but I couldn't get the door open. Then, Dad came out and he was tucking in his shirt. I told him I wanted to get a Granola bar and he said, 'No, Mom's sleeping and you might wake her up.' So we left. I thought the museum was kind of dumb, but Hayden and Thera really liked it. Then we drove out to see a dead whale that was on the beach. We took some pictures and then went back to the house. Dad let me drive."

Nick turned sideways in his seat and studied Marsha's face, which was devoid of expression. "What happened when you got home?" he asked.

"Hayden and Thera were all excited," she said. "Dad told them to go in and tell Mom how much fun they had. Hayden ran into the bedroom and came out screaming. He said, 'There's something wrong with Mom. She's got blood all over her.' Thera was right behind him. She said, 'Mom's all bloody and she's not breathing right.' Dad told me to go in and find out what was wrong with Mom. I came back and told him she had been stabbed. He looked in the bedroom and said we needed to go out on the porch and have a family prayer. After we did that, we went to the Red Cross station to get help.''

Nick was floored. Val's eyes narrowed but he kept them on the highway. They had been reared in a strict church environment and Dan had taken their faith with greater gusto, it seemed, than they possessed, but it struck both brothers as ridiculous that with his wife hanging to life by a thread, Dan would take the time for a formal prayer session before getting medical help.

"You had a prayer before you went to get help?" Nick asked.

"Yeah," his niece said.

The enormity of Marsha's words was stunning. Either Dan was a party to their sister's death or the shock of it had rendered him wholly irrational. Nick had his convictions. Val, outwardly at least, would not rush to judgment. In their weariness, both men were willing to leave the question for another day. Something else, though, had been troubling Nick, and before Marsha leaned back into the sanctuary of sleep, he had one last interrogatory.

"Well, Marsha," he asked her, when it seemed that everything else had been said, "did you get a chance to say goodbye to your mother, to tell her that you loved her?"

"No," Marsha said, tossing off the answer with diffidence. "She died before we could see her at the hospital."

Nick cursed under his breath. It was not the answer he had hoped to hear.

Chapter Four

By the time he started his shift, Sgt. Joe Ruet had already heard about the murder from news reports. There had been a few brief accounts on local radio stations and a more detailed story prominently displayed on the front page of the *Mesa Tribune*.

Gilbert woman killed in Mexico, the headline shouted above smaller type, which read, *Motive remains mystery*.

There was nothing in the text to suggest to Ruet that this was a case for the Gilbert Police Department:

Trish Willoughby, a 42-year-old Gilbert mother of three, was slain in Mexico this weekend after she apparently startled thieves in the affluent Puerto Penasco home her family had rented for the weekend, her husband said Sunday.

Dan Willoughby said he had taken his two daughters, 17 and 10, and 6-year-old son to a show at a museum

Saturday and returned to the Las Conchas area home about 5 P.M. "Upon returning to our home we had rented for that weekend, I found my wife in the bedroom where she had been murdered."

Willoughby said he believes his wife had been taking a nap when robbers forced their way into the home. "I think she surprised them and there was force used in order to obtain what they wanted, which was money," he said. Her belongings were strewn across the bedroom, her wedding ring had been removed, and a few hundred dollars that had been inside her purse were missing, he said.

Willoughby said his wife died on the way to the hospital. He said she apparently had been struck on the head.

The family arrived in Puerto Penasco about noon on Friday and planned to return Sunday.

Willoughby said the Mexican police have been cooperative and have suspects, but the slaying has shocked the community, popular with Americans.

"What they are saying, the story which I believe, is that for years and years and years, they have not had any type of heinous type murder. And in this nice quiet community in which people trust each other . . . so they are extremely upset that something like this should happen to cast a negative picture of Puerto Penasco."

Willoughby said two of his brothers-in-law came and brought his daughters back (to Gilbert) Sunday evening.

"With me is my 6-year-old son who refuses to leave my side. I have told my children that I will not leave Mexico without my wife, and my 6-year-old will not leave without me and he's standing by my side until we all leave."

Ruet read the story with a cop's eye for oddities, but didn't linger over it. Though the victim and her family were prominent members of his community, the crime was out of his jurisdiction.

After the squad meeting that opened each shift, he sat at his desk, which was cluttered with files, and considered which investigation he could advance a little today.

"You know about that murder down in Sonora?"

Det. Patrick McNabb was standing in front of him. Ruet looked up from the file he was reading and nodded. "I read about it this morning," he said.

If the news reports were correct, it was nothing more than a straightforward case of robbery-murder in a country where such crimes were becoming commonplace. Affluent foreigners were increasingly vulnerable in Mexico, just as they were throughout Latin America, where kidnapping and robbery were the fund-raising tools of choice for so-called revolutionaries. But as often as not the crimes were carried out by masquerading thugs and thieves more interested in building a stake to buy into the drug business than in pursuing some professed political agenda.

Ruet intuitively knew that McNabb hadn't stopped by for idle conversation about something that happened two hundred miles away. McNabb was all business to an extent that sometimes irritated Ruet. He had a crisp, military bearing and usually talked in formal legalese and wrote his reports in the same manner. "Dammit, Patrick," Ruet once needled him, "Why don't you write these things in plain English?" But McNabb was a good detective, and Ruet liked him and respected his instincts and abilities.

"We may have a problem," McNabb said.

"What kind of problem?"

"We've had a few phone calls today," McNabb said.

"And?" Ruet asked.

"Looks like this guy had a mistress."

Ruet tossed his lean frame back in the chair and weighed the implications of that nugget of information. He had just been assigned to homicide work after a couple of years in narcotics and could only imagine the difficulty of cutting his teeth on a murder that crossed international boundaries.

His expertise was the drug business and the callous characters who populated it. Four years earlier, he had given up his job with an armored car service in Chicago and moved to Gilbert, a town he had visited once on vacation. In Chicago, he had been a reserve police officer, a volunteer job that offered little that was more exciting than walking a beat and writing an occasional parking ticket. In Arizona, he decided to become a real cop.

When he arrived, Gilbert, a twenty-minute drive from downtown Phoenix, was beginning to sprawl across a portion of the Valley of the Sun that is as flat as fry bread. It was raw desert until the early 1900s, when Roosevelt Dam was constructed up in the Superstition Mountains. Spun off from the resulting reservoir were the Eastern and Consolidated Canals that carried irrigation water that turned the land southeast of Phoenix into green groves of citrus fruit and fields of cotton, alfalfa and vegetables. In 1970, the population of Gilbert was a mere 1,971. By 1980, it had grown to 5,717 and exploded to 29,188 by the end of the decade. It was the fastest growing community in Arizona and, by the end of the century, would be pushing 100,000, following the course of other Phoenix suburbs such as Mesa and Tempe and Chandler. Ranches and orchards would yield to gated communities, and golf courses would become as ubiquitous as Circle K convenience stores.

Arizona, particularly the Valley of the Sun, had become its own kind of melting pot, as retirees, entrepreneurs, hucksters, New Age pilgrims, Rust Belt fugitives and a dozen other varieties of migrants, compelled by their own westward yearnings or wicked pasts, inundated the state.

For a cop, life here might not be as dynamic or as dangerous as on the streets of Chicago, but it would have its challenges, the most prevalent of which was tracking drug smugglers. Arizona's long, remote border with Mexico and the desert's adaptability to hidden landing strips made the state a tempting route for northbound narcotics. South of the border, corrupt police and prosecutors helped keep the valve open, and on the U.S. side, the best interdiction measures probably bagged only ten percent of the flow. No one actually knew.

When high-tech balloons tethered to the desert floor helped fill the radar gap, the traffickers went overland, hiring young Mexican boys as *mules* to move dope in canvas or burlap backpacks that weighed as much as 150 pounds. To intercept them, the U.S. Customs Service deployed a low-tech force of Pima and Papago Indians, who used tracking techniques passed down from their ancestors, to pick up their trails and pursue them on horseback. But nothing dammed the river of opiates and marijuana. Lawmen probably intercepted just enough to keep the market from being oversupplied, thus keeping prices high and the trade highly profitable.

Life in that realm was cheap. For someone like Ruet, the narcolords, driven purely by profit, were not too hard to understand. They produced a product, established a network of wholesale and retail distribution and did business, sometimes carelessly or haplessly enough to get caught, and had no qualms about killing to protect their racket.

In his brief tenure as a cop, Ruet had worked his share of smuggling cases and became adept at the tricky process of building conspiracy charges. He still had a lot to learn about working a murder, but the elements of conspiracy, whatever the crime, were the same. He knew exactly the implications of what McNabb was telling him. If bandits killed Trish Willoughby, that was Puerto Penasco's problem. If Dan Willoughby was involved, that was a different matter. The case could end up in the Gilbert Police Department's lap if it appeared that the murder was planned in Gilbert.

Random killings are much rarer than most people believe, Ruet knew. Most murder victims are killed by someone they know, and if they are married, the spouse is an automatic suspect until his or her alibi has been confirmed beyond any doubt.

"Willoughby had a mistress?" Ruet asked.

"We had one call from a florist. Apparently, he has been going to her shop regularly for a year, sending flowers to another woman."

"Does she have the woman's name?"

Taking a small notebook from his shirt pocket, McNabb flipped a page and said, "Yesenia Patino."

"She has proof?"

"Still has all the sales slips, along with the notes he wrote."

Ruet thought for a moment. A lot of men have affairs. That doesn't make them killers.

"We also had a call from a banker," McNabb said. "He said Willoughby and this other woman have a joint checking account."

That would suggest that the affair was more than a fling, Ruet thought, and it would have to be checked out, but it still didn't add up to murder.

"It sounds like this guy had a pretty good alibi," Ruet said. "The newspapers say he wasn't at the house when she was killed. He was with his children."

"There was another call," McNabb said, as if he had been holding the bombshell for last. "Some guy at Air Express International. Willoughby used to work there. This guy says Willoughby was in El Paso a few months ago asking about hit men."

Now the story was becoming loony. Ruet had seen a lot of dumb criminals, but this tested credulity. A guy carries on an open affair, marked by an abundant paper trail, and goes off to a border town—using his real name—in search of someone to snuff his wife. Not likely.

He asked McNabb to visit the florist and the banker and get everything they had. As preposterous as it sounded, the hired gun story would also have to be followed up. Unless . . . unless the police in Puerto Penasco saved them the trouble by quickly arresting a burglar in possession of Trish Willoughby's jewelry.

He walked to the coffeepot, filled his cup and returned to

his desk, sitting for a long time mulling the possibilities, most of which were not cheerful. Yes, there were intriguing elements to the case, the kind to start a detective's juices flowing, but Ruet knew that his department was woefully understaffed and underfinanced for an investigation that already showed promise of spreading tentacles across state lines and foreign borders. The homicide unit consisted of himself and three detectives, and a budget that hardly foresaw a far-flung case of this nature.

But there was no reason to panic. Ruet still was not certain that the case would be his to solve even if Willoughby did have something to do with it. The murder was carried out in Mexico. If a killer had been hired in El Paso, then the conspiracy occurred in Texas and was someone else's problem. If some acts of conspiracy did occur in Gilbert, Ruet would have jurisdiction, but as far as he knew at the moment, all he had was a guy who may have sent flowers and given money to a woman other than his wife.

For now, he would try to monitor developments in Puerto Penasco from afar and hope the police there found their burglars.

Chapter Five

Thera Huish also read the newspapers that morning, read them through eyes that were bleary from only a few hours' sleep. Nick and Val and the two girls had arrived home after three o'clock and it was nearly four before the car was unpacked and the children were bedded down.

As Nick was leaving, his mother walked with him to the door and asked if Marsha had said much on the drive home.

"She talked a lot," Nick said. "There are some things Danny hasn't told us."

"I was sure of that."

He briefly related fragments of Marsha's story, particularly that part about Dan going back into the house, locking the door and refusing to let Marsha go inside for a Granola bar.

Thera took a deep breath and leaned against the door.

"Nick, you're telling me . . . Danny was in that house with Trish for ten or fifteen minutes."

"That's how long Marsha thought it was. Talk to her in the morning and judge for yourself," he said, turning to leave. He stopped and faced his mother again. "Something else. Trish

was barely breathing when they found her, but before going
for help they went out to the front porch for a family prayer."

"Marsha told you . . ."

He nodded and began to move toward the car. Thera wanted
to hear more, but the fatigue in her son's face told her she
would have to wait. Val, too, was ready to crash. Sterling, Bob
and Arlene had already turned in. She went inside and sat in
the living room, a few steps from the office she had shared
with her daughter, and felt a weariness ooze through her like
a toxic cloud. Her body felt as heavy as steel, but her mind
was racing and her chest burned with an ache she had never
known . . . not grief, something else, something more unbearable. She had lost a husband once, long ago, and a son just a
year and a half ago. She could bear the loss of her daughter,
but not this way, not from this senseless savagery.

Sterling was already asleep when she made her way to the
bedroom. She undressed quietly, slid into bed and surrendered
to her exhaustion.

Because of the stories in the morning papers, the phone
began to ring early. Neighbors, friends, business associates,
church members, were all offering condolences and whatever
assistance they could provide. Between calls, Thera paced the
floor, anxious for the children to awaken. She wanted to hear
Marsha's story. But the morning wore on and still the children
slept.

Dan called to tell them that he was having legal problems
getting Trish's body released from Mexico. Something about
a name being entered erroneously on the death certificate. That
set off a flurry of phone calls. Sterling contacted the office of
Sen. John McCain, who in turn contacted his old friend Grant
Woods, who had just taken office as Arizona's attorney general.

Such high-level intervention was no guarantee that this wrin-
kle could be ironed out quickly. Even without a legitimate
reason to impound Trish's body, the authorities in Puerto Pen-

asco could have been playing the game familiar to visitors to Mexico, where every level of the bureaucracy is mired in a sty of corruption, where every tooth is honed for *la mordida,* the little bite. Need a driver's license? Slip the clerk a few coins for everyone all the way up to the governor to nibble on and you're expedited. Would they end up haggling over petty bribes to get Trish home?

The police in Puerto Penasco did not believe Dan's story—at least they did not believe it enough to leave him at liberty while they awaited the results of the autopsy. Late Monday morning, three officers went to the motel where he was ensconced with his six-year-old son. Speaking in a language the young boy did not understand, they informed Dan that he was under arrest.

Apparently, they had not thought through the matter of what they would do with the child. The American decided for them. He leaned down, scooped Hayden into his arms and said, "You just wrap your legs around Daddy and hold on tight. We'll go to jail together."

Because violent crime was so rare in Puerto Penasco, everyone in town, particularly the Americans who lived or spent extended vacations there, followed every development with morbid curiosity and, in some cases, genuine concern for Trish Willoughby's family. Phone lines buzzed in and between Gilbert and Rocky Point.

The Huishes learned of Dan's arrest, and the jailing of Hayden along with him, from a friend who knew a mobile home park owner in the Sonoran village. The park owner would contact a judge he knew and try to get the father and son released. Sit tight.

Thera's nerves were as raw as road kill by the time the children awoke late that morning. After they had eaten, she took Marsha into the living room. She tried to appear composed, so as not to addle her granddaughter, but her insides were churning.

"Honey, tell Grandma what happened," she said, taking a seat beside Marsha on the sofa.

Again, Marsha related the story she had told her uncles on the trip home, but Thera wanted more detail.

"How was your dad acting that afternoon?" she asked.

"The same," Marsha said.

"Was he with you the whole time you were gone?"

"Yeah." Then she volunteered something she had not previously mentioned. While they were at the museum, which sits atop a sand hill looking down on Las Conchas, her dad made several trips to the second-floor balcony and looked in the direction of their beach house.

"What was he looking for?"

"I don't know. He didn't say anything."

"What about the three Indians who were seen going into the house?" Thera asked.

Marsha looked blank, as though she was hearing of them for the first time.

"I don't know about them," she said, puzzled by the question. Marsha had not read the morning papers.

"When you got back to the house, did you see anyone around?"

"There was a black pickup driving away," she said.

"Did your dad say anything?"

"He just said, 'Don't worry, everything's going to be fine.' "

"What did he mean by that?"

"I don't know."

There were other details she wanted to know, but Marsha couldn't provide them. Thera placed her hand on her granddaughter's arm as a gesture of . . . what? Thanks? Love? Gratitude? Comfort? Marsha did not seem particularly distressed by her mother's death, and she told her story with no apparent inkling that it could incriminate her father. Why should she harbor such horrible thoughts? Until she was adopted by Dan and Trish three years ago, Marsha had known little but the unhappy life of orphanages and foster homes, of rejection and abandonment. By comparison, the Willoughby household, however tense and contentious the past year had been, was a haven of sanity and stability and middle-class comfort. In Marsha's world, Thera imagined, it was easy to rationalize that the weekend in Puerto Penasco was just another of life's curves. *Bad things happen and sometimes they happen to good people.* Why should she suppose for an instant that her father was a villain in the misfortune?

Marsha seemed to tire of talking about it, and Thera was frazzled by the scramble going on around her as her husband and sons worked for the release of Trish's body from Mexico. God, what a nightmare. Dan and his six-year-old son were in a Mexican jail. Trish was laid out in her own cold prison, expropriated by red tape, nearly two hundred miles away.

Thera wanted to lie down.

Leaving Marsha on the sofa, she stood up and began to make her way down the hallway to her bedroom. Everything her granddaughter had said began to coagulate in her head and she felt vapid, out of touch with what was happening around her. She leaned against one wall and then another, stumbled into the bedroom and collapsed on the floor.

Nick was the first to reach her. As he lifted her onto the bed, he screamed for someone to call for a doctor.

Richard Hinton arrived at the Huish home just after the doctor had gone. He was by profession a certified public accountant and by calling the bishop of Trish and Dan's church in Gilbert. Although Thera and Sterling attended another church, one in their ward in Mesa, Hinton knew them well because of his close affiliation with Trish and Dan.

He went into the bedroom and sat beside Thera, who was beginning to feel the effects of the Valium the doctor had given her. He offered condolences and was startled by her response.

"Bishop," she said. "Dan Willoughby murdered my daughter."

That possibility had never entered his mind. Dan had held several high positions in Hinton's ward, including that of executive secretary to the bishop, and was a tireless worker in all of his assignments.

He was aware there had been problems in the Willoughby's marriage—Trish had once sought his counsel for that reason—but in the five years he had known them, he believed that Trish and Dan had a sound relationship and were capable of resolving their difficulties. In the Mormon Church, the bishop of a ward functions much in the same manner of a priest in a Catholic parish. Although he is not a paid professional cleric, the bishop has the responsibility to oversee the operations of the church and see to the welfare of his congregation. That includes counseling in financial, spiritual and family matters. Hinton had dealt often with marital problems and the Willoughbys' seemed far less severe than most.

"Aw, Sister Huish," he said, "you can't believe that . . . Dan is a wonderful man."

"Mark my word, he murdered my daughter. She came to you for help and you did nothing. You didn't take her seriously."

Hinton, thinking she was delirious from mourning or medication, quietly excused himself. Dan Willoughby a murderer? It was wholly unimaginable.

Nick went in to check on his mother and she was still agitated. She told him what she had told the bishop.

"What did he say?" Nick asked.

"He thought I was out of my mind."

Nick's face crimsoned. *A lot of people were going to think that.* Dan had a lot of friends and was beloved by the neighbors and church members he had helped out in one way or another. They didn't know the real Dan Willoughby, Nick thought. But how could they? Even Trish's family had only sparse inklings of his true nature.

Thera reached for her son's arm and squeezed it. "I want you to go to Mexico and get Trish's body," she said. "Don't you come home without her."

Shortly before the mobile home park owner called, Luz Quintero spoke to the Sonoran attorney general and learned that the police had arrested the American whose wife was killed in the Las Conchas beach house, but she doubted the reports that his son was sharing a jail cell with him. She was an experienced lawyer and civil registry judge who understood that the police might have acted hastily in suspecting Dan Willoughby, but some provision besides jail would have been made for his son. So she thought.

This was no ordinary case. It possessed enormous economic implications.

An easy afternoon's drive from Phoenix or Tucson, Puerto Penasco had become the Arizona coast, a slice of Mexico—known as a free travel zone in the vernacular of international trade—where Americans could move about freely without passports or birth certificates or visas or even proof of vehicle ownership.

Because there was never much reason for humanity to trek to this most arid part of the Sonoran desert, Puerto Penasco would not have existed without the lifeblood of gringo dollars. In the early 1900s game fishermen discovered the abundant sailfish in the Sea of Cortez, but the sport fishing traffic was hardly voluminous enough to sustain a village. A semblance of real development began in the late 1920s, when prohibition in the United States offered opportunities for whiskey smugglers. Saloons and night clubs sprang up, along with gambling and prostitution. A modest commercial fishing industry sprouted, and in time a railroad arrived, as did a small airline service.

With the fishing industry now withered almost to the level of avocation and liquor and gambling no longer a novelty, the town lived on U.S. currency, not just tourism, but more importantly the real estate investments that flowed from the north. The term "planned community" infiltrated the local lexicon and miles of once deserted beaches were being spaded into retirement villages for American and Canadian squatters.

For hundreds of Americans, Rocky Point had become a permanent residence, and thousands more—snowbirds who arrived for the winter—camped in motor home compounds strung along the beaches. They, along with the weekend sun seekers who roosted in the hulking new hotels that rose out of the sand, gave Puerto Penasco the visage and texture of a U.S. colony.

Rather than guard against the intrusion and cultural influence of foreigners, the local government went to generous lengths to further the Americanization of their town, even to the unofficial acceptance of the Anglo name by which northerners knew it. It was a rare vendor who did not price his goods in dollars rather than pesos.

Crime wasn't unheard of, but Americans were made to feel as safe as in their own backyards. From the border crossing at Lukeville—known widely as Gringo Pass—the sixty-mile stretch of two-lane blacktop to Rocky Point was patrolled by the Green Angels, a federal force that offered motorists not only emergency assistance but assurance of safety and security as well. It is said that would-be criminals in Rocky Point get the message early: Rob or assault or burglarize an American and the police may be the least of your worries; the nearest merchant is more likely to beat you senseless.

Now the town had on its hands the grisly murder of an American tourist. Not good for business.

With the arrest of the American husband, tourism officials in Rocky Point swiftly engaged in damage control, issuing statements to the press disputing the suggestion—made solely by Dan Willoughby—that his wife was killed by local bandits. Contrary to Willoughby's statement to reporters the previous day, the Mexican police said they had no suspects, at least not three Indians who were said to have been at the scene. There was no question that everyone in Puerto Penasco was eager to shift the blame north of the border and reassure tourists and investors that murderous thugs were not loose on the resort town.

The judge's fears were confirmed as soon as she entered the holding area of the small police station. The sight of a child in the cell infuriated her.

"Get them out of here," she told the jailer. Following a hurried huddle of police officials, Dan and Hayden were released and Quintero walked outside with them. At the request of the Sonoran attorney general, who had been in contact with his counterpart in Arizona, she was prepared to help put this matter in other hands.

"Come to my office," she told Dan, "and I'll help you with the papers you'll need to take your wife home."

For half an hour, while Hayden fidgeted in a wooden chair, they shuffled and signed the legal documents necessary for the removal of Trish's body from Mexico. Something about Dan Willoughby repulsed her. He did not have the demeanor of a man whose wife had just been murdered, none of the sadness of a new widower. Rather, he possessed the swagger and cockiness of a surfer, a beach boy on a lark. But it was not her job to pass judgment on inscrutable gringos. She just wanted him gone.

"You'll have to arrange for a mortuary here to take the body across the border and be transferred to another hearse on the other side," she said, handing him the documents.

Dan nodded and thanked her. Then he leaned across the desk and, speaking just above a whisper in the Spanish at which he had become so proficient, said, "If I come back sometime, will you have dinner with me?"

Rising from her chair and leading him toward the door, she shook her head slowly and said, "I don't think so, Mr. Willoughby."

Chapter Six

Hours before receiving word that Dan was cleared to leave Mexico with Trish's body, the Huishes had arranged for the Bunker Family Mortuaries to send a hearse to the border. Val would make the trip again, this time accompanied by Bob. At the funeral home, they met with Randy Bunker, the mortician, and a driver, and were on the road by two o'clock. They would rendezvous with the Mexican hearse in Lukeville and transfer the body. Trish would come home in the Bunker hearse; the two brothers would ride in the van with Dan and Hayden.

Neither knew just what they would say to their brother-in-law on the long ride back. Their parents and Nick were convinced that Dan had something to do with Trish's death. They were hesitant to make that leap, at least for now. For several years, Val's swimming pool construction business in California had prospered and prevented him from spending much time in Phoenix. Bob worked full time in the air freight business and sold swimming pools on the side, so he too had not been exposed to the family tensions that existed in Arizona.

They were tentative for other reasons. It was Val's nature

to be patient, to wait for the facts to be sorted out, to require some convincing preponderance of evidence before deciding that anyone—especially his brother-in-law—was a killer. It was Bob's nature to see the best, believe the best. The fourth born of the clan, he had always been the family conciliator. Disinclined to confrontation, he took it upon himself at an early age to restore calm when tempers flared in the household. When he was six or seven, the family often watched a weekly television variety show hosted by the King Sisters. Each program closed with the old Mormon hymn *Love At Home,* and Bob had carefully learned the lyrics. Occasionally, if there was an argument or loud discussion in the house, whether it involved his parents or his brothers and sister, he would amble through the room, hands in his pockets, eyes straight ahead, softly mimicking the King Sisters warbling about the beauty of love at home. As he exited the room, the arguments usually dissolved into laughter.

Earlier that Monday, while the household was in turmoil over Hayden being jailed with his father and the legal snag in getting Trish's body released, Bob and Arlene had gone for a walk. They talked about his parents' state of mind and Nick's anger and the bizarre turns of the past forty-eight hours.

"Wouldn't it be something if Danny was involved?" he said, still unable to find the capacity to believe such an absurdity. Danny had been his brother and his buddy. Danny had brought him into the air freight business and taught him the ropes, and there was no better teacher. Danny was an extraordinary salesman and scored fat bonuses wherever he worked. Bob had heard the rumors of his brother-in-law's ethical lapses—and he knew from personal experience that Danny was not above swimming outside the buoys of business virtue—but he mostly chalked them up to the sour grapes of jealous competitors in a business known for fierce, if not cutthroat, competition. *Wouldn't it be something* . . .

Arlene considered his question. "That would be weird," she said.

* * *

For both brothers, the death of their sister had seemed almost an abstraction, a distant, speaker-phone mirage. But as the hearse turned into the general store parking lot in Lukeville, their perspectives were jolted.

Their vehicle pulled alongside the one that had already arrived from Mexico. Nick's van was there, too, with Dan and Hayden inside it. Everyone got out and stood by as the rear doors to the two hearses swung open and the fragile-looking wooden box with a cloth lining was transferred from one to the other. Bob found himself thinking, *It's real. Trish is in that box. This is really happening.*

Randy Bunker signed a form acknowledging receipt of the body, and the transfer was completed. Without delay, Dan and Hayden climbed into the back of Nick's van. Val got behind the wheel and Bob slid into the front passenger seat. The two brothers were tense and reticent at first. Something told them it was going to be a long and uncomfortable ride home.

They didn't quite know what to say, or if anything should be said in Hayden's presence. It was Dan, more than they, who was unnerved by the silence. He shifted forward to the edge of his seat and began to retell the story they had heard several times. As before, he omitted significant details—that he had left the kids in the van and gone back into the house alone, the delay in going for help—and underscored the part about the three Indians in the dark pickup truck who were seen near the house.

Since he had opened the door to this dialog, Val and Bob peppered him with questions, but were careful not to appear accusatory. *How long were you gone? Was the door locked? Was Trish asleep when you left? What was the name of the doctor who tried to help?*

Dan suddenly became irritated.

"How many times do I have to tell this story?" he snapped.

Bob said, "Danny, our sister is dead. Mom's daughter is

dead. Your children's mother is dead. You'll tell the story as many times as it needs to be told until everybody is satisfied."

Dan's face flushed. "I've told you everything I know. I've told you everything that happened. What more do you want?"

Bob, slow to anger and slower still to challenge, decided not to press the issue. He turned to stare at the road ahead.

Silence again engulfed the van, but not for long. After a minute or two, Dan leaned forward and asked, "What's Mom going to do with the business?"

Startled by the question, neither brother responded.

"I don't know what we're going to do for money," Dan said. "I don't know where the money is. Trish handled all the money."

He waited for a response and, receiving none, rephrased the question. "Is she going to sell the business?"

Val was beginning to come around to Nick's way of thinking.

"Danny," he said. "I don't know what Mom's going to do with the business. She hasn't discussed it. Her daughter has just been murdered. I doubt that she has given it a second's thought."

Long periods of awkward silence accompanied them back to Phoenix and the two brothers were relieved by the sight of the city lights. They followed Interstate Highway 10 through downtown, veered south toward Tempe and turned onto Superstition Highway for the straight shot to Gilbert. At the Gilbert Road exit, they drove south and turned right just past the large Church of Jesus Christ of Latter-day Saints the Willoughbys attended. Fanning out around the church was the kind of languid neighborhood where Wally and the Beav would have felt at home: tidy, clean, green, exhaling an air of suburban innocence and bounty.

At the brick house on the corner, landscaped with a lush array of desert foliage, the van growled to a stop at the curb beside the garage. Bob surveyed the place warily. Only four days ago, it had been the scene of a happy and memorable farewell party, but now it seemed stark and ghostly. His sister didn't live here anymore.

"Will you pick up Marsha and Thera and bring them home?" Dan requested.

Val nodded. He wondered how the children would feel here, knowing that their mother would never return. Like his brother, he thought the house looked cold and dead, but there was no reason Trish's children should not be here. They would have things to talk about, and in their own familiar surroundings, they might more easily work through whatever they were feeling. He wondered what exactly were they feeling. No one, not Dan, not his children, had demonstrated any particular symptoms of bereavement, only conspicuous indifference. Maybe this had been two households—the one the family and neighbors saw, the joyful, rock-solid, churchgoing middle-class paragon, and another one, perhaps one that harbored secrets no one had fathomed.

That dreary hypothesis hung in the air like noxious fumes. When they finally knew everything about Trish's death, would they know more than they wanted to know about her and the man she had married?

Chapter Seven

Tuesday, February 26

Sterling put his hand over the telephone's mouthpiece. "Thera, this is Danny," he said.

"And?" she said.

Both knew they would have to face their son-in-law today, but neither had looked forward to it. Since Sunday, Thera's disdain for Dan had turned to icy loathing and she was unable to conceal her feelings.

"He wants to come and see you," Sterling said.

"I won't see him," she said. "I won't talk to him."

"You've got to talk to him, Thera. We've got a funeral to plan."

She thought for a second and said, "The only way I will talk to him is if his bishop comes over with him."

Sterling relayed the message to Dan and hung up the phone. "He's going to call Bishop Hinton. If he's free, they'll be here in an hour."

She had given little thought to how she would handle her

first confrontation with Dan, but now an idea arrived from nowhere. Thera went into her office, unplugged the tape recorder she often used in business to tape important phone calls or dictate notes to herself, and took it into her bedroom. She sat it on the nightstand, turned it on and set it for voice activation. If anyone entered the room and began talking, their words would be preserved.

Returning to the kitchen, she poured a cup of coffee and waited for Dan and Bishop Hinton to show up. She wasn't sure why she had insisted on Hinton's presence. Maybe she was uncertain of what her own actions would be and wanted an outsider there to keep her in check. She was still sitting there, on a wooden chair at the kitchen table, when the doorbell rang and she heard Sterling inviting the visitors in.

She braced for the encounter, but still flinched at the sight of her son-in-law. When she had last seen him only four days ago, he was tanned and hearty and gregarious. Now, as he strode into the kitchen, the bishop trailing in his wake, he appeared sallow and perspired profusely. His shirt was damp and beads of sweat ran down his temples and jowls. He reeked of terror, and the stench filled the room. He reached for her hand and began to kneel at her side.

"Don't you touch me," she snapped. "You get up and come with me."

She strode down the hallway, Dan in tow and Sterling close behind. When they reached the bedroom, she turned and faced her son-in-law.

"I want to know everything that happened," she said.

At first Dan didn't see the recorder.

"It's like I've been telling you . . ." his voice trailed off when he finally noticed it. "What's that for?"

"Just tell me what happened," Thera insisted.

"Is that for the police?"

"That's for me, Danny."

Standing by the nightstand, Sterling reached for the recorder and said, "I'm going to take the voice activation off."

Thera struggled to control her emotions. What she felt about the man in front of her was based more on intuition than hard fact. In her heart, she was positive that he was somehow involved in her daughter's death, but in her head there was only a jumble of fragmented details. It was possible that the murder happened just as he said, that the confusion and stress that he and the children experienced could explain the inconsistent accounts they had given.

Part of her hoped that Dan's story would be convincing, that it would resolve the incongruities that had troubled the family. Though she and Nick had profound suspicions of him, her other sons, as well as her husband, had been notably more forbearing. Perhaps her judgment had been colored by the unhappy things she had witnessed in the past year. She truly did not want to believe that her daughter had been murdered by this man, who had been a close part of the family for fifteen years.

"I want to record it, Danny, because I . . . my mind is not in such a state as to be able to comprehend anything," she said. "I want to be able to comprehend everything. I have never heard the whole story from you, Danny, and I'm going to ask you to tell it."

"You want to hear it all?"

"Everything."

"It's hard to talk about," he said, his voice breaking. "It was awful."

"I want to know, Danny. I have to know. I don't care how gory the details are, I have to know every detail of this thing before I can put it to rest in my mind."

Dan seemed to shrink in size and grow older in front of her, as though the cartilage were being sucked from his body. He shifted his weight and tried to avoid her eyes, scanning the room like a cornered animal searching for a passage out of this place, away from this woman.

Her voice filled the pause. "There's this one problem . . . the thing I can't get out of my mind is why did I not hear about the death of my daughter until eight-thirty Sunday morning when she apparently was dead at six o'clock Saturday,'' she said. ''Why didn't you call me then and tell me?''

Dan was still silent. Wiping the sweat from his face with a bare hand, he looked toward Sterling but found no ally in his father-in-law.

''This is our daughter we're talking about,'' Sterling said.

''I know that,'' Danny said. ''I'm the only one who was there . . . to tell you.''

''There are just a lot of things, Danny, that we don't know,'' Sterling said. ''We have bits and pieces from you, but we don't have the whole story. We have a little from Tom Jaunerena. We have a little from Senator McCain's office, but not very much. We're having a hard time connecting the bits and pieces. Somebody says this, somebody says that and sometimes what one person says doesn't jibe with what somebody else says.''

Dan looked down at the floor and said nothing.

''Thera's confused and she's hurt,'' Sterling continued. ''We're all hurting deeply. We don't understand why fourteen hours elapsed between the time Trish died and when we heard about it.''

Finally, Dan broke his silence, but his words bumped together in incoherent gibberish. ''You don't understand, see, because . . . I understand the questions and the concerns . . . because truthfully . . . we were going out to the museum . . .''

''Danny,'' Sterling said. ''Start back at the beginning, before you went to the museum. Was she asleep? Had she been asleep for a period of time?''

''No,'' Dan said. ''She had spent the day reading a book. We went out to the beach and sat for a while. It was overcast, real hot. Trish didn't like to sit in the sun, you know, but it was overcast, so it was enjoyable most of the day, just a very quiet and relaxing day. So, a little bit before four, I said, 'Well, it's time to go to the museum.' Trish said, 'Do you mind just taking the kids. I really would like to nap.' That's what she told me, Thera. She said she had some hectic weeks ahead and she really needed some peace and quiet. I said, 'Well, honey, just lie down and take a nap.' ''

As he spoke, Dan seemed to regain some of his confidence, regressing back to the old Dan Willoughby, the garrulous pitchman who could sell sand in the Sahara. The words tumbled from him like a studied spiel to a reluctant client as he retold the tale of gathering the children into the van—this time adding the part about going back into the house for his passport—the two-hour excursion to the museum and the site of the beached whale.

Thera absorbed every detail, measuring them against the stories she had been told by her grandchildren and by friends in Mexico who had made inquiries. Her questions still were not being answered. Why had he not called as soon as Trish was found? Why did he return to the house for a passport in a region of Mexico where neither a passport nor a birth certificate is required of American visitors? Why had he locked the door if he was only going to be inside for a few seconds? Why did he keep Hayden in Rocky Point with him?

More troubling than the unanswered questions, though, was his voice and his mannerisms. *He has rehearsed this a hundred times,* she thought. Dan Willoughby was working, selling, selling himself, selling his story. Whatever emotion and remorse he revealed was, to her, contrived, like the minimal inflections of a tired actor with an old script.

He told of buying T-shirts for Thera and Hayden, of photographing the dead whale and letting Marsha drive back to the rented house.

"We didn't get back until six or six fifteen," he said. "Hayden was all excited because in the museum they had sharks that were in formaldehyde and a lot of other stuff. The kids ran into the house to tell their mom what they had seen. I mean, they burst out the door of that van. Thera went in the bedroom and came out saying, 'Mom's got blood on her head.' Hayden was right behind her. He said, 'Dad, Mom's not breathing very well.' ''

Dan paused and mimicked the gasping sounds his son had made.

"I went to the bedroom. There were no lights on and the drapes on the window were closed, so there was a minimal amount of light, so Hayden didn't really see what had totally happened to her. I went in there and . . . you want to hear it all?"

Thera said, "All of it."

"I went up to her and there was a towel draped over her head and I moved it up a little bit and it was drenched in blood. There was a . . . a kitchen knife . . . stainless steel . . . not a serrated, just a regular . . ."

"Table knife," Thera said.

"Table knife. It was sticking out of her head, the right side of her head. You couldn't see much because of a mass of blood and hair. She was gasping for . . . for . . . breathing real hard. I ran outside and grabbed the kids and got them in the van. I had noticed a Red Cross station outside the guard gate. I pulled in there and told them what had happened to my wife. There must have been four, five or six guys there. They moved so fast, I couldn't believe it. They had their lights on and we drove down that road at eighty-five miles an hour."

As he spoke, Dan's eyes darted back and forth, from Thera to Sterling, as though he might discern their credulity from their expressions. Both were as stolid as statues, neither moved by his account.

He had said nothing of holding a family prayer before going for help, or of letting Marsha drive the van to the Red Cross station. And in Marsha's version, her father had never entered the room where his wife lay dying. Wisely, Thera and Sterling did not cross-examine him. She let him tell his version for the tape recorder. If they asked too many questions, he might deduce things they already knew and try to tailor his story to explain them away.

He hadn't called from the beach house, he said, because there was no phone there. After Trish died in the hospital, he moved the children into a motel, but there was no phone in the room. He asked the desk clerk to place a collect call to the Huish residence at nine o'clock, he said.

"The operator came on the line and said, 'I'm sorry but they will not accept the call because it's an answering service. I knew you had all gone to Sterling's performance."

"Danny," Sterling said. "We were home by one. You could have kept trying."

"I must have passed out from exhaustion."

Having already concluded that he had made no effort to reach the family that night, she moved to another matter.

"What about this black truck?" she said. "Who actually saw somebody go to that house?"

"The guard at the gate going into Las Conchas told the police that he saw a black Toyota with Arizona plates. There were three Indians in it. They make a clear distinction in Mexico of who's Indian and who's Mexican. It's a cultural thing. Las Conchas is also patrolled by the police. They told me that they saw that same Toyota at five in the afternoon. It was parked right beside the house. They told me that someone saw a man . . . saw someone get out and go to the back door, and shortly thereafter it apparently drove off. That's been verified by two or three people . . . the black Toyota . . . the three Indians . . . and a fella was seen entering the back door."

"Was it locked?"

"Thera, I honestly don't know."

"Okay. Now I need to clarify this: Marsha said when you went back into the house you were gone a very long time. She said when you came out, she wanted to go back inside and get something, a Granola bar or something, and you wouldn't let her because her mother was sleeping and she might wake her. You see, Danny, there are so many things . . ."

"Let me explain that, okay?"

"Okay."

"It couldn't have been three minutes. I went to the bathroom, got my passport. As I was going out the door, Marsha was coming through it. I said, 'Where are you going?' She said, 'I want to get something.' I said, 'Come on, we're going to be late for the museum, and your mom's sleeping.' I never told her she couldn't go in, not at all. I simply said we were going to be late. That's all I can tell you."

For a few seconds, the room was silent, but Thera wasn't finished. She took a deep breath and exhaled slowly.

"I'm having some very real struggles, Danny, and I'm going to be real up front and tell you that this last year you have been very cruel to Trish. I have watched you break her spirit. I have heard you say things to her that have just broken my heart. I asked her why she tolerated those things and she said, 'Mom, we had a celestial marriage and I have to make it work.' Trish always had to do everything to please you, Danny, and—"

"That's not true, Thera."

"Trish would come to work just beaten down, literally beaten down, and Janie and I would look at each other and we knew what had gone on."

"Over the past four or five months, you couldn't say that."

"Yes, I could."

"I . . . I went through a change and you saw it. Sterling saw it and her brothers saw it. I had knots to get out of me and I wasn't a nice person."

"I know."

"I didn't even like me."

"The kids would call and they didn't know where Daddy was and Trish never knew where you were or what you were doing."

Dan bristled at the mention of the children.

"Who got up every morning and fixed their breakfast?" he snapped. "Who put the scriptures out for them to read every morning? Who picked them up from school and took them to gymnastics or to their plays?''

"I understand that," Thera said.

"No, no, Thera, you're wrong."

"Trish didn't tell me everything, but I heard things and I knew you were talking to marriage counselors."

"How long ago was that?" Dan said.

"About ten months ago."

"Almost a year ago. You're not hearing everything. You're not seeing anything. You're going back . . . too far back."

For the first time, Thera was on the defensive. Dan was convinced that he had carried out his fatherly and household duties commendably.

"These last few months, I have done everything for Trish," he insisted. "I did laundry, cleaned the house, vacuumed, everything. Maybe . . ."

"But, Danny . . ."

". . . she didn't tell you those things."

". . . I'm talking about the mental abuse you gave Trish. Your ego has to be satisfied and you always have to be the boss, the power . . . like when you ripped into her for writing that two-thousand-dollar check and she said—"

"Ripped into her?"

"I heard the conversation, Danny."

"Ripped?"

"I heard Trish say, 'What is the problem—' "

"Ripped?"

Finally, Thera gave in. "Well, you confronted her," she said.

"I loved her," Dan said. "Believe it or not, I loved her with all my heart. I know you have mixed feelings. You two were so close every day. You thought the same, breathed the same air, walked the same path. There's nothing wrong with that, but there's another side that involves me. We have a life, another life."

"Absolutely."

"We have a family life."

"Absolutely."

Dan had commandeered the conversation and steered it into private areas his in-laws had visited only lightly, if at all. There was little the Huishes could accomplish by debating the marital difficulties of their dead daughter. He rambled on about his love for Trish and their children until Sterling interrupted.

"May I ask a question?" he said, looking at his wife.

"Yes," she said.

Waving his hand toward the tape recorder, he said, "Have you got enough on there to satisfy you?"

Thera wasn't sure what she had, just that she had her son-in-law's story, with whatever lies, truths, omissions or embellishments it contained. For whatever it might be worth, she had a permanent record of it.

Dan shifted his weight from one leg to the other, back and forth, no doubt hoping the ordeal was over, and waited for her reply.

She nodded, and Sterling turned off the recorder.

Bishop Hinton had waited patiently in the other room, talking with Val and Bob. Knowing Thera's feeling toward her son-in-law made for guarded conversation, but this meeting would be relatively brief. When Dan came out of the bedroom, he was in no mood to linger. He moved quickly toward the door and Hinton, with hasty good-byes to the family, followed him outside.

When they were gone, Thera took the tape out of the machine and gave it to Nick. "Put this in a safe place," she said.

She insisted that Sterling drive her to the funeral home. Dan had said the intruders had cut her daughter from her pelvis to her throat. She had to know exactly what had happened.

The embalming had already taken place and Trish was being

readied for a coffin, but Randy Bunker complied with her request to inspect the body.

The only signs of damage to Trish's torso was a large bruise over the rib cage, just below her right breast, about the size of a fist.

Chapter Eight

Phone calls concerning Dan Willoughby continued to stream into the Gilbert Police Department. Tuesday morning, the local newspapers had reported that, contrary to Willoughby's initial comments from Mexico, the Puerto Penasco police had no suspects—except perhaps Willoughby himself, who had been briefly detained there. Sgt. Joe Ruet may have been inexperienced in homicides, but this case had an odor he couldn't ignore. The thin, tenuous suggestion that the husband may have had a hand in the murder emboldened more and more citizens to offer what they knew.

Ruet began to wonder if there was anyone in Gilbert and Mesa and Scottsdale who didn't know about Willoughby and his mistress. The banker and the florist were just the beginning. Calls came in from apartment managers, bartenders, health club trainers, all manner of anonymous Good Samaritans bearing truths. Each phone called carried the tacit plea: *Check this guy out.*

Fred Dees, a police chief who still had the keen intuition and hard eye of a street cop, listened to Ruet's summary of the information he had received. "Put McNabb on it full time," he told the detective. "If you need another investigator, you got him."

"I can use another one," Ruet said. "What about the county attorney? This will take a lot of work and we could use some help from his office."

"You can try," Dees said.

He met with McNabb and told him to pursue every phone call, every lead. But he sensed that the case was going to get bigger than the Gilbert Police Department very quickly. The newspapers were reporting that the police in Puerto Penasco were not commenting on the case and, because he was not in direct communication with them, Ruet had no knowledge of whether or not they were conducting a vigorous investigation. If the victim and their only suspect were back on American soil, they might feel little compulsion to dig further because even if they found evidence that incriminated the husband, they might never be able to prosecute him. In that case, the murder of Trish Willoughby could easily be relegated to an unsolved case file. *Like hell it will.* Ruet placed a call to the Maricopa County Attorney's office and asked if an investigator was available to meet with him.

For a while, at least, the animosity between the Huish family and Dan Willoughby had to be put aside, the suspicion and anger suppressed long enough to bury the dead.

Dan seemed to slip into a mode of meekness, of passive resistance. At the funeral home, he took no part in the selection of a coffin.

"Whatever you want," he shrugged when the others asked his opinion.

"It's for your wife," Thera said, trying to inject a measure of sympathy into the words.

"I don't have any money, Thera. I don't know how I can pay for any of this."

Her patience wearing thin, she snapped, "I'll pay for everything, Danny. Just help us make a decision. It's your responsibility, too."

He shrugged and said, "Whatever you want."

At the cemetery, there was another decision to be made. Would they buy one plot or two?

"I guess one," Dan said.

Thinking that possibly he was being guided more by uncertain finances than true preference, Val said, "Dan, don't you think you might want to be buried next to Trish?"

For a moment, his demeanor shifted from indifference to blunt, if boorish, candor. "Well," he said, "I might remarry."

In their meeting with Bishop Hinton to plan the funeral service, Dan turned sullen again. Was there a particular song he wanted played? *Not really.* A favored prayer? *No.* Trish's parents and each of her brothers would deliver a personal eulogy. Thera and Sterling would sing a special song. Marsha would read a Mother's Day poem written a couple of years ago by little Thera. Did Dan want to say a few words? *No . . . I wouldn't know what to say.*

Exasperated by his detachment, the others proceeded without him. To them, it seemed that he had already removed himself from his deceased wife and everything that had been connected to her. His attitude and actions made no sense to anyone in the Huish family. He professed his love for Trish but recused himself from her funeral arrangement. He knew the family, especially his mother-in-law, suspected that he had a hand in Trish's death, yet he was unable to maintain even the facade of a grieving widower.

They all kept up their shields of civility, but with each passing hour the armor became more and more translucent.

A wake was scheduled for Wednesday night and the funeral would be at eleven o'clock on Thursday morning. They would have to contain themselves until Trish was buried. What they would do next depended on developments, if any, in Puerto

Penasco. Surely, they all believed, somebody was doing something to find the murderer. Surely.

Joe Ruet met for an hour with the investigator from the county attorney's office, explained the phone calls the Gilbert police had been receiving and the need for experienced assistance. He was not encouraged by the response, which was mostly a pained expression on the face of the county sleuth. Ruet understood. This investigation could be a quagmire. Even if they had the budget, which neither did, they did not have the jurisdiction to charge into Mexico to question witnesses and gather physical evidence. They could face a mountain of international treaties, reams of protocol, State Department channels, language barriers and God knew what else. And, for all they knew, the crime scene had already been tainted, if not obliterated.

The answer Ruet got was what he expected. Maricopa County would pass on this one.

Perhaps he could interest the county sheriff's department. Ruet made a phone call, talked to a homicide deputy and got a quick answer. Nope. Didn't happen here. It's Sonora's problem.

He went back to Chief Dees and they weighed their options. Alone, their small department could muck around in this case forever and not bring it to a close. Yet they were disinclined to walk away from it.

"Try the AG's office," Dees told him. "They've got some good people and they've got the resources."

"Anyone in particular I should talk to?"

"Ask for Kay Lines. He's a good man."

Ruet nodded, wrote down the name, and went back to his desk. When McNabb came on duty, he briefed him on the conversation with the chief and said, "Do you know this guy Lines?"

"No."

"Wanna give him a call and tell him what you've got? If they won't help us, this one's going to fall through the cracks."

"I don't think the AG is going to assist us. If they're interested, they'll want the case."

"Fine," Ruet said. "We'll assist them. Just try to get them interested."

Chapter Nine

Wednesday, February 27

Considering the way she died, an open casket for the traditional public viewing might have been out of the question. But the morticians completed their task skillfully. The contours of her forehead and scalp were reshaped with wax and the blond wig closely matched her natural hair. The makeup, which masked the trauma to her fair skin, was heavily applied but not objectionably so. Her head was tilted slightly to the side to conceal the one blemish the undertakers could not, and her hands were folded across her midsection, hands that were almost luminous against the soft white fabric of her temple robe and burial gown.

Standing beside the metallic rose coffin, Thera Huish was pleased that her daughter seemed almost natural, as lovely as she had been in life. She reached for little Thera's hand and tried to draw her toward the casket.

"See how pretty Mommy looks," she said.

"I don't want to look," her grandaughter said. "I don't want to see her."

"Come on, honey," the grandmother pleaded. "Look at Mommy's hands. See how pretty they are . . . just like they always were."

This was how she wanted little Thera to remember her mother—at peace, at rest—and not the way she had last seen her in the darkened bedroom of the beach house in Mexico, lying in a bed drenched with blood, a knife protruding from her skull.

What the children may have seen troubled Thera nearly as much as the murder of her daughter. Two children, innocent of life's hardships, let alone its horrors, had been thrust suddenly into a grotesque reality that could become the stuff of their dreams for the rest of their lives. She wanted desperately to erase all of that.

For all her pleading, though, the child refused to look into the coffin, and as guests began to arrive, Thera put the effort aside for a later time. The family took its place beside Trish, forming a receiving line that guided visitors past the head of the casket first, in a direction that would minimize their view of that side of her face that was most severely damaged.

For two hours, the procession of somber faces shuffled past, offering handshakes and hugs and tears and, now and then, smiles as they recalled fond times spent with Trish. They were friends and neighbors who knew her from her work in the church, from her roles in community theater productions and from the hugely successful business she had built in partnership with her mother. They were shocked by her death and the circumstances of it, they assured the family. *Who would do such a thing? Why?* they wondered aloud. *And in Rocky Point, of all places. Was there a safer place in all of Mexico for Americans to hang out?* They were full of compassion for the children, and for Dan, who had been a loyal friend to most of them.

Thera, tall and slender and possessing the same smooth skin

and light coloring as her daughter, found herself going through the motions of this ritual in a distracted, mechanical way. She had become preoccupied with Dan and kept a cautious eye on him as the faces of the visitors blurred past. He was erratic, pivoting from grief-stricken to glad-handing and back again. He fidgeted and moved away from the other family members, moved alongside the casket as if to block the view of his deceased wife.

As the drone of condolences and reminiscences became a distant buzz in Thera's head, she turned to Nick and whispered, "See if you can do something . . . keep him in line here with the rest of us."

Nick, too, was deep in his own thoughts and in no mood to baby-sit his brother-in-law. Earlier, he had stood alone by his sister's body and felt a seething rage rise within himself. Trish had died alone in a foreign place, far from those who loved her, and that chewed at his insides.

It was he and Trish who had been at the hospital bedside when their brother Rick died of liver and kidney failure just eighteen months earlier. Rick's life had been tormented by alcoholism and brushes with the law, but the family always stood by him. When he checked into the hospital for the last time in the summer of 1989, his family was a constant presence as his life drained away. Trish held Rick's hand that day when the doctor told them the time was near, and Nick leaned over his brother and spoke quietly. "We all love you and we're going to miss you," he said, "but we understand that it's time for you to go. We can accept that." Rick's eyes opened briefly and the pain seemed to drain from his face. He looked at Nick, then at Trish, and then his heart stopped beating.

As difficult as that moment was, Nick felt a sense of relief and blessing that his brother had died in the presence of loved ones. His sister, who had clung to Rick's hand long after his passing, had no such comfort in her final moments. Her last vision was not of her children or her parents or her brothers, but that of a killer's eyes and some instrument of iron or wood hurtling through the shadows toward her temple, a knife slicing a dark arc toward her brain.

When the last visitors had left the church, the family of Tricia Willoughby gathered once more at her coffin, said a brief prayer and then they, too, filed out into the chilly desert night.

Nick lagged behind and returned to his sister's side. Before the morticians closed the coffin for the last time, he took a pen and paper from his pocket, wrote a short note and placed it in her hand.

"Sis," the message said. "I promise I won't rest until the people who did this have been caught."

He hurried to catch up with his parents and brothers who were waiting beside their cars. He told no one about the note. It was a private oath, the final covenant between brother and sister.

Thursday, February 28

At daybreak, shallow clouds streaked across the sky over Phoenix and a light rain pelted the rooftops and broad flat streets of the valley. At his home in Mesa, Nick was awakened by the raindrops tapping against his bedroom window. He sat up in bed, looked out at the somber, gray morning and groaned. *Not today, please,* he thought.

He had spent a fitful night, drifting in and out of sleep as the past few days buzzed in his head like a swarm of insects. He checked the clock and lay back down, hoping for an hour or two more of sleep, but to no avail. He slid out of bed slowly so as not to wake Cara, went into the kitchen, made coffee and toast, and sat alone at the table thinking of what he would say about Trish at her funeral.

The church would be filled; he already knew that. Trish had many friends in Gilbert, people she knew from the church and her children's schools. But others, associates and friends she had made through her business, were arriving from as far away as Canada and Hawaii. What could he say to them, those who had known her for only a short time? A life cannot easily be reduced to words, especially a life so filled with contradictions.

He had found it amusing that one newspaper headline identified her as a "socialite," a term that, to him, oozed pretension and pomposity—characteristics absent from the Trish he knew.

More often, he thought of her as a classic dumb blonde, a persona projected by her tendency to become absorbed in her own thoughts. *Dumb like a fox,* he thought. With their mother, she had built a $2 million business that was raking in $40,000 or more a month. Again, the food fight rushed back to him. He smiled to himself and decided that was the Trish he would eulogize.

By midmorning, the sun had burned away the clouds and filled the valley with a golden light that seemed almost liquid, rich and thick, spilling out of the pastel heavens and down the distant mountains, washing across the desert floor and clinging to everything it touched.

Sterling Huish dressed in his best suit and sat now with a mug of coffee, staring out the kitchen window at the luminous day. Thera was not yet ready. She had spent the morning meticulously applying her makeup, touching up her hair and selecting the dark blue and orchid dress she would wear to the funeral.

Sterling, too, contemplated his eulogy to the stepdaughter he had always considered complex, if not enigmatic. He decided he would share the story of the defiant little girl who stood in the backseat of his car and dared him to steer her off balance. It spoke volumes about Trish, who had dropped out of high school, flirted with the counterculture and recreational drugs, endured an abusive first marriage and then regained her equilibrium, rediscovered her family and her church, bore one child

and adopted two others and became one of the most successful
businesswomen in her community. Yes, she was complex.

The casket was pushed from the viewing room to the church,
where the hum of a plaintive Mormon hymn arose from the
lips of forty members of the Phabulous Phoenicians, who stood
behind the altar facing the crowd of more than six hundred.
Then the family entered, Dan first, followed by Hayden, then
his two daughters, then his in-laws. For a moment, he stood
in the aisle by the first pew and extended his arm, as if to invite
Thera to his side. She ignored him and took a seat beside her
husband, her three sons and two granddaughters.

One by one, the friends, business associates and family members went to the altar and delivered brief eulogies. Dan remained
seated and said nothing. Anyone who noticed his absence from
the service could easily have attributed it to the grief he surely
felt. He had many friends in the church that morning, friends
who had no reason to believe that his life with Trish had been
anything but ideal.

One of them was Brent Hatch. In the Mormon organizational
structure, each church serves a ward, presided over by a bishop.
A cluster of wards forms a stake, presided over by a president.
Hatch was the president of the stake that included the Willoughbys' ward. He was the last to speak and he spoke directly to
the widower.

"Danny, remember that beautiful morning in the spring of
'78 when you knelt at the altar and those having the power
and the authority to do so sealed her to you to be your eternal
companion? Danny, not 'til death do you part, but forever and
for eternity."

Willoughby showed no emotion and the nod of his head was
barely perceptible.

"And then in November of 1989—Hayden and Marsha
joined that forever family, never again, Danny, to be separated," Hatch said. "What greater blessing, Danny? There was

no talk of divorce. There was no unfaithfulness. There was none of what we see so much of in the world today. How blessed you are to have that memory and not question what lies ahead in eternity.''

When they stepped outside the church, rain clouds again were gathering quickly over the desert. As the hearse led a procession of two hundred cars out of the parking lot, north toward Mesa, the sky opened up and water fell in blinding torrents. As the procession turned east toward the Superstition Mountains, toward the cemetery on the edge of town, the drivers hunched forward, barely able to see the road or the cars in front of them.

At the cemetery, the funeral director, drenched despite a large umbrella, approached the family limousine with bad news. The grave was filled with water, making burial impossible.

''We'll have to wait until it dries up,'' he said. ''Probably tomorrow.''

Braving the elements, Sterling's brother, Bruton Huish, got out of his car, walked across the soggy turf and said a blessing over the open grave, officially rendering Trish's body unto the earth. Then the procession turned and headed back toward the church, where a meal was waiting. Trish's body was taken to the funeral home. She would be buried inconspicuously, without audience, early the next morning.

When the guests had been fed and had gone back to their lives, Trish Willoughby's family gathered at her parents' home to ponder what happens next. None know, but they knew their nightmare was just beginning. The murderer was still at large.

PART TWO
The Journey

Chapter Ten

Life was hard in those days, as hard as the rocky soil on Promontory Summit, as hard as the salt flats where the great lake had receded. In a good year, it might rain eight or ten inches, barely enough for the dry farmers to bring in a thin crop of alfalfa or winter wheat, hardly enough to entice a city boy back to the land. But on the streets of Ogden, Joseph Nicholas had seen worse.

As the Great Depression wore on, he grew weary of standing in bread lines to feed his family, weary of the spiritual malaise that hung like a dirt cloud over nearly everyone he knew in town, weary of that heartclot of powerlessness that arrived with each sunrise. The hills and flats north of the Great Salt Lake had never been a land of plenty anyway, and now it was as dismal as the Dust Bowl. Construction ground to a halt after the stock market collapse of 1929 and factories and mines shut down. Farm crops brought only a fraction of pre-Depression prices and sometimes it seemed that everyone was out of work.

With the election of Franklin Roosevelt and the advent of the New Deal, he picked up occasional employment through the Works Progress Administration, but he resented the money as much as he needed it. However it might be disguised, it was still a handout, a federal dole in the cloak of meaningful labor. Like many of the Mormon pioneers and their descendants who had civilized this inhospitable territory, he was too proud, stubborn, independent and self-reliant to be taken in by the makework of the New Deal. Programs such as the WPA may have been important—even essential—cogs in the machinery of economic deliverance, but to Nicholas they still reeked of charity.

That the entire country was suffering was no consolation to Nicholas. In time, he found himself contemplating the unthinkable.

He was not an accomplished farmer, but his father owned land in the hardscrabble deserts and prairies that stretched west from the Wasatch Mountains toward Nevada. Thanks to the diligence of the Mormon settlers who began arriving here in the mid 1800s, irrigation had rendered many places in the Utah wasteland arable. The plains of Promontory was not one of them. It was fit only for the dry farming of hardy grains that could survive on whatever rainfall the fickle skies chose to provide. But Nicholas had seen worse.

After persuading his father to cede forty acres to him, he went to the WPA with a proposition.

"Give me enough money to get to Promontory and I'll never be dependent on the state again," he said.

With the deal struck, he loaded his wife, son and few belongings into his old car and set out for a town that had never taken root, a town that had been little more than an illusion, a ghostly blip on the radar of history.

It was at Promontory Summit in 1869 that America was united geographically. Two railroad lines, one pushing west from Omaha and the other proceeding east from Sacramento, met at this place of desolation, and the first continental railway was complete. The cultural and economic implications were enormous, as coast-to-coast travel was cut from months to days and the West truly belonged to the nation. A tent city sprung up at the site where the tracks connected and a more permanent village followed. But Promontory, the town, was soon the habitat of apparitions and memories. Perhaps it was too remote or too harsh, but whatever the reason, the population drifted west or back toward the Wasatch Mountains or to the Valley of the Great Salt Lake. Those who remained were scattered in sparse pockets across the farms and ranches that were being established.

To call the Nicholas's new home a farmhouse would be to test hyperbole. It was a two-room shanty set on a patch of high, dusty prairie. There was no electricity, no running water, no indoor plumbing. But it was a place where Joseph and Doran could practice self-sufficiency and teach it to their children, who would eventually number seven.

There would be no slackers in this household. When Joseph's stern voice bellowed reveille, no one dared ignore it, else a second summons would be issued in the form of a glass of cold water in the face or on the back of the neck. There were chickens to be fed, cows to be milked, butter to be churned, fields to be tilled, a garden—the source of virtually all the family meals—to be tended, and school to attend.

When the alfalfa was harvested, each member of the family participated in culling the seeds for resale in town. In a good autumn, the seeds would fetch perhaps five dollars—enough for a three-month supply of kitchen staples and Christmas gifts for all the children. It was a lean and arduous subsistence from which the Nicholas children longed to be liberated.

Thera Nicholas was particularly impassioned in her yearning for freedom. As one of the eldest siblings—the second born— she shared responsibility for her younger brothers and sisters. Even at the one-room school they attended she was often as much instructor as pupil. Regular teachers came and went, but almost without exception they were young, single and female— much to the liking of the local cowboys. It was not unusual for a wrangler to stop by the school, spend an hour or two chatting with the teacher or take her for short horseback rides.

On those occasions, Thera was usually left in charge of the other students—a dozen or so spread across eight grades. She read to them, conducted their music lessons and helped with their penmanship.

By the time she went off to high school in Tremonton, eighteen miles away, she was mature beyond her years and she had learned well her parents' gospel of hard work and self-reliance. Still, the journey to the outside world was frightening. Compared to the environment in which she had grown up— the drab, parched emptiness, the daily toil and long, muted nights—Tremonton was a head-turning metropolis, a place filled with unfamiliar faces and modern wonders. Its streets were paved and its emporiums, diners, salons and offices were lit by electricity.

It even had a movie house, the Liberty Theater, run by a young man named Dorian Toland, who had joined the Army fresh out of high school but, before completing his hitch, was forced to apply for a hardship discharge. His father had suffered a disabling stroke and his mother was unable to manage the family business alone.

As in many small towns of that era, the movie theater was an important center of community life, almost as important as the church in fashioning the social interactions and sensibilities of the local adolescents. It was there that Thera and Dorian met and became fast friends. Soon they were dating and talking about marriage. She was only sixteen, and he just a few years older, but both had borne the weight of responsibility at a tender age and it was not unusual for them to contemplate such a serious step. Teenage wedlock was common then, and these two seemed as suitable for it as any.

To Thera, marriage offered an escape from the farm and an opportunity for a life in more promising surroundings. Her husband would have a reliable business—not one that ebbed and flowed with the elements—and she could help with it. They could have a home, children, neighbors, friends.

The vows were exchanged in 1946 in a small Mormon church and within a year, Thera gave birth to a son, Val. Patricia, called Trish from the beginning, was born eleven months later. The theater provided an ample livelihood, but Thera and Dorian, like many young people bearing fresh memories of the Depression, were ambitious and eager for greater security. Dorian was casting about for new business ventures.

He planned to be gone only a few days. In his single-engine Cessna, he would fly his father up to Wyoming and drop him off to spend a few days with relatives. From there, he would make his way to Seattle, stopping at small airfields to refuel, and after attending to some business, he would pick his father up on the return trip.

They never made it to Wyoming. Soon after they were airborne, a howling Pacific storm blew across the Cascades and lashed the Great Basin with a fury. Dorian lost his bearings and the small craft was tossed about like paper. On-board instruments were spare in those days and small-craft pilots flew by vision and instinct more than anything else. By the time he picked up a radio signal and fixed his location, Dorian and his father were well over Idaho. He managed to land and refuel at Kooskia, but decided to push on because the town had no facilities to provide for his invalid father. He stopped again in Kamiah, a few miles up the Selway River, took on more fuel and decided to try to reach Lewiston.

"Fly low and follow the river," the airport supervisor told him.

The next time anyone saw the Cessna, it was wreckage.

Either the weather had thrown her husband's craft into a spin, or it had clipped a canyon wall above the river and crashed just outside of Lewiston. At the age of eighteen, Thera Toland was a widow with two infant children.

* * *

After serving a wartime hitch as an Air Force enlisted man, Sterling Huish went back to Utah with a life plan. He would enter Brigham Young University, earn a degree and an ROTC commission, and return to the Air Force as a career officer. During the summers, he worked at whatever jobs were available, and in the postwar economic expansion, they were plentiful. There were houses to be built, factories to be retooled, and modern amenities to be extended to the rural backwaters. He was a member of the work crew that laid the first electric lines to the farms and ranches around Promontory.

He also had a passion for singing. In his spare time, he performed with a barbershop quartet that sometimes entertained at the Tremonton high school Thera attended. But they did not meet until after Thera had married Dorian Toland and Sterling began dating Dorian's sister. Many nights, he hung around the theater, sitting with Thera in the ticket booth while waiting for her sister-in-law to get off work.

After Dorian's death, that friendship quickly turned to romance, but Sterling would soon graduate from BYU and begin the nomadic life of a military officer. Thera still worked at the Liberty Theater when she could find time from caring for two infants, but she felt more and more adrift as the weeks passed. When Sterling proposed marriage, she accepted.

For the next two decades, Sterling's assignments took them to Germany, back to Provo, to Okinawa, then back to Utah. Along the way, Thera gave birth to three more sons, first Rick, then Bob, then Nick.

Trish was not only Thera's sole female progeny, she was the most enigmatic of the brood. By comparison, her sons were eminently fathomable, each with his distinct personality but none possessing the bewildering qualities of her daughter.

She learned to speak later than most children and depended

on her older brother, Val, with whom she shared the kind of mystical bond often found among twins, to interpret her infantile gibberish for her parents. "She wants a drink of water," he would tell his parents. Or, "She has to go to the bathroom." If she finished her dessert first, it took only a longing look and Val would share his with her.

To her parents, that seemed to be the limit of her reliance. By the time she was three, she showed every sign of having inherited the independence and resoluteness of her forebears.

She liked to ride standing up in the backseat of the family car, as if to prove that she could defy the turns and swerves that might have sent less purposeful tots sprawling across the seat or tumbling into the floorboard. Watching her in the rearview mirror, Sterling sometimes gave the steering wheel a slight jerk in one direction or another to see if he could tip her off balance.

"Stop foolin' around," she would growl through tight lips, her eyes fixed hard on him. *You're wasting your time,* the look said, *you can't make me fall.*

It was also at an early age that she began to reveal evidence of a secluded place inside her, a room to which she would retreat on a whim. Playful and frisky one moment, she would suddenly withdraw into herself, her detached gaze forming a protective curtain around her. In those moments she was uncommunicative, and no one, not her parents or her brothers or her playmates, could enter her restricted zone without invitation.

When she entered that private room, Thera would wonder where her daughter had gone. And she would wonder if she would ever find out.

Chapter Eleven

Understanding rebellious children is one of the impossibilities of parenthood. Trish had inherited much from her mother—striking good looks, a strong will, a precocious sense of responsibility—but as she passed from childhood to adolescence, she acquired an attitude of unknown origins. Thera was perplexed and troubled by it. There was little overt hostility between them, just a diminishing degree of communication.

Trish was twelve when John F. Kennedy took office in January 1961, and the new decade was building toward a force that would slam into America like an asteroid, scattering fallout from the mushroom cloud of campus revolution, sexual revolution, civil rights revolution, the Vietnam War, space flight, political assassinations, women's liberation, flower children—the whole glob of psychic shrapnel that marked the sixties. It was a period of great creativity and, concurrently, equally enormous havoc—the destruction of innocence, the renunciation of authority, a loss of reverence for tradition, the demise of unquestioning obedience to parental dictates.

If their elders recoiled from that chaos in fear or anger, the

young were drawn to it, and their developing sensibilities—
still malleable to the sculpturing grit borne by the winds and
tides of their times—took forms that were inexplicable to their
parents.

The young Thera Nicholas had been restless, too, but to
liberate herself from the dead-end alley of poverty, isolation
and dreariness. Trish never knew such things. Instead, she was
hell-bent on escaping a life of comfort and opportunity. Her
generation luxuriated in the harvest of an earlier generation's
sacrifices and, yet, it feasted on an inscrutable arrogance, the
compulsion to raze the old order and raise a new one founded
on . . . what? The noble pursuit of greater equality, personal
liberty and accountable authority may have been the compact,
but would it be consummated in a chemical fog? *Do your own
thing, baby. Turn on, tune in, drop out.* Thera didn't understand
it.

Given that the counterculture consisted largely of middle-
class kids challenging their parents' values, Trish was a likely
candidate to drift under its spell. In fact, she could have been
the flower child prototype.

Growing up on and around military bases, in the insular and
autocratic environment of rigid rules and chains of command,
is enough to render any child of spirit and curiosity vulnerable
to the allure of insurrection. A military society simply is not
the real world of rowdy democracy, contentious discourse and
unfettered locomotion. If you've got wings, spread them someplace else.

Life in Utah was nearly as restrictive, especially for those
of the Mormon persuasion. It is a religion of communal obliga-
tion and continuing redemption wherein salvation is found
through one's works and not just one's faith. Stopping by the
church or temple for an hour of prayer and worship once a
week isn't enough, as in less stringent denominations. Genuine
adherence calls for selfless immersion.

If the military is a peculiar institution—the least democratic
segment of America charged with the defense of democracy—

the Mormons also are a singular slice of the American experience. The religion didn't even exist before 1830, when Joseph Smith, the twenty-five-year-old, Vermont-born son of an impoverished farmer, wove it from threads of Judaism and Christianity, spun together with his own visions. He called it the Church of Jesus Christ of Latter-day Saints and its guiding text was not only the Bible, but also Smith's Book of Mormon, his translation of writing on golden plates which he excavated, according to his account, from a hill near Manchester, New York, after being directed there by the angel Moroni.

Non-Mormon scholars usually dismissed the tome as a collection of Indian legends, autobiography and Smith's commentary on political and religious controversies of the mid-nineteenth century, but his followers accepted the Book of Mormon as a sacred account of God's dealings with the ancient tribes of the American continent, tribes believed to have descended from Hebrews who traveled from Jerusalem to North America six hundred years before the birth of Christ.

Smith's essential teaching was that God evolved from mankind and, therefore, present mankind likewise could transmute into godliness. Jesus Christ was sent to earth to save mankind, Smith believed, but personal salvation was conditional upon the quality of the individual's life. Thus, his church would have no professional clergy; the functions of a bishop (the LDS version of a priest or minister) would be shared by all members of a ward. Males could become deacons at the age of twelve, teachers at fourteen and at sixteen could be inducted into the priesthood. At eighteen, they could be assigned to missionary work, which they carried out at their own expense. Women were consigned to less significant roles, an arrangement that may have grated on Trish, as it did on many women in the age of liberation.

Probably no religious faction in America suffered the persecution the Mormons did, partly for Smith's revision of Christianity but largely for his advocacy, in the early days of the church, of plural marriages. It was that persecution that drove

Smith and his followers from New York to Ohio, then to Missouri and to Carthage, Illinois, where Smith was murdered in jail. His successor as leader of the Mormons was Brigham Young, who led the flock on to Utah. There, they built a city beside the Great Salt Lake, a shallow inland sea of such high saline and mineral content that it would support no life, save the brine shrimp and larva of the brine fly.

Historians have noted that of all the Western states, Utah was the best organized and disciplined. Under Brigham Young, the persecuted exiles formed a theocratic government—the Provisional State of Deseret (the word means "honeybee" and was chosen for its allusion to the iron work ethic of those first settlers). Cooperatively, they laid out streets, built schools and temples and turned the Great Salt Lake valley into an irrigated garden that would lure thousands of others of like faith. From 1850 to 1880, the population of Utah multiplied twelve times.

Rather than abating, the controversy surrounding the church heightened after 1851, when Brigham Young was elected governor and officially instituted the practice of polygamy. Over the next decade, Congress voted to outlaw the lifestyle and President James Buchanan ordered Young's removal as governor (federal troops were sent to Utah to enforce the eviction). By the mid-1890s Mormon control over Utah had officially ended, and to achieve statehood the church hierarchy renounced plural marriages.

Polygamy didn't disappear, but continued in isolated pockets of the nation, mostly in the West, under condemnation of the LDS Church (engaging in polygamy was, and still is, grounds for excommunication). Thus, the church's journey toward the American mainstream was tedious and often stigmatized by something that had been an official part of its culture for a relatively brief time.

Those were the roots of the young girl entering high school in Bountiful, Utah, and the roots of her parents and grandparents and great grandparents, roots that were enduring and tried by ordeal, and they collided with the world that was exploding beyond the Great Salt Lake valley.

Thera endeavored, without success, to understand what was going on in her daughter's head and in her heart, but the chasm between them seemed to widen with each passing year: a mother's aspirations on one precipice, a daughter's unfledged yearnings on the other. In the excitement of the sixties, Bountiful must have been as dreary to Trish as Promontory had been to her mother.

Her travels and exposure to the world, even through a military prism, had endowed Trish with an enthusiasm and worldliness that served well her academic and social lives. She participated in school bands, gymnastics teams, cheerleading and drama. The frequent moves were not a hindrance. Her classmates, after all, were in the same boat. Making new friends and adapting to new surroundings was second nature to them.

It wasn't until the Huish family settled in Bountiful, after a stint in Okinawa, that Trish began to feel out of place, began to feel a step or two behind her peers. Trends in popular music and fashion had, to some degree, bypassed her. While she had once been in command of her environment, she now felt shunned by the popular groups in school. She was not an oddball, just misaligned, just enough of an outsider to make those grand days of high school a time of discomfort.

She dropped out of school in her senior year and moved into an apartment with a girlfriend. Thera cajoled and pleaded for her to return to school, but Trish's stony gaze drew the curtain between them and she retreated into that private place inside herself. If there was an encouraging side to their rocky relationship, it was that Trish seemed to be willing to accept the responsibility that independence demanded. In the spring, she landed a job with the Mountain Bell Telephone Company and was, from all appearances, excited about it when she shared the news with her parents.

On the Monday that she was to have reported for work, the

Huishes received a telephone call from her supervisor. Trish was a no-show. Did they know where she was? Concerned that she may have been ill, Thera drove to her apartment and, in talking to her roommate, learned that what afflicted her daughter was worse than a stomachache; it was wanderlust. Over the weekend, without telling anyone, she had caught a ride with friends who were traveling to the West Coast.

Depending on one's point of view, California was either the center of hell or the golden incubator of the New Order. Places such as Berkeley, Watts and Haight-Ashbury were steady date-lines for the national press's diet of violence, protest and drugs, and Thera imagined that her daughter was skidding toward the clutch of Lucifer himself.

For two panicked weeks, she and Sterling hounded Trish's friends and tried to enlist the resources of the police, who had no interest in an adult woman who chose to move out of state. She had not been kidnapped or coerced into flight, so she was a "missing person" only to her parents. She was, after all, of legal majority and free to move about as she chose.

"Even if we find her," Sterling finally acknowledged, "we can't force her to come back."

Through clenched teeth, Thera uttered what would become a familiar vow over the next several years: "I am not going to lose my daughter."

At last, through bits and pieces of information gleaned from Trish's friends, the search led them to Venice, a beach town on the Pacific coast west of Los Angeles. As best they could determine, she was living in what sounded to them like a hippie commune, sharing a house with other young people who supported themselves by making clothing and crafts for sale on the beach.

They went back to the police, who were able to obtain a phone number for the house in Venice, but were unable to do much besides verify that Trish had not been kidnapped.

"I left of my own free will," she told the officer who telephoned her. "I'm here because this is where I want to be."

It was not where her mother wanted her to be. Thera could only imagine the life her daughter was living. Hippie communes had become commonplace and the images of them presented by the media were confounding. On one hand they were a collection of young men and women searching for spiritual meaning, independence and emancipation from the shackles of values they no longer accepted. On the other hand, they seemed to be places where autonomy was surrendered to the group, where individual identity seemed lost to the cause, where religious order seemed dictated by drug-crazed gurus. He had not yet come to public attention, but Charles Manson was loose on the land at that time and was forging his own cult of zombies who would one day kill upon his command.

Not knowing their daughter's exact address, Thera and Sterling thought it pointless to make a trip to Venice. And they had no reason to believe they could persuade her to return home with them if they did. All they had was a telephone number and motivation fed by a strong measure of panic.

Almost daily, Thera called the house in Venice. When she was told that her daughter was not there, she wondered if that was true or if Trish was merely avoiding her. When they spoke, Trish was aloof and taciturn, sometimes icy. Their conversations were brief: the mother pleading for her daughter's return and the daughter demurring with inimical finality.

After their talks, Thera would convey the results to her husband and often she would repeat an old affirmation: *I am not going to lose my daughter*. Trish was her blood, not his, and Sterling could offer little but encouragement to his wife. Though he had raised Trish as his own—he never formally adopted her or Val—he could be more objective about her nature. She was a complicated young woman, perhaps a match for her mother in a duel of obstinacy. The outcome of this tug-of-war for the soul of Trish Toland was far from certain.

As the weeks passed and the telephone discourse wore on, Thera began to detect a change in her daughter. She was less eager to cut short the conversations, less inclined to interrupt her mother's pleadings. Maybe, Thera began to hope, the hippie life had lost its allure, the novelty had worn off and dreariness had set it. At times, she sensed a longing in Trish's voice—homesickness?—that emboldened her to press harder. Careful not to appear demanding or domineering, she nudged her daughter gently. She coaxed and encouraged, and when she hung up, she prayed.

Summer settled gently over the State of Deseret and Bountiful was just that—clear and dry and filled with the renewal carried forth from a prodigal spring.

Elsewhere, the country was in turmoil. The previous summer, riots had broken out in Watts and the urban violence had stretched far into 1966. James Meredith was felled by birdshot marching across Mississippi, and Stokely Carmichael first spoke the immortal words that sent chills through middle-class white enclaves from coast to coast: "We . . . want . . . black . . . power." The Vietnam War was tearing apart both the country and the presidency of Lyndon Johnson, and college students were tearing apart their campuses. The whole damn county was under siege, but in Bountiful, it was turning into a promising season.

Early one evening, Thera spent an hour on the phone with her daughter, and for half that time, it was mostly a one-sided conversation. Trish was still aloof, but less defiantly so, and as they talked she revealed the first crack in her shell. Life among the flower children of Venice had long since lost its luster, she confided at last. She didn't know what she wanted but she didn't want this any more.

Thera hung up the phone, looked at Sterling and nearly shouted, "She's coming home."

Chapter Twelve

Because of Sterling's affiliation with Brigham Young University—he taught ROTC classes—Trish was able to enroll there in the fall despite her lack of a high school diploma. Along with the basic freshman courses, she studied accounting, a field that had appealed to her since high school.

Her relationship with her parents remained strained, for no reason they could decode, but most of the acrimony had vanished. For the time being, it was enough for Thera and Sterling that their daughter was away from the clutches of a culture they feared and loathed and was now on a course that made sense to them.

In their presence, Trish often stayed within herself, secluded behind her own curtain of privacy. She could be buoyant and outgoing, especially with her brothers, but her mood could change quickly, and it was rare that she revealed her deepest thoughts or feelings.

Thera tried to reassure herself that Trish just needed time, that as she matured her adolescent chemistry would find its balance, that her youthful compulsions—the wanderlust and adventurous itch—would recede.

Three months into the fall semester, Trish finally confided in her. As the Utah days shortened and the nights turned long and cold, she sat in the warmth of her parents' house, surrounded by familiar things, and let the curtain fall.

"I'm not happy here," she told her mother. "This is not what I want to do."

Not completely surprised by the revelation, Thera sat silently and let her daughter continue.

"School just doesn't interest me, Mom. Can you understand that?"

"I guess I can."

"I want to be on my own. I want to work and get on with my life. I'm just treading water here."

For a change, Trish was talking about her feelings, and Thera considered that tremendous progress. At least she didn't hitch a ride and slip away without warning as she had done before.

"Trish," Thera said. "You're not thinking of going back to that house in Venice."

"No, but I'd like to go back to California. I like it there, Mom. I guess I wasn't cut out to be a hippie, but I'm not happy here and I'm not happy in school."

Thera would not be able to change her daughter's mind, not for long anyway. If she tried, the curtain would go back up. Trish looked at her with eyes that seemed to plead for understanding, maybe even for encouragement. She would not ask her mother to help, but her face spoke for her. It was the pleading face of a child veiling the willful adult within.

If she were going to leave again, and there was little doubt about that, Thera would seize the opportunity to help define the terms. She would call her brother in San Francisco and arrange for Trish to stay with him and his family until she found a job and was able to live on her own.

Tony Crano had the dark, chiseled good looks of a soap opera heartthrob and Trish told anyone who would listen that she fell instantly in love with him. They were married just shy of her twenty-first birthday, only a few months after they met at a nightclub in San Francisco. He was a couple of years older than she and, in the fashion of the time, wore his sable hair well past collar length. His attire, though, was more mainstream than the counterculture uniform that prevailed in San Francisco.

The Huishes liked him well enough, even though they were convinced that he would never be a close part of the family. Like Trish, he was moody and standoffish, not necessarily secretive, just unwilling, or unable, to bond with his new in-laws.

No matter. If Trish was happy, that was enough for Thera. Communication between mother and daughter was still tenuous, but Thera was encouraged—and hugely relieved—by the turn Trish's life had taken in the two and a half years since she returned to California. She had assisted in that relocation with no small pang of anxiety.

Early in 1967, Haight-Ashbury had been glutted with flower children kneeling at the altars of the ragged gods Joplin and Hendrix and Garcia and Leary, and God only knew how many other prophets of decadence. The Haight, as the district was known, was awash in psychedelic chemicals, casual sex, interracial sex, homo sex and dropout philosophy—*I don't know. I don't care. It doesn't make any difference*—and the summer of love was riding the surf toward San Francisco. Everything about the place was anathema to middle America and it made Venice look like Ozzie Nelson's patio.

She had fully understood the risk of dispatching her daughter to those environs, and Thera could only pray that the presence of family would be a prevailing influence. Trish moved in with her uncle just after Christmas, and to everyone's relief, The Haight apparently held no attraction for her. She possessed the usual youthful zest for fun and socializing, but if it had a destructive edge, her family was oblivious to it.

What they saw was a young woman intent upon finding her niche, who landed an entry-level job in the bookkeeping department at Barclay's Bank, worked hard and learned the numbers craft well—well enough, in fact, that she eventually found a better job with a company that ran a large chain of ice cream parlors in northern California, and she quickly worked her way up to head bookkeeper. She moved into an apartment with a girlfriend and, by sharing expenses, practiced the lessons of frugality her mother had drilled into her.

Then she met Tony in 1969. The courtship was brief, too brief, in fact, for Trish to truly know the man she had wed. After a few months, the union began to unravel. Beneath Tony's handsome and charming exterior was a flaw that only revealed itself over time—an aversion to steady employment, an obsessive hankering for credit cards, particularly those that had been issued in his wife's name, and an eye for women to whom he was not married. While Trish struggled to hold the wolves at bay, her husband partied and philandered on her plastic.

As the months passed and the debts piled up, Trish took second jobs, usually as a waitress in restaurants or cocktail lounges, but she could not make money as fast as Tony could spend it. He left it to her to fend off the creditors, and he became increasingly abusive as the relationship deteriorated into almost daily confrontations.

After a year, Trish kicked him out of the house, moved back in with her old roommate and filed for bankruptcy. She did not, though, immediately file for divorce. Tony was out of her life, and while he had left her credit rating in ruins, she was in control again. Since she had no plans to remarry, she did not feel compelled to tidy up the legal loose ends until she had dealt with her debts and was back on her feet, emotionally as well as financially.

More than miles continued to separate the mother and daughter. They were not estranged in the true sense of the word, merely detached from one another. Because of that, Thera knew scant details of Trish's failed marriage, but she was neither surprised nor terribly disappointed by that outcome. During that year, they communicated mostly by telephone, cursory conversations in which Trish revealed little, but in which Thera sensed more than she heard.

Many times, she wanted to take her daughter into her arms and hug away the pain that Trish could not completely conceal, but she was unwilling to risk further alienation by intervening in Trish's life without an invitation, which was not forthcoming. Besides, she had other children to attend and her own financial future to think about. Val was grown and gone from home. Rick, Bob and Nick were teenagers, but old enough now that they required less of her time, so Thera began to assess her interests and abilities with an eye toward enhancing the family income. Sterling would soon retire from the Air Force, and while military pensions were adequate, they were hardly princely.

The daughter of Joseph Nicholas had never forgotten the lean years and had no yen to revisit them. She also realized that waiting tables or working behind a retail counter was not the route to financial security. She had limited education, limited work experience and limited capital to invest in a business. The most obvious option left was one that did not displease her.

She had most of the attributes that success in sales demanded. She was attractive, articulate, extroverted, amiable and as persistent as a forest fire. It didn't take an MBA to understand that selling on commission was tantamount to self-employment— the purest pursuit of Darwinian economics, survival and prosperity of the fittest wit—and she was aware that many great fortunes had been amassed in just that way. A good salesman could sit at the table with the barons of oil and real estate and manufacturing.

She signed on with the Figurette Bra Company and began pounding the sidewalks. To the women's liberationists, who were trying to knock down much larger corporate doors and glass ceilings, peddling custom-fitted bras door to door might not have seemed particularly glamorous, but after a few weeks, Thera Huish realized she had found her niche. That discovery came on an afternoon when she rang the doorbell of a woman endowed with brusque sales resistance.

"Hello," Thera said politely. "I wonder if I could talk to you about—"

The door slammed in her face. After pondering her next move for a moment, she went to the rear of the house and knocked on the back door. The woman appeared with a scowl that would stop a rhino in its tracks.

"Hi," Thera said with a broad smile. "I've got something I think will interest you, and I hope you're not as cantankerous as the woman who just answered the front door."

For an instant, the woman seemed poised to slam the door again, but something, maybe the audacity of this caller with the sample case, or maybe her cheerful insistence, cracked her defenses. She grinned, shook her head and pushed the door open wider. "I guess you'd better come in," she said.

Thera left twenty minutes later with an order for three Figurette custom-fitted bras.

Her career as a saleswoman filled her days and many of her evenings, but not the hole in her spirit, the place left vacant by her daughter. After her separation from Tony, Trish seemed to settle back down to her old routine, and Thera no longer worried that she would drift astray. She only worried that they would eventually drift irrevocably apart.

Trish simply seemed not to want or need her mother in her life. When she could slip away for a couple of days, Thera would fly to San Francisco, sometimes taking Nick with her. The visits were odd, almost maddening to her. Trish would pick her up at the airport and, after greetings that were stilted and perfunctory, they would drive in silence to Trish's apartment. For the duration, the younger woman would go about her routine of cleaning and cooking with minimal conversation.

Except when Nick accompanied her. The first time he visited his sister's house was in 1968, shortly before her marriage to Tony. He was nine years old and to him the West Coast was a place in a movie or a song or a newsreel. It was exotic and full of mystical notions and customs. In his young mind, his sister, simply because she was here, was a figure of hip sophistication, someone firmly in possession of herself and her era.

He entered her apartment that day and a song called "California Dreamin' " was playing on the stereo, and it completed his transport to Fantasy Island. Nobody would write a song called "Utah Dreamin'." California was a special place and had been since the time of the Spaniards, a land of dreams and plenty, a land of opportunities and second chances, of wealth and wickedness and everything else that strummed the strings of America's westward longing.

While that song resonated in his head and his imagination, Trish hugged him and kissed him on the cheek. She fussed over him and offered him soft drinks, and before the visit was over she gave him a pair of her black go-go boots, just like the ones he had seen on television. As a souvenir, they were both a token of his sister's affection and a trophy of sorts. The kid from Bountiful had been to the mountaintop and come down with the sacred talisman.

Thera was delighted when Trish showed such tenderness for her brothers, but she always wondered why it ended there, why that affinity and attachment were withheld from her parents. She and Sterling had been strict disciplinarians, to be sure, but so were most of the parents they knew. Trish was no longer a mutinous teenager, yet she seemed incapable of putting away childish things and coming to adult terms with her mother and father.

Try as she might to reopen the channels, Thera began to fear that her own efforts would never be enough, that some exterior catalyst would have to come into play. She never would have imagined—certainly never wished—that the bridge that would one day span the chasm between them would be made of the stone and steel of a jail cell.

Chapter Thirteen

Spring 1973

With the rack of suits standing against one wall and the floor covered with cardboard boxes—large, bulky cartons of the type in which Kleenex or Bounty paper towels are shipped to supermarkets—the place looked more like a wholesale shipping dock than a residential garage.

Dan Willoughby had brought him out here for a reason, Sterling Huish assumed, so he waited for an explanation.

"Look at this," he said, unfolding the top flaps on one of the boxes.

Sterling looked down at the contents: basketballs, soccer balls, volleyballs, balls of every sort. The significance of it eluded him.

"Where did all this stuff come from?" he asked.

"I have guys that owe me," Dan said with a whiff of swagger.

He looked toward the street and saw a young boy walking along the sidewalk. Reaching into the box, he pulled out a cheap rubber basketball.

"Hey, kid," he yelled, "you want a basketball?"

The boy stopped and eyed him suspiciously. His mama had warned him not to take candy from strangers. She didn't say anything about basketballs. He waited, like an audience anticipating the punch line.

"Here," Willoughby said, tossing the ball down the driveway. It bounced as if it were filled with helium, but the price was right. The kid caught it, said a cautious thank you and dribbled on his way.

Dan Willoughby must be the most popular man in the neighborhood, Sterling thought. If he felt a twinge of discomfort, it was because of the suspicion that what he had witnessed was a scenario played out for his benefit. Maybe his daughter's new boyfriend merely wanted to demonstrate his generosity. While he wasn't certain what it was, Sterling felt that Willoughby had revealed something more.

He was an ingratiating fellow, tall, handsome and as glib as a carnival barker. He always had a smile, an embrace, an amusing story to tell, and he went to great lengths to make Sterling and Thera feel at home when they came to visit. With Trish, he was affectionate, even doting at times. He was thirty-three, nine years older than Trish, but he seemed a far better match for her than Tony had been. From all appearances, he was a steady worker who paid his own way, and in fact was more than willing to help Trish through the financial hardship that followed her life with Tony.

The Huishes liked him almost immediately. That he had been reared in the Catholic Church and, in his early years, educated in Catholic schools was of no consequence. They wanted very much for their daughter to find her way back to her Mormon footing, but they did not view Dan Willoughby as an obstacle to that. Like Trish, he had drifted away from his church—he sometimes referred to himself as agnostic—but he had a solid religious grounding and therefore, they reasoned, was not likely to corrupt any roots that might still tether Trish her to her faith.

He was young enough to have ambition and goals and he was too old to be a hippie. It could be worse.

Dan Willoughby was a friend of Trish's roommate and that is how they met in 1972. It would have been hard for her not to fall in love with him. Older, more mature and more stable than most of the men she had dated, he was a hefty counterbalance to the tatters of her own life. He knew things and how to arrange things. Sure, he was college educated, but his savvy went beyond that. He was streetwise and seemed to know people who were willing, even eager, to do favors for him. Whatever the need, Willoughby seemed to have the fix.

And he courted her with style and passion. She sent frequent missives to her mother, brief notes that gushed with the delight of finding a man who sent flowers for no particular reason, who wrote love poems to her and who spared no expense in pleasing her. After dating for several months, they decided that they were in love and that they would live together while they tidied up the loose ends in Trish's life.

Willoughby rented a small house on a hillside behind the Cow Palace in the San Francisco suburb of Brisbane. He hired a lawyer to obtain Trish's divorce from Tony and dipped into his own pocket to settle old debts and remove some of the taint of her bankruptcy. For the first time since she left home at the age of eighteen, Trish was not wholly on her own. She had a partner and a protector, a man who exuded such confidence and intellect that the Huishes could find little grounds on which to object to the relationship. In fact, they put away most of their concerns about their daughter's welfare.

Trish seemed happier and more at ease than they had ever known her to be, but she inexplicably maintained her emotional distance from her parents. Their visits to California were infrequent, but Willoughby occasionally brought Trish to Utah to spend a few days with them. Those reunions were cordial, but, as before, the wall that Trish had built was impenetrable.

By comparison, her new companion was starkly and refreshingly extroverted, a profuse conversationalist who made them feel that they were important to him. But as they came to know Willoughby better, it occurred to Sterling and Thera that they actually knew very little about him. For all his loquacity, he revealed little about himself aside from the skeletal tidbits of biography he would mention, almost as asides, to complete a rudimentary sketch of himself.

He was born in Watseka, Illinois, on May 28, 1939, but moved to California at a young age when his father gave up a struggling jewelry business for the more secure life of a civil servant maintaining delicate military electronics equipment at McClellan Air Force Base near Sacramento. His mother had taught school for nearly twenty years before fleeing the classroom to work in a Sacramento department store. He had an older brother, about whom he spoke not at all. While he usually portrayed his childhood as ordinary—firm but loving parents who gave him a life of neither abundance nor want—Thera and Sterling sensed there were long and deep tensions in his family that he simply chose not to divulge.

What they knew of his adult years seemed innocuous and routine. He attended Sacramento Junior College, he told them, but dropped out after a year to enlist in the U.S. Army, which resulted in a stint in Germany where he watched the construction of the Berlin Wall. Back in civilian life, he returned to college, grew restless and dropped out again to travel around Europe with a couple of friends. Eventually, he said, he returned to California with a strong interest in foreign languages and earned a bachelor of arts degree in German (with a minor in Spanish) from Sacramento State College and later spent six months studying Spanish at the University of Saltillo in Mexico.

It was hard not to admire the young man for his intellectual curiosity and conspicuous ambition. He had studied bacteriology and chemistry and, after returning from Mexico, he said, he moved to Phoenix to study international business relations at the Thunderbird School of International Management. As best the Huishes could determine, he pursued all his varied interests at his own expense, as his parents were of modest means and his aging father was in poor health.

By almost every objective measure, he was exactly what Trish needed at this stage of her life. Even on a subjective scale, the debits were minor. Sometimes he seemed too good, too right, too lucid and accomplished, too eager to dabble at, but never fully complete, his self-portrait—all of which cloaked him in a Gatsbyesque veneer, a man trailing a silent and invisible wake that could only be sensed.

He was eager to do favors, lend money, fix problems, soothe wounds, right wrongs—but he never seemed to forget, or to hesitate in pointing out to others, the good deeds he had done. He often told of a college incident in which an Asian student was denied membership in a fraternity. In a show of indignation and moral courage, Willoughby took to the soapbox and shamed the frat boys into reconsidering.

Never articulated, but always implied, in his tales of selflessness was that he had earned someone's undying gratitude. *I've got people who owe me,* he had said in explaining the boxes of cheap toys in his garage. The burden of gratitude is backbreaking and Sterling often found himself wondering if Dan always let his beneficiaries off so easy, let them settle their accounts with a few trinkets. Why was it important to him, important enough that he would boast of it, to have people indebted to him?

A psychiatrist might ascribe that behavior to a compulsion to control others, but Sterling saw no evidence of that. More plausible, to him, was a simpler motivation: Dan just wanted to be liked.

At that, he was very successful.

Chapter Fourteen

With her daughter ensconced in a routine that resembled normalcy, Thera was able to concentrate more fully on her sales business. Form-fitting bras, she had found, were a product for which there was a hearty demand. The possibilities were limited only by the number of doors she could knock on in a day—but she always found time to knock on more doors than just about anyone else in the sales force.

As the seasons came and went, her hard work began to pay generous financial rewards and to attract the attention of her corporate bosses. She was not just a top-notch saleswoman, but an efficient organizer and tutor, sharing her experience and expertise with other salespeople, adept at broadening her territory and developing new markets.

By the summer of 1975, while Dan and Trish were making plans for a September wedding, Thera was getting feelers from the home office about a possible promotion, a major one that would require her to relocate. There was nothing binding her to Utah. Sterling had retired from the Air Force and was free to live wherever he chose. Their youngest son, Nick, had only a couple of years of high school left, then he would be off to college. For the right offer, she would soon be in a position to uproot and accept a new challenge.

After living with him for nearly three years, Trish felt that she knew enough about Dan to marry him, even though some of what she knew made a sham of the swell-guy face he always presented to her parents. He wasn't evil, but he was no Boy Scout.

Before they met, he had confided to her, he had a few run-ins with the law. All were unfortunate mix-ups, he assured her. He had been the victim of bad timing or was guilty mostly of trying to protect a friend.

Like that 1970s drug bust: He had stopped by a friend's house and the police arrived only minutes afterward. They found "dangerous narcotics" which belonged to the friend, not Dan, but he was booked anyway. Or that time he was traveling with friends to Auburn, California, and they were stopped by police. The suitcase containing the marijuana belonged to one of the other guys. And that rap for credit card fraud: He was only using plastic that belonged to a friend who owed him money. He did his six months without complaining. Shoplifting? Hell no. He was at a mall with a girlfriend and he suspected that *she* was stealing. He took possession of her shopping bag to prevent her from stuffing it with pilfered goods, and when a store detective stopped them, he took the rap and the four months in jail while his girlfriend was not so much as taken downtown.

He could be devastatingly persuasive. Trish may have been so taken by him that she was blinded to the recurring theme of his confessions: the fault was never his; circumstances always wrapped themselves around him. Besides, she was hardly pure. She and Dan often smoked marijuana together and occasionally had toyed with other recreational drugs. It was no big deal.

Practically everyone they knew did it. Dan's earlier misfortune had simply been to get caught.

Any reservations she might have had about marrying him bore more on his line of work than on his rap sheet. Before the credit card conviction, he had worked for Bank of America, using his education in international business relations to maneuver toward an overseas position with the company. After serving his time, he was hired by Nick Eden Enterprises, an advertising and public relations firm. He was away from home a lot, entertaining clients well into the night or disappearing for days at a time to promote entertainers in Reno and Las Vegas.

It was the kind of glamorous, charged and schmoozing life that Dan seemed to thrive on, but the routine grated on Trish. She felt that her soul mate had a life apart from her. While she toiled in the comparatively mundane and arcane fields of balance sheets and cash flow reports, he hobnobbed with high rollers and celebrities.

During his absences, Trish took to spending evenings now and then with friends she knew from work or the neighborhood. Movies, dinners or drinks in a Bay Area bar were the staples of their outings, but one such excursion, on March 18, 1975, resulted in an incident that may have been pivotal in her life and the lives of everyone close to her.

She spent the night in the Redwood City jail.

Bar hopping their way down Highway 101 that evening, she and a couple of friends reached Redwood City soggy with gin and tonic and in the mood to raise hell. The barroom got noisy, then rowdy and someone called the police. Trish and her friends were arrested for disorderly conduct.

Having no money for bail, she remained behind bars until Dan could pay her thirty-five-dollar fine the next day.

After that, they talked often about the direction their lives were taking, the drug and alcohol current that carried them along, the absence of anything permanent to lean against. They were not kids anymore. Trish was nearly twenty-seven and Dan thirty-six. Maybe it was time to rethink their life plan.

On Labor Day 1975, six months after her arrest, they slipped down the coast, past Monterey Bay, to Carmel-by-the-Sea and were married.

Change did not come easily or quickly. Despite her frequent urging that he look for another job, one that freed him from the obligations of travel and entertaining, Dan was reluctant to abandon the high life. It wasn't just the money—Trish's income was adequate to guarantee they would not descend into insolvency—but also the excitement, the people, the addictive tempo.

As the new year approached, though, he faced one of those milestones that often usher men into a period of self-assessment. A few weeks before Christmas, myelofibrosis claimed his father's life. They had not been close—the fact that Dan's older brother did not even attend the funeral spoke loudly of the degree of dysfunction in his family—but the premature loss of a parent is a sobering reflection of one's own mortality.

On January 2, 1976, Dan and Trish drove to Sacramento to bring back some personal belongings his father had left to him. Most prized of his inherited possessions was a twenty-year-old Ford pickup truck, which his father had kept in good running order while sorely neglecting the paint and body. With a little restoration, it could become a collector's gem.

Driving it back to Brisbane, Dan was arrested for drunk driving. A month later, he was arrested in San Mateo and charged with assault and battery after an altercation at a restaurant. An unhappy and unsettling pattern was starting to develop.

She wasn't sure why the time felt right, but it did. She had waited years for instinct or intuition to guide her and all that time, her daughter slid further and further away from her. Many times she had repeated the vow—*I am not going to lose my daughter*—but the repetition gave the words a hollow timbre. She simply didn't know how to close the gap.

Now, looking through the material that had arrived from the

Figurette Bra Company, she was gripped by an irresistible urge, an impulse as strong as a snakebite. She picked up the telephone and called Trish.

"Hi Mom." The cheer in her voice was uncharacteristic. "What's up?"

"I want you to do something," Thera said. "My company's having its convention in Colorado this year. I want you to go with me."

"Well . . . why?"

"I just want you to come away with me. It's only for a few days."

"Isn't Papa going with you?"

"He doesn't have to. I want you to go . . . just you and me."

"I guess . . . I guess I could do that," Trish stammered. It was evident that she was taken aback by the invitation. If she wondered about her mother's motives, she didn't inquire. "Sure. I'll go."

"I'll pay all your expenses," Thera said, barely able to contain her excitement.

"You don't have to do that."

"I want to. I'll make the arrangement and let you know the schedule."

They met at Stapleton International Airport in Denver, rented a car and set out on Interstate Highway 70 for the spectacular climb toward the Great Divide and Breckenridge just on the other side. The conifer slopes of the jagged peaks, thrust skyward eons ago by the cataclysmic buckling of the earth's crust, swallowed them up, and the drive at first was marked by long periods of clumsy silence. Their destination was a resort hotel high among the Rocky Mountain ski meccas, but neither woman knew exactly where this drive was taking them. Possibly nowhere.

The convention calendar was crowded, and as one of the rising stars of the company, Thera would be expected to participate fully. Trish could observe, or she could pass the time shopping or horseback riding or availing herself of other off-season offerings of the town. Surely they would have some time alone with each other, but Thera feared those moments would be strained or, at best, tolerable but nonproductive.

As they ascended the mountains, though, she became encouraged by her daughter's attitude—not exactly ebullient, but more affable than Thera had seen her in years. Conversation began to flow easier. Trish talked about her job and about Dan's career change—he had left public relations and was managing a restaurant—and the difference marriage had made in their relationship. She asked about her brothers—Val was the only one with whom she had stayed in close contact—and about her mother's work. She seemed thrilled by Thera's success and potential advancement.

By the time they reached the hotel, Thera was more than encouraged. She was certain that the next three days would be some kind of turning point. Gone was the adolescent petulance that had followed her daughter well into adulthood. In its place was a maturity that gave the mother cause to believe they could, at long last, speak to each other from the same ground.

They checked into the hotel and Thera signed in at the convention desk, gathering up the armload of materials that was dispensed to each participant. In their room, they quickly unpacked and settled into two large chairs beside an oval table near the window. They had a couple of hours to rest before dinner and the cocktail party and socializing that would precede the convention's official opening.

As the sun dimmed outside their window, the mountains seemed to rise up around them like dark ramparts holding the outside world at bay. They were alone in their own cocoon, surrounded by nothing and no one. They talked well past the dinner hour, ordered room service meals and skipped the evening party. The next morning, they had breakfast in the hotel restaurant, and Thera made a perfunctory but brief appearance at the convention opener, but the business of form-fitted bras was far from her focus. She felt an urgency to return to her daughter. They had warmed to each other the night before, and she was terrified that if left unattended the flames would go out again.

Returning to her room, she found Trish sitting by the window. They talked some more. Thera felt like a blind woman feeling her way along a wall. If she said the wrong thing, she might drive Trish back inside herself, but as the morning wore on, she realized this was the time for the full, unlimited, unmodified hang out. Trish was coming out of her shelter, talking about her life, her childhood pains and resentments, about her marriages and the void she had begun to feel from having abandoned her church. Mother and daughter hugged each other and cried and talked some more.

Downstairs, the convention proceeded without Figurette Bra's pre-eminent saleswoman. She was sequestered with her daughter on a mission worth more than a lifetime of commissions. Lunch was ordered in and the dialog evolved into a marathon. For three days, they rarely left the hotel room. Years of pent-up emotions found the form of words. The dam had broken and all the anger, resentment, anxiety, distrust, all the love, regret, pain, all the suspicion, secrecy, bitterness, all of it spilled out.

When it was over, both felt exhausted and exhilarated. The bond that had formed between them, Thera believed, was unlike any that had ever existed, even when Trish was a child. She had no doubt—almost none, anyway—that it had an iron permanence. When they parted after those days on the mountain, Thera hugged her daughter and told her she loved her.

"I love you too, Mom."

They spoke by phone often, and over the next few months they had a lot to share with each other. Trish was thrilled to learn that her mother had accepted the job of national sales manager for Figurette, a position that would require her and Sterling to relocate to Phoenix. Thera was ecstatic that after returning to California from the Rockies, Trish had contacted the Mormon bishop of her ward and was renewing her ties to the church.

Even Dan was taking an interest in her religion. After leaving the public relations rat race for the restaurant business, he was home every night and their lives were beginning to resemble suburban normalcy.

One night, she even confided to her mother that California had lost some of its charm and she was not averse to leaving.

"I'd like to be closer to you and Papa," she said.

Chapter Fifteen

Like Utah, Arizona was raw and rugged, its deserts and mountains as immense as the sky and nearly as untouchable. In the canyons and valleys, on the peaks and plateaus and along the rivers and flatlands, ancient Indian cultures had risen for two millennia or more and then vanished without explanation. More modern tribes would inherit the turf and, later, European settlers would voraciously exploit it, but none could quite subdue it.

At the end of the Mexican–American War in 1848, Arizona became United States territory, and the nation was washing westward in a great tide. Frontiers are always settled by misfits and renegades and outcasts, and Arizona's was no exception. Like most of the West, its territorial history of land grabbers, con men, gunfighters, loners and hungry profiteers—the human residue that could not or would not coexist with polite society back East—imprinted the state with a birthmark that is still visible today.

Arizona meant freedom and opportunity, but freedom frequently was interpreted as leave to define the law as merely a suggestion, and opportunity did not always come affixed to an unfailing ethical compass. Scoundrels would populate the state's lore—none more grandly than James Addison Reavis, a master forger who spent years after the Civil War creating a fraud of epic dimensions.

Under the terms of the 1848 Treaty of Guadalupe Hidalgo, which was signed at the end of the Mexican–American War and ceded Arizona to the United States, the government was required to honor all legitimate claims by the Spanish and Mexican citizens who had owned the land under colonial rule. Altering and falsifying centuries-old Mexican and Spanish land documents, Reavis created generations of a fictitious family and made it the *rightful* owner of ten million acres of Spanish land grants—an area that included Phoenix. Naturally, the land passed to Reavis's fictitious family and then to Reavis himself, and before his racket was exposed in 1890, he milked it for a large fortune by charging rent and taxes to the individuals and corporations that occupied it.

Other scam artists, though hardly as clever and audacious, would follow Reavis in sufficient numbers that by the 1980s it stunned no one when a Phoenix savings and loan owner named Charles Keating became the poster boy for that decade's massive S&L fraud scandals. The swindlers were abetted by the cultural bedrock of the frontier, a fierce independence that disdained governmental authority and glorified individual initiative, even when it taxied along the aprons of legality.

That same mind-set spawned a political order that was hard at its conservative core but spongy at the ethical edges. As the twentieth century wound to a close, Arizona governors routinely left office under indictment, and lesser scandals bubbled up through the bureaucracy like mineral springs.

More legitimate pursuits, of course, left an equally pronounced imprint on the sensibilities of the state. Rich deposits of gold, silver and copper were the stuff of feverish dreams, so much so that Mark Twain once quipped that all that was required to create an instant town in Arizona was "a rumor and a hole in the ground."

Prospectors found, however, that the land did not surrender its treasures without a struggle. Boomtowns died as quickly as they were born. Fortunes came and went, but hope was a powerful and omnipotent narcotic. To this day, ranges such as the Superstition Mountains east of Phoenix breathe tempting legends of lost mines, fabulous wealth discovered and then misplaced by some drunken Dutchman or solar-deranged desert rat.

Those legends dangle like a hypnotist's pendant to more than a few who have heard them, and modern immigrants to the state often exhibit signs of having been singed by the same flame as their territorial predecessors, incited by the same fantasy, propelled by the same lust, seduced by the same promise: dig and ye shall find.

When Sterling and Thera Huish arrived in 1978, Arizona was in the frenzy of the Sun Belt population explosion. The suburbs of Phoenix were pushing out into the desert at full throttle. Wide boulevards and walled communities and golf courses proliferated on tracts where caravans of camels had carted cargo a century ago. By comparison, Utah had been sedate, and they found themselves invigorated by the boisterous bazaar they had landed in. The towering palms and golden sunlight suggested an island leisure, but that was a thin veneer. The place fairly hissed with an electric energy. The dreamy-eyed, spirit-starved New Age ruminators were an acute minority; everyone else was in a hurry.

Now in her early forties, Thera felt a quickness in her own pulse, an eagerness to succeed in her new position and explore the limits of business. She and Sterling bought a house in Mesa, a Phoenix suburb that had been settled by Mormons and had retained much of that religious influence, including a temple that served several wards.

Business was good, so good in fact that Thera was able to exercise some of the authority that came with the increased responsibility of being an executive. She might be able to finesse the reunion with her daughter she had thought about for years.

Trish talked more and more of leaving California and being near her parents. Dan had left the restaurant he managed and was doing well in his new sales job at a company called Cutter Air Freight. It was a crowded and highly competitive business—companies such as Cutter functioned as the outsourced shipping department of industries with high volumes of products that had to be distributed directly to numerous customers. Since they compete on service more than price (the airlines set the same rates for everybody), they live and die by the talent of their sales force. Dan, it turned out, was one hell of a salesman—indefatigable, ingratiating and as smooth as motor oil. His track record at Cutter was impressive enough, Trish told her mother, that he could work just about anywhere. Every major city had a yellow page full of shipping contractors.

For her part, Trish felt limited in her job and more than a little bored by it.

"Why don't you come here and work with me?" Thera asked.

Dan and Trish had barely settled into their new home in Mesa when Thera got the bad news: Figurette Bra was purchased by another company, and in the restructuring, she was deemed superfluous. Downsized.

While disappointing, it was not a major crisis. With her savings and Sterling's military retirement income, she had breathing room to find another business.

Trish and Dan certainly faced no financial hardship. He had found a job with C.F. Air Freight in Phoenix and quickly established himself as the company's top salesman. His income was more than adequate for the two of them. After a year and a half, he left that company for a higher paying job at Burlington Air Freight and was becoming well-known in the industry.

Financially, they were secure enough that they began trying to have a child, and Dan offered to help provide the financing if she and her mother found another business in which to invest.

After their years of near estrangement, the mother and daughter grew closer than Thera had ever dreamed possible. With Sterling and Dan's help, they plunged into a couple of business ventures that were successful, but not spectacularly so. For a time, they ran a job placement service and then formed a company they called Safe In America that conducted crime prevention classes. At the end of each presentation, they sold tear gas canisters to the attendees.

Even when business lagged, Trish was endlessly effusive and optimistic. She had ceased retreating to her private inner space, and along with being her mother's business partner, she was also her best friend. They spent many hours together and their personalities seemed to converge and meld into one. They bought their clothes from the same dress shops, were coiffed at the same salon, had a taste for the same music and drama. Nick would often remark to his mother that they had become like identical twins; no, he would correct himself, like clones.

If there was a forlorn shade to this new life in Arizona it was that Trish had been unable to conceive a child. She was frustrated by the failed efforts, but Dan seemed especially eager—almost frantically driven—to start a family. He was good with children, enjoyed talking to them on their own level and valued their respect and affection.

At his urging, they applied to the state Department of Economic Security in January 1980 to be certified as adoptive parents, a procedure that requires a lengthy and detailed background investigation. Friends, neighbors and coworkers are routinely interviewed. Financial ability to provide for a child is established. Court records are examined for criminal histories. The task can take months.

Brenda Holmes drew the assignment and set about gathering

the most fundamental data. At first blush, the couple appeared
ideal. Their income was sufficient. They were becoming deeply
involved in their church and were well-regarded in the community. Most of the initial information was provided by Dan and
Trish, but as the caseworker peeled back the layers and looked
deeper into their lives, she began to have reservations.

Trish told her about the 1975 arrest in Redwood City, but
it did not show up on the FBI report she requested. Dan was
vague about some periods of his life and appeared to have been
less than candid about his employment record. He had left C.F.
Air Freight in 1979, he told her, because a headhunter had
recruited him for a better job at Burlington Air Freight. In truth,
he had been fired.

Sam Bowser thought the name fit perfectly. Dan Willoughby
had the smoothness and flair that caused him to be known as
the James Bond of the air freight industry. He lived on the
edge of something those around him could not perceive and
he seemed to view the world as his backyard. He was a smart
dresser, physically fit, well-groomed and supremely confident.
There was no customer he couldn't get, no crack he couldn't
patch.

When Bowser went to work for him at C.F. Air Freight,
Willoughby took him under his wing, taught him the business
with a brashness that left an enduring impression. He was at
work by five each morning and spent his days on the phone to
customers or pounding the sidewalks looking for new ones.
Bowser liked him and admired him.

But before Willoughby's year and a half stint with C.F. Air
was over, Bowser began to discern his dark side, a deviousness
that went beyond competitive necessity, a manipulativeness
that was not justified by the ends it achieved. If a customer
called complaining about overdue freight, Dan had a quick
excuse. The driver was involved in an accident, he would say,

or he would fabricate some equally audacious excuse. Once, he told a customer the plane carrying his goods had crashed.

Still, he brought in the business. He was named salesman of the year, an accolade that came with a large bonus and company-paid trip to Hawaii. Before he could claim the prize, however, his superiors learned at least one of the secrets of his success. He was a natural salesman, to be sure, and he worked overtime to keep his customers satisfied. But he had a problem with honesty. To recruit new accounts, he had been forging routing slips to take business away from his competitors.

It was not a complex scheme, but it was one that could not be concealed for long. It worked like this: Company A ships gizmos to Company B, which pays for the freight and, therefore, designates the carrier. After forging the name of Company B's traffic manager to a routing slip authorizing C.F. Air to be the new carrier, he would take the document to Company A's traffic manager and say, "We received this in the mail. They want us to handle their freight." Company A would switch to C.F. Air and, as long as the service was good and the price didn't increase, Company B wasn't likely to complain—at least not immediately. There are dozens of small air freight companies. The competition is intense, if not cutthroat. Some companies don't survive and new ones spring up to take their place. Who had the time to check every little detail?

Practiced too often, though, a scheme such as Willoughby's was bound to be exposed—either by a competitor or even a jealous fellow employee, someone not raking in the fat commissions and bonuses.

When Willoughby was caught, his bosses informed him they were taking back the salesman of the year award and canceling his trip to Hawaii. His response was classic late twentieth-century American: he threatened to sue. Moreover, the threat spoke to a slice of Willoughby's dark side, that fragment that spun noble rationales for all of Dan Willoughby's lapses and transgressions. He had only acted in the best interest of the company, he believed.

Negotiations ensued and a compromise was reached. He could keep the Hawaii trip and resign from the company when he returned.

Not just James Bond, Bowser thought, but J.R. Ewing to boot. He regretted the departure of his boss and mentor, but something told him Dan Willoughby would land on his feet and the air freight industry would hear more of him.

There were other bits and pieces of information Brenda Holmes could not substantiate or reconcile, inconsistencies that led her to feel that the Willoughbys might not, at that time, measure up to the standards the state set for adoptive parents. In March 1980, her investigation far from complete, she learned that Trish was pregnant. It was an opportunity to table the adoption process.

Dan and Trish had acknowledged that during the first five years of their relationship they had indulged in recreational drugs. That ceased, they assured her, when Trish reunited with her church and Dan followed. Since that time, they vowed, they had even adhered to the Mormon restrictions against alcohol. Holmes knew a little of their brushes with the law, but not enough. Though they seemed happy, well-adjusted and firmly anchored, she could not be sure. She moved to terminate the application.

Her report suggested relief that the process would go no further:

> Interviews with the Willoughbys left many, many questions unanswered and some level of mistrust about portions of the information provided. After conferring with my supervisor, Gladys Warren, it was decided that we would request that the family withdraw. We felt that they needed time with the new baby ... and that they may change their minds about wanting to adopt once they have a child of their own. We also recommended that they

allow for time to go by from the dealings and problems of
the past. The Willoughbys agreed ... if we would hold
all the information and documents gathered in their file
in case they decided to reapply for adoption at a later
time.

Because adoption service records, particularly background
investigations, are highly confidential, Holmes's note and mis-
trusts were consigned to a file cabinet, tucked away for future
reference but nonexistent to anyone outside the agency. Perhaps
Trish knew all there was to know about Dan, but her parents
and her brothers knew none of it. Her neighbors and fellow
church members knew only what they saw, and in the minds
of many of them, Dan Willoughby bore no blemishes.

Chapter Sixteen

The children were always excited when Dan Willoughby stopped by. As often as not, he brought toys or candy, but to their mother his messages were his greatest gifts. If her children were sad or apprehensive or lethargic, Dan always knew exactly what to say to cheer them up or motivate them or to calm their inner storms.

He was psychologist, priest, Santa Claus, surrogate father and fix-it guy all in one wise and self-assured bundle. Among his admirers, and there were many in Gilbert, Judy Richfield stood at the top of the list.

Her marriage was in tatters when she first met the Willoughbys, just after they moved from Mesa into a large, new house a few blocks from the Houston Ward LDS Church, which she attended. To her, and to everyone else in the church, the Willoughbys were irreproachable, wholly devoted to each other and to their daughter, Thera, who was about to turn four. And they were devoted to the church.

Dan's involvement in the work of the church accelerated rapidly after the move to Gilbert, and in a short time, he was being called upon for all manner of tasks, which he tackled with tireless gusto. He taught Sunday school, supervised Boy Scout troups, performed baptisms and blessings, served as executive assistant to the bishop. If the church needed anything—tables and chairs for a banquet, athletic equipment for a youth team, anything—he was the first to volunteer to handle it. But he was at his best in his role in the priesthood, a male cadre designated to see to the needs of other church members. In that capacity, he became a home teacher, something like a caseworker, to whom specific families with needs were assigned.

The needs varied. Some families had relationship problems or money shortages, and others had psychological and spiritual snags that weighed upon them. Judy Richfield's family seemed to have all of them. When her marriage ended, the full responsibility for her six children fell to her. Dan Willoughby was more than a home teacher. He became her guardian and protector and sometimes, she felt, her savior.

"You're a better father to my kids than I am a mother," she often told him.

She was amazed that he would spend so much time with them, dropping by after school to see how their day went, to listen to their endless stories of classroom adversity or playground folly. He always heard them out, as though he were genuinely interested in the minutiae their lives. He bought shoes and clothing for them, and if one of them had a worn bicycle, it would be replaced when the next birthday rolled around.

Dan seemed to have not only the financial means to provide for her family's needs, but the connections. If her washing machine broke down or a screen door frayed, Dan would dispatch a handyman to make the repairs. If her car sputtered, he got it fixed. She never knew how those things were being done, because Dan didn't want her to know.

"Dan, where is the money coming from for all this?" she had asked him in the beginning.

"Don't you worry about it," he said.

"But . . . let me help pay for it."

"It's all taken care of," he said, seeming offended that she was uncomfortable with his altruism.

She stopped asking and accepted his favors as the gestures of someone who truly cared about others. She had never asked for anything; he was observant enough to know her family's needs with no cue from her.

When her house began to show the wear that six children can inflict, he assembled his priesthood group.

"I want to remodel, or redecorate, the Richfields' home," he told them. "It needs some painting and fixing up."

It was not a large home, but the cost would not be insignificant.

"How much money will this take?" he was asked by one of the members.

"I'll supply paint but I need you to supply the manpower," he said, thereby removing the cost factor from their decision.

On those terms, they could hardly refuse.

Willoughby coordinated the project and made sure all the materials—paint, brushes, rollers, lumber, nails, hardware— were available and the work was completed in a couple of weeks.

Judy Richfield was certain that Dan had paid the bill. But she never asked.

Paul Delon and Dan Willoughby were friends from the moment they met. They were next-door neighbors and both spent a lot of time outside with their children, playing ball in the street or swimming in the Willoughbys' pool or slipping away in Dan's car for ice cream cones.

Delon was a bricklayer by trade, and by the mid-1980s, the construction frenzy that had swept the Valley of the Sun had started to cool. Beneath the surface of what had been a golden economy, rust spots were starting to appear—slower growth, weakened real estate prices and careless or overly optimistic lending institutions holding mammoth uncollectible notes.

Willoughby knew his neighbor was in a bind. One evening, he stepped next door with a $500 check.

"Don't worry about paying it back," he said.

"Dan, I don't know when things will pick up," Delon said.

"Whenever you get it, you pay it. I'm doing fine," Willoughby said.

It took a few months, but Delon repaid the loan. It turned out the money had provided only a short reprieve.

"What's the matter?" Willoughby asked, ambling over to his neighbor's yard. "You look down in the dumps."

"Yeah ... well ... work's slow again, Dan. I'm afraid I'm going to lose my house."

"What would it take?" Willoughby asked.

Given the culture of the LDS Church and the way members counseled and assisted each other, it did not seem an inappropriate question. Personal travails were commonly shared and, if possible, remedies arrived at within the church community.

"I don't know ... I'm probably two or three payments behind."

Their children showed up, pestering them to play with them, so the subject was dropped.

That evening, Delon answered the knock at his door and found Dan Willoughby.

"Come in, Dan," he said.

Instead of entering, Willoughby handed him a small piece of paper. "Hope this will help," he said. It was a check for $2,000.

Delon hesitated. *This guy doesn't know me THAT well,* he thought. *How does he know I'm not lying about my financial bind or about losing my house?*

"Dan ... this is a lot ..."

"When you get the money and you feel comfortable giving it back, fine," his friend said.

* * *

Duke Boggs not only attended church with the Willoughbys, but lived across the street from them. Like nearly everyone in the neighborhood, he knew of Dan's generosity—not just toward church members but, occasionally, casual acquaintances or even complete strangers—and was himself the beneficiary of his neighbor's largesse.

He too was in the masonry business and was suffering through the economic slowdown. His debts were not huge, but he couldn't pay them and his creditors were impatient. Bankruptcy appeared to be the only way to buy time to get back on his feet. Although bankruptcies were rampant in the 1980s, especially after the collapse of oil and real estate markets, it was a painful step and not one that Boggs contemplated lightly.

Dan Willoughby's helping hand was never far away. When Boggs's truck broke down, Willoughby saw that it was repaired. He helped out by hiring Boggs to do masonry work on his house and, when it was completed, was complimentary of his craftsmanship. They talked about the business slowdown Boggs was experiencing and his impatient creditors.

"How much would it take to make your business solvent?" Dan asked him.

"About $5,000," Boggs sighed, as though he were speaking of all the money in the world.

Willoughby said nothing more about it until a few days later, when he appeared at Boggs's door with a cashier's check for that amount, a loan to hold the wolves at bay until business picked up again.

As was his practice, Willoughby asked for nothing in return, not even a promissory note. "You can pay it back when you can," he said.

While $5,000 was not a fortune, it was no small gesture and Boggs was overwhelmed. Dan brushed aside his expressions of gratitude. "You'd do the same for me," he said.

Work was still hard to come by, but over the next six weeks, Boggs settled up overdue accounts and slept a little sounder. Then Willoughby showed up again.

"I hate to ask this, Duke," he said, "but that loan . . . I kind of need the money back."

Floored by the request, Boggs explained that he had spent most of the money on his business and wasn't sure when he could scrape that amount together. Was Dan having a problem?

"Not really," Willoughby said, "but I need it to pay my tithes."

For the first time in the years they had known each other, Boggs had an uneasy feeling about his neighbor. He knew that Willoughby had loaned money to others, and he had never known him to press for repayment. Why would he give someone such a large sum and ask for it back so soon? Maybe his own business was suffering, Boggs thought, but there were no outward clues to that. Recently, Dan had even talked about buying a new Jaguar.

Boggs didn't buy the tithing story, but he was in no position to equivocate. He owed the man money.

"I'll see what I can do, Dan," he said. "I mean, I can't come up with it overnight."

Again, Willoughby apologized for asking for such quick repayment. He was tense and avoided eye contact.

"I'll do the best I can," Boggs assured him.

He nodded, turned and walked back across the street. Boggs watched his silhouette, as silent as fog, glide through the glow of a street lamp and disappear around the corner of the garage. What disturbed him most was not the money, but Dan Willoughby, his friend and fellow Mormon. Something was amiss, he felt, but he had no idea what it could be.

Chapter Seventeen

By the time little Thera was two years old, Dan and Trish were trying to have another child, but, as before, she was unable to conceive. In February 1984, they renewed their application to become adoptive parents and were given temporary custody of an infant boy, whom they planned to name Hayden (Dan's middle name) Sterling Willoughby.

After completing the paperwork and being fingerprinted at the Maricopa County Juvenile Court Center, they could only wait while the lengthy process began anew. It would take more than three months for records of the Federal Bureau of Investigation to be searched.

In the meantime, Brent Darmer, their caseworker, began his work by reviewing the investigative file Brenda Holmes had compiled several years earlier. Though incomplete, it was valuable groundwork and it pointed to issues he would have to probe more thoroughly. Blemishes on an applicant's record do not necessarily mean automatic disqualification, but he would have to be certain that any untoward conduct or attitudes were firmly in the past.

Next, he undertook a series of interviews with the Willoughbys to develop a more complete picture of their backgrounds.
His impressions largely were positive. They were, in every
sense, a charming and congenial couple. Both longed for a
larger family and finances were no obstacle. As in his previous
job, Dan Willoughby had made his mark at Burlington Air
Freight, bringing in clients by the truckload and being paid
accordingly. He was earning $4,300 a month, plus bonuses of
as much as $70,000 a year. Both portrayed childhoods that
were normal and happy, despite strict and demanding parents.
Trish was candid about the rebellious period in her life when
she was drawn to the counterculture and all that implied, her
failed first marriage and her return to the Mormon fold. Dan
discussed his poor relationship with his brother and his own
penchant for childhood mischief—and the black paddle wielded
by his father on such occasions—but he appeared to have few
scars to bear or skeletons to conceal.

Except . . .

"The period of 1970 through 1976 appears to be somewhat
sketchy," Darmer recorded in his notes, "and involves various
jobs where he became more and more associated with 'nefarious
people' in order to make successful deals. During the majority
of this time, he was working for Nick Eden Enterprises, which
was a Madison Avenue type advertising and public relations
company and allegedly a subdivision of G. Walter Thompson.
Through this, he wined and dined clients and promoted entertainers in Reno and Las Vegas. Dan does not appear to be
proud of this period of his life and portrays a peripheral association with organized crime. In the later part of 1977, Dan made
a decision to change his lifestyle and disassociate himself from
the questionable people and activities that he had been involved
in."

On May 15, 1984, the results of the FBI's research of Willoughby's fingerprint file were returned to the juvenile court

center and passed along to Darmer at the adoption services office. He didn't like what he saw.

> *12-13-62 FP, Dir of Fed Police Innsbruck, Austria. Dan Willoughby, suspicion of theft, four months imprisonment, probation until 2-1-66.*

> *7-11-69, SO, Redwood City, CA. Dan Hayden Willoughby 62664, auto theft, RSP, forgery, conspiracy.*

> *7-10-69, PD Daly City, CA. Dan Hayden Willoughby 12768, 496 PC 484 F2 possession of stolen property and credit card fraud, three years eight months, CO Jail, restitution, jail stayed to 2-20-70.*

> *8-6-69, SO San Rafael, CA. Dan Hayden Willoughby 36945, 484f.2 PC theft, imposition of sentence suspended, supervised probation for two years, 60 days Marin Co Jail concurrent with his confinement in San Mateo Co make restitution in amount of $268.12 to Emporium San Rafael.*

> *10-7-70 SO Sacramento, CA. Dan Hayden Willoughby 124465, possession of dangerous drugs, dismissed.*

> *5-19-71 PD Palo Alto, CA. Dan Hayden Willoughby 33876/SCC 350363, shoplifting, possession of stolen credit cards, four months couny jail.*

> *12-20-71, SO Auburn, CA. Dan Hayden Willoughby 20784, 11910 H&S possession of dangerous drugs, dismissed.*

> *8-23-72, Redwood City, CA. Dan Hayden Willoughby 62664 SID 1 225, forging credit cards, illegal possession*

*of credit cards, one year prob and serve 70 days county
jail.*

*11-2-72, SO Marysville, CA. Dan Hayden Willoughby
A45837, kidnapping, dismissed.*

*3-13-76, PD San Mateo, CA. Dan Hayden Willoughby
62310, 240-242 PC Citizens arrest assault and battery,
dismissed.*

*1-2-76, SO Sacramento, CA. Dan Hayden Willoughby
124465, misdemeanor drunk driving on highway,
acquitted.*

Trish's arrest at the Redwood City bar also turned up on her
FBI report and it, along with the information on her husband,
put a particular burden on the caseworker. Rap sheets have
been known to be inaccurate or incomplete and, in the case of
old offenses, the original police reports may not be available
to flesh out the details. Except for the assault and kidnapping
charges, both of which had been dismissed, the FBI material
did not suggest that Willoughby had a violent history or was
a major league criminal. Booze, drugs and small-time thievery
seemed to be his style, and even those offenses had occurred
a long time ago—the last was nearly a decade old.

Darmer wanted to hear Willoughby's explanation of those
incidents before deciding whether that behavior was truly
behind him. Another home interview was scheduled for early
June and Willoughby was fully aware of what the discussion
would be about.

He was as engaging as always, but there was in his demeanor
a lump of anxiety barely concealed by the thin facade of poise.
He leaned forward in his chair while Darmer fished the rap
sheet from his briefcase.

"This is what came back from the FBI," Darmer said, handing him a copy of the document.

Willoughby nodded his head in quick, nervous jerks. "Yeah ... you see ..."

"Let's go through this from the beginning," Darmer said. "Some of these could be serious. Tell me about the 1962 theft in Innsbruck."

"That was unfortunate," Willoughby said. "See, after I got out of the Army, I went back to Europe with some friends. Remember, I told you earlier we worked our way over on a French cruise ship and bought this VW bus ... just knocked about every county in western Europe, you know, working as ski instructors or on fishing boats. Well, in Innsbruck we ran into this guy on the street who wanted to sell some skis, so we bought them and later another guy saw us with them and said they had been stolen from him. So we were arrested. They held us in jail for four months. Then the guy who sold them to us was found and he admitted he had stolen them. So, we were found not guilty."

Darmer interrupted. "This says you were placed on probation until February 1966."

"Uh-huh. See, they deported us and said we couldn't come back to Austria until 1966."

Being unfamiliar with foreign courts and legal procedures, Darmer accepted the explanation—for the time. But another inconsistency lay buried in his notes. Earlier, Willoughby had told him he was discharged from the Army in 1964 and returned to Europe with friends a year or so later. In actuality, he was a soldier when the ski theft occurred, not a student on hiatus from his studies. Having not yet cataloged all of his notes, Darmer was not immediately aware of the discrepancy. Military records might have told him more.

"Okay, let's move on," he said.

For half an hour, they went through the list and Willoughby had a convincing defense for each.

Auto theft, forgery, possession of stolen property and credit card fraud? The plastic belonged to a friend who owed him money, as did the car he was driving. Possession of dangerous drugs? He just showed up at a friend's house at the wrong time, a time when the friend was about to be busted. Shoplifting? His girlfriend did it and left him holding the bag. Kidnapping? Look, a friend was running away with another man's wife and stopped to spend the night with him. The angry husband planted marijuana in his apartment and accused him of kidnapping his wife and, well, the whole thing got out of hand but the pissed off husband didn't show up for the pretrial hearing so the charges were dropped. Assault and battery? Nah. One night at the restaurant a belligerent customer had to be tossed out and punched out.

Because his explanations seemed reasonable and the offenses were in the distant past, they did not necessarily disqualify him from being an adoptive parent. All of this raised one important question: Knowing that the information would surface in an FBI records check, why had Willoughby not voluntarily disclosed it sooner?

"I thought those records might have been expunged," he told Darmer. "I've had a lawyer working on that for more than a year. I was hoping to erase that period of my life."

Darmer carefully studied the man leaning toward him. He was now forty-five years old, rushing toward middle age, and the years hung over him like the Sword of Damocles, the thread fraying as the clock ticked faster. He wanted a larger family but his wife could not conceive. Should he be penalized for youthful indiscretions, some of which were no worse than what thousands of young people experienced in the sixties and seventies?

"I'm not proud of a lot of things I did," Willoughby continued, pressing his case with a nervous zeal. "You see, a lot of things made me stop and take a look at where I was headed."

"What things?" Darmer asked.

"Mostly Trish, and her reinvolvement with the church. I liked the changes that I saw in her and I didn't like what I saw in myself. I began to see my faults in a new light. So, I started breaking off contact with people I'd been associating with. I changed jobs and started going to church with Trish. I found acceptance there . . . you know . . . and it sort of brought out my old beliefs and values.''

As he spoke, he seemed to sense that Darmer, who occasionally made notations in his notebook, was sympathetic. In fact, he was. Willoughby could have stopped there, but instead was compelled to go further.

''I can tell you more,'' he said, ''but it would have to be in strictest confidence.''

''Everything I learn is kept in strictest confidence,'' Darmer assured him.

''Well, after I joined the church I became friends with a church member who was with the FBI. I talked to him a little about my past and he was a great help to me. At that time, I guess I wanted to make up for a lot of things, do something to atone for the bad things I had done. So I went down to the Brisbane Police Department and met with the head of detectives. I knew him on a personal basis and he knew about some of the people I used to associate with . . . you know . . . I told you about some of the people I met when I was promoting entertainers.''

''I remember.''

''I told this detective that if I could be of any help to him, I would. He asked me if I knew a mob guy named Jimmy Fratianno. He's the one they called Jimmy the Weasel. I told him I had done some socializing with Jimmy. He asked me if I would cooperate with the FBI in San Francisco. They were trying to build a case against Jimmy. I agreed to do it.''

Now the story was spinning into left field and Darmer hurtling along behind it. Still he took detailed notes as Willoughby, no longer edgy in discussing his past, let the tale unwind.

''I spent . . . I guess it was about nine months looking up the guys in Fratianno's crowd and getting to know them and getting to know Jimmy again. They kind of took me into their group . . . I even got a job as chauffeur for Fratianno. I had access to everything—his home, his office, his personal phone

book. I installed some listening devices where the FBI wanted
them. Every once in a while, I would meet with someone from
the Organized Crime Task Force and pass the info along to
them.

"So one day I happened to be at Fratianno's office and
heard him put out a contract on two Teamsters Union guys in
Cleveland. I taped the conversation. Well, the two guys were
killed and the hit man was caught, and to save himself, he
fingered Fratianno. With his testimony and my tape, there was
a pretty good case against Fratianno and he was arrested a
couple of weeks later. I got out of the organization and moved
to Arizona not long after that."

Darmer didn't know what to make of the yarn. In the murky
world of the Mafia, anything was possible and *something* had
turned Jimmy the Weasel back in 1977. More than likely,
though, it was fear of the mob more than fear of the feds that
made him one of the celebrated informants of his time.

Fratianno had an erratic career in organized crime. He was
born into poverty in Cleveland in 1913, grew up hustling on
the streets, and was doing time for armed robbery in his early
twenties. By the end of World War II, he had drifted to Los
Angeles, which was not prime mob territory, but a pretty good
place to hustle. There, he hooked up with Johnny Roselli, an
Al Capone lieutenant who had been sent west to try to muscle in
on the L.A. gambling operations controlled by Mickey Cohen.

Over the years, the L.A. gang became known as the Mickey
Mouse Mafia because it was a weak and often bumbling country
cousin to the powerful crime families of New York and Chicago
and Kansas City. In fact, it was the only major crime family
that did not stake a claim to the casino lode when modern Las
Vegas was born in the late 1940s. No depth, no resources,
Fratianno once said of the L.A. family, adding, "They didn't
have nobody to kill people."

Jimmy the Weasel stepped up to fill that void and before
long was known as the Mafia's "West Coast executioner."
But being a hit man was like being a brain surgeon. It paid

well enough, but your services weren't needed every day. And, with Fratianno's reputation, legitimate work was even more hard to come by. When he wasn't in prison, he was scuffling to stay solvent. Following his release from prison in the late 1970s, he was made acting boss of the L.A. family and soon thereafter cut a deal with the feds to turn state's evidence. The reason? He always maintained that it was because he learned that rivals for the top mob job had put out a contract on his life. He was getting old, sixty-four at the time, too old to scuffle anymore.

He sat down with federal prosecutors and cleared up more than a dozen murders, some of them thirty years old. He identified Mafia leaders around the country, exposed their business practices and connections. For nearly a decade he was trotted around the country to testify in a string of murder and bribery cases. He was credited with sinking a mob skimming operation in Vegas by telling the feds how the books were cooked. From him, America learned that Teamsters President Jackie Presser was controlled by Cleveland Mafia boss James Licavoli. His testimony bagged Roy Williams, Presser's predecessor, for trying to bribe Sen. Howard Cannon of Nevada. In all, he put twenty-five mobsters in prison and was the most prolific government Mafia informant since Joe Valachi opened his veins to Senate rackets hearings in 1963.

Along the way, he became a national celebrity, authoring two books on his life of crime and appearing on television shows to promote them. He also pocketed a million U.S. tax dollars before the Justice Department decided, nearly ten years after taking him under its protective wing, to cut him loose.

Was Dan Willoughby present at the creation of this prosecutorial bonanza? And if he were, why would he reveal it with such candor now?

"Don't you worry about what would happen if organized crime people found out about your involvement?" Darmer asked.

"Nah," Willoughby said. "I'm small stuff. After Jimmy started working with the FBI, he was a much bigger target."

He seemed pleased with himself, a little cocky. He had inserted himself, heroically, into an epic moment in law enforcement history, had righted all his wrongs, had cleansed himself in the blood of underworld sacrifice.

"Is it possible for me to verify any of this?" Darmer asked.

"I'm afraid not," Willoughby said. "A lot of it is pretty top secret. The FBI won't talk about because it might endanger me or some of their undercover people in California."

After more discussions with the Willoughbys' friends and family members, Darmer's initial positive feelings toward the couple were reinforced. The past was past. In his report to the juvenile court, dated July 10, 1984, he concluded:

> Dan and Trish have been married for nine years and during this time they have developed a strong, loving and stable marriage relationship. The applicants both experienced troubled times in their past and have attempted to make amends. They have been open, although somewhat embarrassed, regarding their past lives. Their remorse seems genuine and the dedication to a new life sincere.
>
> Seven years have transpired since their commitment to a new life and no further problems have arose. They have grown in their relationship and found solace in their religion. During this time they have been blessed with a child that is thriving within this loving, nurturing home environment. It is felt that this is the best recommendation of all.
>
> From all information gathered in this investigation, it is clear also that the applicants are morally and emotionally suited to being adoptive parents and will be able to provide easily for the child's physical and emotional needs.

After Hayden became an official member of the family, Trish spent more time at home, letting her mother carry a bigger load in the pepper spray business they were trying to build. Business had not been spectacular anyway, and it appeared it might soon peter out.

Besides, Dan had done very well with Burlington Air Freight. His rise to district manager had been nothing short of meteoric and he had even helped finance her own struggling enterprises. She could easily afford to spend more time with her family.

"I quit Burlington," Dan announced one day.

"You quit your job?"

"I got a better offer from A.E.I," he said. Air Express International was a major competitor of Burlington's. "It's a chance to make a lot more money."

Because he had done well since their move to Phoenix, Trish had no reason to be concerned. He always seemed to know what he was doing, always seemed to make the right move.

Dan neglected to mention that the move was not voluntarily. He had been fired again.

Chapter Eighteen

As the two young women, escorted by an older man, made their way across the bar, Phil Cantrelli felt called to play the game again. They were Hispanic and he knew all too well that Dan Willoughby liked all things Mexican—the country, the culture, the music, the beer, the women. Willoughby had often talked about wanting to move to Mexico and, that being out of the question immediately, had once asked Cantrelli to find him a Mexican woman.

Willoughby, too, noticed the two young women. In fact, he had not taken his eye off of them since they entered the bar. Cantrelli anticipated the competition, the chance to one-up his pal in yet another contest of cocksmanship. And he could do it in front of an audience. He and Willoughby and Susan Bach, another salesperson at Air Express International, were entertaining an out-of-town client, and Willoughby had been a strutting rooster all evening, full of himself and full of his usual crap. *Screw him.* Excusing himself to go to the restroom, Cantrelli circled by the bar to the waitress station.

''See the older guy with the two babes,'' he said to the waitress, who was waiting for a drink order to be filled.

''Yeah.''

''You know them?''

''Yeah, they come in occasionally.''

''Is he their boss or something?''

''He's their father,'' she said.

Returning to his table, Cantrelli, as well as Willoughby, studied the Hispanic trio. Time after time, a male approached one of the women, asked her to dance, and slinked the long walk back to his chair. Nothing collapses the ego like being rejected for a dance with every eye in the room boring in on you. No stranger to the barroom hustle or to Hispanic culture, Cantrelli felt supremely confident.

''Watch this,'' he said, leaning to his side and whispering to Susan. ''I'm going to make a chump out of Willoughby.''

''What are you going to do?''

''Dance with one of those Mexican women . . . the untouchables.''

''Fat chance,'' she said.

''Bet you a double scotch.''

''Okay.''

As soon as the next song began, he rose, winked at Willoughby and walked with studied nonchalance to the table of the three Hispanics.

Without looking at either woman, he bowed toward the father and asked, ''May I dance with your daughter?''

Smiling, the father nodded his approval. The daughter nearest him accompanied Cantrelli to the dance floor. When the music stopped, he escorted her back to the table, not to her chair, but to her father, who was duly impressed by this rare show of deference to parental pre-eminence, this respect for archaic etiquette.

In the way that friends and friendly rivals understand such things, Willoughby knew he had been challenged, and he quickly accepted. He asked the other daughter to dance. With a polite smile and a shake of her head, she sent him on that long walk of humiliation. He sat at the table, gripping his drink glass with both hands and avoiding eye contact with his companions.

Cantrelli leaned toward Susan and said, "Wanna make another bet."

"No, thanks," she said. This did not appear to be a good night to bet against her coworker. She also was not sure she wanted to be present when her boss was provoked beyond his tolerance.

"I just don't want ol' Dan to think the first time was a fluke," he said. "This'll chap him."

Revisiting the table across the room, he again asked the father's permission and danced with the daughter who had just refused Willoughby's invitation. As they scooted around the hardwood floor, even in the darkened room, Cantrelli was certain he could see the blood rushing to Willoughby's face.

Theirs had always been a tenuous friendship, an odd one marked by remarkably intimate conversations and a saw-toothed rivalry. When they first met in the late 1970s, Cantrelli, then the traffic manager for a company that shipped with C.F. Air Freight, was Willoughby's client. Their relationship was purely professional, and it wasn't until they worked closely together at Air Express International a few years later that they became pals and confidants. If Willoughby's swagger did not impress him in the beginning, at least it did not repulse him.

From mutual friends and industry scuttlebutt, he knew that Willoughby had been fired by C.F. Air for ethical lapses in 1979, but had gone on to bigger things at Burlington Air Freight. Fired from that job after a few years, he was quickly picked up by Air Express International. Cantrelli had heard the stories of the devious means Willoughby employed to acquire new accounts, but also how he was quick to share the bounty with his subordinates. The word was that Willoughby routinely kept only half of his bonuses and doled out the rest to his coworkers, all the way down to forklift operators in the warehouse. At the same time, Willoughby had earned a reputation for an explosive temper. He would curse at anyone who displeased him and once punched a warehouse worker and knocked him off the loading dock.

Joining him at A.E.I. at the end of 1984, Cantrelli was at first guarded in their professional dealing. In a short time, though, he discovered they had something in common—an eye for women. Though both were married, neither could resist the chase, a catalyst that was both a bond and a wedge between them. In the office and in watering holes around Mesa and Chandler and Scottsdale, they shared secrets with each other, discussed their lusts and ambition, and their pasts.

Willoughby made references to Mafia connections he had in San Francisco. He boasted of his ability to manipulate others with intimidation, kindness and impenetrable layers of mendacity.

"If you insulate yourself with enough people around you, you can never be caught," Willoughby told him on more than one occasion. "You can manipulate the world. If you tell enough lies, no one can figure out the truth."

At work, Cantrelli observed him tutoring other salesmen in the fine art of forging routing slips to obtain new business. He heard Willoughby make promises to his subordinates that he could not possibly keep—or had no intention of keeping. He watched the temper tantrums—Willoughby scattering files over his office floor or hurling glasses filled with iced tea across the room—and the buck passing. When there was a screwup or irregularity, Willoughby artfully shifted the blame to someone else. Dan Willoughby, he came to believe, not only lived a lie but believed his own lies. *A legend in his own mind,* Cantrelli often thought.

In time, he grew weary and wary of Dan Willoughby, weary of listening to his boasts and bluster and wary of his own vulnerability to Willoughby's schemes. Well he should have been, for Willoughby was anything but discriminating in whom he shafted.

All of Trish's brothers were fond of Dan, but none more so than Bob. He thought of his brother-in-law as a big brother and enjoyed hanging out with him. Dan was wise and smooth. Dan made him laugh. Dan made the world look rosy and conquerable. If you were in need, Dan would take off his shoes in a snowstorm and hand them to you.

"There's good money in air freight," Dan told him not long after he arrived in Phoenix and was working for C.F. Air Freight. "I can help you get started."

"How?" Bob asked. He was in his early 20s and was having trouble finding his niche, getting a toehold in a field that was both interesting to him and offered a future for him and his wife and the family they were planning. Selling real estate had been paying the bills, but it did not seem to be his calling.

"Pickup and delivery," he said. "You could work for yourself and contract out to us. There's a lot of demand for that right now. I can teach you the business and if you want, you can work up to salesman, or higher."

"What do I have to do?" Bob asked.

They could be partners, Dan explained. He would line up the customers and send the hauling work to Bob in exchange for a ten percent commission. West Phoenix was wide open, plenty of business there. All he needed was a light truck.

Jumping at the chance to team up with his *brother*, Bob agreed. With Dan's help, he formed a company called H&H Freight, acquired a couple of used trucks, which he painted in the C.F. Air colors, and was soon handling the company's cartage for all of west Phoenix. As Dan had promised, business was good, and Bob made regular commission payments to his partner.

As he learned the business, he also came to the unhappy realization that his arrangement with his brother-in-law was unique, that it was not standard procedure for cartage companies to pay commissions to freight salesmen. Checking around, he discovered that C.F. Air's pickup and delivery guys in east Phoenix were not paying kickbacks to Dan or anyone else.

For weeks, he fretted over the predicament. To end the compact, he would have to confront his *brother* and let him know that he knew that he had been scammed. He would rather eat a live tarantula. The pain of being duped by his *brother* eventually gave way to anger and the courage to initiate the inevitable confrontation. He would not only stop paying commissions, he would insist that Dan return the money he had already received.

"Why should I do that?" Willoughby asked him. "We had a deal. I got you the business. I earned my cut."

He doesn't get it, Bob thought.

"You weren't selling for me," Bob said. "You were doing what you had to do anyway. You were getting business for yourself, for the company. Somebody had to do the hauling and you weren't going to get commissions from anybody else. Why would you take them from me?"

"That was our deal."

Doesn't get it. "It's not right, Dan."

Rather than risk provoking a bitter family feud, Bob let the conversation end there. Later, he went to Trish and told her what her husband had done. She knew about the commissions, but thought it was standard procedure for that industry.

"I'll talk to him," she said.

A few days later, Dan, without apology or acknowledgment that he had in any way done anything unprincipled, repaid the commissions, and the matter was never mentioned again. They remained friends and *brothers,* and Dan later helped him land a better position in the air freight business in Denver.

Despite their rivalry of sexual conquest and his growing reservations about Willoughby—his prancing and preening, his capacity for deceit and inveiglement, the ease with which he screwed his friends when it served his purpose—Cantrelli continued to carouse with him and, curiously, they continued to reveal much of themselves to each other.

When Tina Roush joined the company as Dan's personal secretary, Cantrelli tried, without subtlety or discreetness, to seduce her, as though to demonstrate that Willoughby's territory was not inviolate. The more she shunned his advances, the harder he persevered, even calling her at home and leaving suggestive messages on her answering machine.

Willoughby was fully aware of his chase, but for once seemed uninterested in making it a duel. He and Tina had become good friends. He helped her out when she needed a car, and he encouraged her to come to him with any other problems. In turn, she offered a sympathetic ear when he felt the need to unburden himself, which he did with some regularity.

He told her about his love of Mexico and his wife's dislike of the country. He wanted to move there some day, but Trish would never agree to that. He liked scuba diving and his wife hated it. What he revealed, initially, was not so much a man in a miserable marriage, but a man in middle age with diminishing options, a man whose longings were thwarted by a wife who did not share them.

Willoughby also bent Cantrelli's ear with his tales of personal unrest. He was crowding fifty and appeared to be sliding into the jaws of a full-blown midlife crisis. His wife had embarked on yet another speculative business venture—this one showing early promise—and they spent little time together. The marriage seemed to be on the skids, yet Willoughby talked of adopting another child. He berated his subordinates in the morning and shared his bonuses with them in the afternoon. He made house calls for the church on Sunday and chased skirts on Monday.

He was an enigma Cantrelli had no inclination to decipher. He listened to Willoughby's grumbling, but was less than sympathetic. Like most of the other employees, he didn't really like Willoughby, who had begun wearing electric blue blazers and shirts with open collars to expose his chest and the gold chains hanging from his neck. The others sneeringly referred to him as Disco Dan.

One afternoon at the office, after a long session of bitching about his marriage, Willoughby leaned back in his chair and sighed, "I just want out of it."

"File for divorce," Cantrelli said.

"I can't do that," Willoughby said. "She knows enough about me to make my life hell."

"Well, why don't you knock her off?" Cantrelli said, with deep-friend sarcasm.

Willoughby gazed past him, gazed off into some tenebrous fissure of his own psyche. "That's an option," he said.

Chapter Nineteen

As epiphanies go, this one was off the scale, as intense as a religious conversion, raw and soul-stirring, the light and the way revealed. It came in a bottle, with a taste as strong as medicine, and it changed her life forever. Just in time.

In the summer of 1987, Thera Huish was in need of a life change. She was weary, depleted and frustrated that her business undertakings, however promising they began, had all ended in the scrap heap. She and Trish had plunged into two multilevel marketing ventures, and when the last one folded, they vowed never to amble down that alley again.

Multilevel marketing has a spotty history, partly because it is a pyramid operation whose success depends not just on pushing the product, but constantly recruiting new distributors, who buy into the operation. You begin as a distributor and earn commissions on the product you sell. But the big money is made by recruiting new distributors because you also earn a lesser commission on what they sell. As they recruit others, you earn from them also, building a downstream flow of revenue that can compound to spectacular heights.

Too often, the emphasis is placed on recruiting distributors rather than pushing the product, and for those who get in early, the rewards come easier. When the market becomes saturated with distributors, the pyramid tends to collapse, or at least stop growing. It is a business fueled by grand promises and, in many cases, presided over by charlatans.

Thera lost one business after she was injured in an automobile accident and was unable to work for several months. Another collapsed when she discovered the manufacturer was stealing from its distributors. Still suffering the effects of her car accident and the string of surgeries that followed it, she was ready for lower-voltage pursuits.

"We can find something else," she told her daughter when the pepper spray business folded, "but it won't be multilevel marketing. I've had it with that."

Trish, her own health flagging that summer—partly from work stress and partly from the demands of rearing two children—readily concurred.

So it was with little enthusiasm that Thera listened to Kathleen Peters sing the praises of an odd-sounding nutritional supplement called Km. Her old friend wanted to entice her into another multilevel marketing operation, and she wasn't interested.

"Just try some of it," Kathleen prodded. She knew of Thera's sales prowess, but also knew she had to sell her on the product and not just the job.

"I already take potassium," Thera said.

"Not like this."

Undeterred, Kathleen took a videotape to Trish's house. "Just do one thing for me," she said. "Watch it with your mother. I'll pick it up tomorrow."

Neither was in a mood to spend the evening watching a promotional tape about a company they had never heard of, particularly one with the bombastic name of Matol Botanical International Ltd. But, in deference to their friend, they watched—half watched, really—and absorbed little of it.

Kathleen stopped by the next day to pick up the tape and gave Thera a $35 bottle of Km. "Try this and let me know if you feel a difference," she said.

In less than two years, Thera Huish would be making her own promotional tape for Matol. Trying the supplement for the first time, she said in that endorsement, "I felt something from the top of my head to the bottom of my feet. I could feel it in my hair. I felt it had to be either illegal or immoral, it felt so good."

Trish's initial reaction was similar, and within a few weeks, under the name T&T Distributors, they were full-blown agents for Matol, back in the jaws of multilevel sales. They sold and recruited with a missionary ardor, and within a few months it was obvious to them that they had found their Holy Grail. By the middle of 1988, they were raking in $14,000 a month or more and the potential seemed limitless.

Watching the young girl on television, they both felt a tugging in their chests, but Dan spoke first.

"Why don't we look into this," he said.

They had talked about adopting another child, but as Trish's business grew and travel became an essential part of it, they had let the notion slide. They had also watched "Wednesday's Child," the weekly television feature offered as part of the evening newscast, but the children profiled posed particular problems. Most came from dysfunctional or abusive families or had been abandoned to a series of foster homes. Some had mental or physical deficiencies and others showed their scars in hostile or antisocial attitudes.

Some, like Marsha, had simply moved beyond the age of adoptability. She was fifteen and had spent her life bouncing from one foster home to another. She was a beautiful young woman, but as the broadcast pointed out, she needed a patient and loving environment to overcome her troubled past. Dan and Trish were confident that they were up to the challenge. A phone call to the show's producer set the adoption process in motion.

Trish soon began to have reservations. Their Matol business was exceeding their rosiest expectations and placing enormous demands on their time. Thera and Sterling bought a large house in Mesa and converted one room to an office. They even hired an assistant, Janie Clepp, to help with processing the orders, shipping, filing and occasionally tending to Trish's children after school. Things were happening at a dizzying and fatiguing pace, and Trish suddenly found the prospect of enlarging her family somewhat daunting.

"I just don't know about this adoption," she said, arriving for work after toiling well into the previous evening.

"What's the problem?" Thera asked.

"I'm just not sure it's a good idea . . . not right now, with everything else we've got going on."

Her daughter's abrupt resistance surprised Thera, and she suspected the cause of it ran deeper than Trish was revealing.

"Marsha seems like a sweet child," she said.

"She is," Trish agreed. "It's just that, well, she needs so much attention right now."

Marsha had been in their care pending formal approval of the adoption by the juvenile court, and Trish had quickly grown fond of her. If she had expected a rebellious teenager, that notion was quickly dispelled. Marsha was quiet and well-behaved, and had blended easily into the household. Her physical appearance was such that, upon first meeting, one would have no inkling that she was not Trish and Dan's natural child. She helped to tend the two younger children and was eager with household chores. Referring to Thera as "grandma" came perfectly natural to her. Considering Marsha's smooth adaptation to her new home, it seemed more likely to Thera that the problem lay elsewhere, perhaps with the marriage itself.

As their business grew, she had noticed a subtle change in her son-in-law, a testiness and a surliness that suggested resentment of Trish's success. He was losing control of his domain, was being reduced to a secondary player in a game he needed to quarterback. Trish was away from home more and more, and he was assuming a greater share of the household responsibilities while his regal stature of breadwinner was being diminished. His wife was drifting away, drifting closer to her mother and business partner, closer to independence, and worse, her income far eclipsed his own.

Thera began to overhear snippets of phone conversations which indicated that Dan's resentment had taken the outlet of harassment and taunting.

"I'm running late," Trish said one evening when he called their office. "I'll be there soon."

"That's all right," Dan said. "We can do just fine by ourselves." In an aside to his children, he added, "Can't we kids? We can cook our own dinner. We don't need a mommy, do we?"

Given the direction their relationship seemed to be drifting, another adoption seemed imprudent to Thera.

"Maybe you should put things on hold for a while," she suggested.

"Oh, I can't do that."

"Why not?"

"You know how much Danny wants this," Trish said. "If I balked now, there's no telling what he would do."

Dan did, in fact, possess a zeal for fatherhood that sometimes bordered on the obsessive. Children were important to him, validated him, made him whole. He packed them around him like protective armor, a buffer against the less wholesome side of his nature. They were the anchor and keel of his other side, the righteous, benevolent, devout, churchgoing family man, who slipped into a different skin each day when he left his neighborhood. On weekends, it took little prodding from the neighborhood kids for Dan to pile them into his car and take them for ice cream. In church, after he had taught his children's Sunday school class, he would join his family in the sanctuary and gather them around him in a pew. Usually, Marsha and little Thera sat between him and Trish while he held Hayden on his lap.

But even as his insistence and enthusiasm propelled the adoption forward, the middle-age crazies wrapped around him in bold ways.

Nick's first thought was, *What's a young babe like that doing with that gray-haired old guy?*

They were lying in the bright sunlight on the grass of a small park in downtown Phoenix, while all around them a St. Patrick's Day celebration was in progress. Nick had gone with a few buddies to toss down green beer and check out the girls.

It was the young, baby-faced blonde who caught his eye first. She was leaning on one elbow kissing the old guy, whose back was to Nick. *Hell, she's not even my age,* he thought. *She must be young enough to be his daughter.*

When the young woman broke from the embrace, the old guy rolled over, and Nick found himself staring straight into the eyes of his brother-in-law. Abashed, he turned away quickly, hoping that Dan had been looking past him rather than at him, and tried to lose himself in the crowd.

A short distance away, he turned to look back. The young woman had gotten up and was walking down a side street with Dan close behind. Confident that Dan had not been aware of his presence, Nick followed as they turned into an alley and, peeking around the corner of a building, he watched them embrace and kiss again.

He slipped quickly back down the street to rejoin his friends, but the party mood had deserted him and in its place was a quandary he did not want to address. Should he tell his sister? Should he confront Dan? Should he butt out?

The least painful option prevailed, and Dan apparently never knew he had been caught. Like many roving husbands in mid-life, blinded by the chase for vanishing youth, he had become, in his own mind, either invincible or invisible, or both.

Or he just didn't give a damn anymore.

PART THREE
The Obsession

Chapter Twenty

October 1989

The Jag purred to a stop at the intersection and even through the blaze of an incandescent sky ricocheting off its silver hood, Dan Willoughby immediately spotted the two women coming out of the Circle K convenience store. They were young, thirtyish, Hispanic and dressed for the warm autumn day.

One in particular caught his eye. She had long dark hair, high cheekbones, a wide, full mouth and ebony eyes that glinted in the sunlight. She wore a cheerleader-length skirt that revealed strong, tanned legs, and she walked with the bounce and brashness of a majorette. Gliding past the gas pumps, she casually tore open a Reese's Peanut Butter Cup, took a bite and let the wrapper flutter to the sidewalk.

Through dark glasses, Willoughby's eyes were riveted to them as they crossed the street and took a seat at a bus stop. *Two young babes on foot, women likely to be impressed by a racy new Jaguar.* When the light changed, he cruised by them slowly, smiled and waved. The one in the skirt waved back.

He changed lanes, hung a U-turn and pulled up to the curb in front of them. With a press of a button, the tinted window disappeared into the door well and the two women were staring at him like children at a puppet show.

"We have laws against littering," he said.

The one with the skirt stood up and approached the car. "What did you say?"

"I said we have laws against littering. I saw you throw that candy wrapper on the sidewalk."

She tossed her head to one side and let her thick tresses fall across her shoulder. "I guess I wasn't thinking," she smiled, a coquettish grin that let him know she knew he was not interested in solid waste disposal. "I forget I'm not in Mexico."

Their eyes locked for a moment and Willoughby said, "You two need a ride?"

"Yeah."

"Where are you going?"

"Los Arcos Mall."

"Get in. I'll take you."

"Sure," she said without hesitation. While Willoughby leaned across the console and opened the door, she signaled to her friend, who climbed into the backseat. The skirt rode up front with him.

Pulling into traffic, he reached for his car phone—another gesture certain to impress his passengers since car phones were not then common fixtures—and said, "I've got to make a call to cancel my meeting so I can take you ladies to the mall."

After a short conversation, he put the phone back in its holder.

"My name's Dan," he said, turning his head toward the front-seat passenger and taking in the brown flesh of her thighs.

"I'm Yesenia," she said. "She's Lisa."

"Going shopping, huh?"

"Yeah . . . maybe," Yesenia said. "Sort of hang out. We don't have anything else to do."

"You don't work?"

"No . . . Not right now." Her voice was childlike but her eyes were sensuous coals. She turned slightly toward him.

"What do you do?" she asked.

"Air freight. I manage an air freight company."

She cocked an eyebrow and glanced at her friend in the backseat. They were duly impressed. Willoughby also liked what he was seeing and hearing. A dish on foot, no job, idle time and Mexican to boot.

At the mall, he stopped at the entrance and Yesenia got out and held the seat back to facilitate her friend's exit. Lisa stepped away from the car, but Yesenia lingered at the door.

"This is my number," Willoughby said, handing her his Air Express International business card. "Call me and we'll have lunch or a holiday drink."

"Okay. Sure."

He winked, revved the Jag and pointed it toward the boulevard.

Trish had given him the car for Christmas in 1988, perhaps in hopes of ameliorating some of the tension her work had placed on their marriage. Dan had long lusted for a Jaguar, and that holiday season they could easily afford one. Her business had taken off like a dragster and by that December T&T Distributors' income had leaped to $20,000 to $25,000 a month, most of it pure profit. In a year and a half, mother and daughter had become Matol's top sales team and the company was sending them on frequent trips around the country to promote the product and speak at motivational meetings for new recruits.

Occasionally, their husbands accompanied them, but more often Dan stayed at home to care for the children. He relished the Jaguar and other financial freedoms Trish's income afforded him—he joined a health club and frequented tanning salons, had his hair styled and his fingernails manicured and his clothing tailored—but it all came at a price, a loss of ego and macho equilibrium.

"I'm a kept man," he grumbled to Phil Cantrelli.

The gift of the car had done little to put the marriage back on track. Less than a year after presenting it to her husband, Trish was consulting a marriage counselor.

"Hi."

Willoughby recognized the voice.

"You want to take me to lunch?"

"Yes, I do. Where can I pick you up?"

She gave him her address at the Dartmoor Apartments on Alma School Road.

Before leaving A.E.I., Willoughby disappeared into the bathroom and emerged a few minutes later, the sweet aroma of Brut cologne trailing him through the office and out the front door to his car.

He picked Yesenia up at noon and drove north to Scottsdale, away from the paths normally pounded by his wife.

Over drinks and a three-hour lunch, they sized each other up in that slow ritual of sexual appraisal and risk assessment. He told her he was married and unhappy. She told him she was married, for the second time, and unhappy. He told her he had three children, two of them adopted. She told him she had one adopted son, who lived with her first husband in Oregon. He was stylish and prosperous. She was saucy and poor. He was fifty. She was thirty-three. They agreed to see each other again.

After lunch he dropped her off at the Fiesta Mall in Mesa and gave her $100.

"What's this for?" she asked.

"To buy clothes, so the next time I see you you'll have on a new outfit," he said.

His obsession with her was swift and astonishingly reckless. The next day, he sent a dozen roses to her apartment, knowing that her husband might be there when she received them. They saw each other a couple of times a week, and he sent flowers nearly as often. Once, en route to pick her up, he received a call on his car phone.

"Don't come," Yesenia said. "My husband is here. He came home early."

A month after their first meeting, Dan wanted to take her to his house, a proposal that caused her to wince.

"I want you to meet my kids," he told her.

She balked. Because their relationship had not yet been sexual, had not advanced much beyond the footsie and light smooching stage, certainly had not involved talk of commitment, she was more than a little confounded by his motives.

"What about your wife?"

"She's away . . . on a business trip."

While Yesenia was uneasy about going to his house, his insistence demonstrated a daring streak she found titillating. She liked excitement, action, even a little danger, anything that pricked the adrenal glands. This was a bold and swashbuckling gesture on his part, a thumb against the nose of convention, wicked abandon.

She agreed.

"Kids, this is Victoria, my Spanish teacher," Dan said, introducing her by the name she had used when she lived in Oregon.

Hayden, Thera and Marsha made hurried and superficial acknowledgments and returned to watching television. They were polite and at ease with her presence, but Yesenia was not comfortable. She knew full well where her relationship with this man was headed, and circling so close to his family momentarily unnerved her. There had been many men in her life, dozens, probably hundreds, and many of them had been married, but this was different. The families of her previous lovers had been nameless and faceless. These children were real people.

They stayed only a short time, as though Dan wanted merely to inoculate his children to her, to establish her as a peripheral presence, a bit player they would encounter from time to time.

On the drive back to her apartment, she began to cry. Irritated, Dan turned onto a side street and stopped the car.

"Why are you crying?" he asked.

"You have three beautiful kids and I . . . I don't want to be the cause for your marriage to fall apart."

"You're not the cause," he snapped. "You can't fix something that's already cracked and getting worse. She's a bitch, always bossing me around, pushing me around. She treats the children like shit. I've had enough."

Yesenia wiped her eyes, not knowing how to respond to his tirade. He had whined about his wife and his marriage, but never had he expressed his feeling with such vitriol.

Just as suddenly as his temper had flared, it abated and his voice softened.

"I would like for you to be my wife and the mother of my children."

"I don't know . . ."

"If you won't, I'll find someone else who will."

"Well, I'll keep seeing you," she said, not wanting to risk ending the relationship over that issue, not now. She was not in love with him, but he possessed a quality she coveted. He was a very big spender.

Two days later, Willoughby told his wife he had to make an out-of-town trip for Air Express International. Yesenia told her husband she was going to Oregon to visit her son. Dan picked her up in the Jaguar and they drove two hundred miles up Highway 93, checked into the Colorado Bell Hotel in Laughlin, Nevada, and made love for the first time.

Chapter Twenty-one

Yesenia Patino was not one to be domesticated, as Abel Ramon clearly recognized. He married her anyway, married her knowing she had never divorced her first husband. She had that effect on men. They wanted to possess her, to own her, and her unbridled nature may have been part of the appeal.

Yesenia's appetite for men equaled theirs for her. Abel Ramon wasn't blind and he knew of her lusts when he married her. She liked to go out at night and stay late. She liked to drink, raise hell and spend money, someone else's money. The fast life did not lend itself to gainful employment. She worked briefly at a couple of department stores, but the working life was too close to domestication.

There were other ways, easier ways, for her to provide herself with minor luxuries. Men would gladly pay her to spend time with them. Or she could steal.

Six months before she met Dan Willoughby, Yesenia was arrested at the Sears store in the Fiesta Mall for shoplifting. Two months later, she was pinched again for stealing from an

ABCO Market. She didn't bother to keep appointments with the courts—life was too short for such frivolity.

Ramon was aware that his wife had found a new sugar daddy, and no minor leaguer either. She had money to prowl the streets while he worked. The apartment was never without the scent of fresh flowers. Her wardrobe was expanding, spreading through the closet like kudzu. Though they lived in a decent apartment and usually stayed ahead of the bills, Ramon felt like a pauper. His woman, his wife, was sliding under the spell of a prince.

In reality, Yesenia believed she loved her husband and had no real feeling for Dan Willoughby, whose magnetism, to her at least, resided in his plastic and his checkbook. It was not her inclination, though, to choose between two men. She could have as many as she wanted. If they couldn't accept that, they could walk. Ramon had always accepted it. He didn't like going out, and Yesenia stayed home with him often enough to placate him. A couple of months into her affair with Dan Willoughby, though, he felt pushed to the wall of desperation.

"I could give you a better life," Ramon told her. "I could give you as much as him."

"How?" she asked, almost taunting him.

"Drugs. I could get into that and make a lot of money," he said.

Instead of discouraging his notions of criminal activity, Yesenia encouraged them. Danny was spending a lot of money on her. If her husband wanted to compete, why not? She had no aversion to being kept by two high rollers.

"Fine," she said. "Go ahead."

Less than two months later, Ramon was arrested just south of the border on charges of drug trafficking.

Nothing in her past deterred Dan Willoughby, at least nothing he had learned so far. That she had married Ramon without divorcing her first husband was, in the fires of his obsession, inconsequential. That he could not be certain that she was faithful to him was almost as immaterial. That she was a thief mattered not. He would be her Henry Higgins. He would dress her in finery and teach her table manners, mend her promiscuity, tame her, domesticate her, make her a proper mother for his children. *Dan the Fix-it Man.* She might be a challenge, but she could be conquered. When Dan Willoughby wanted something as bad as he wanted Yesenia Patino, he usually got it.

"Since you never divorced Jack, your marriage to Abel was illegal anyway," he told her after her husband was jailed. "We can probably get you a quick annulment."

"What is that?" She had never heard the term.

"It's like you were never married. The marriage is terminated and never existed. I'll get Fuller to take care of it."

Dan was wound like a pocket watch. With Abel gone, he could command all her time. Her apartment could be their love nest. Yesenia understood that, but she did not understand the urgency he felt for the annulment. All these strange legal exercises were irrelevant to her, not to mention boring.

"If we are going to get married in the future, we want that out of the way," he explained.

The mention of marriage usually touched off an argument. Yesenia was not bending gently to his finishing school tutoring. She was not yet ready for the matronly look, the matronly touch, and she told him so. She wanted to be wild, wear sexy clothes and light up the night.

A child of itinerant Mexican farm laborers who followed the crops up and down the West Coast and across the Southwest, she had lived most of her life in the United States on a green card, and was on her own and on the streets from an early age. She was twenty-two and still hustling when Jack Mulkins, a Portland firefighter older than her father, found her in a bar, felt sorry for her, took her off the streets and, like most men she encountered, fell in love with her. They were married and lived together for eight years, but Yesenia never wore the chains of matrimony well. In her moral macrocosm, a husband was just another lay, another good time in a world full of good times.

Knowing all that, Willoughby still selected her to be his wife and the mother of his children. The mention of it, though, always provoked her.

She never rejected the idea of marriage outright and was prepared to go through with it, if necessary, to secure the creature comforts Willoughby lavished on her. He was now paying her apartment rent and allowing her to sign his name to checks she wrote on his account. She used his cash and credit cards freely, dined in restaurants she could not afford on her own, and scooted through the good times in a silver sports car. A wedding ceremony would be small dues to pay for that ride.

Recognizing that his hold on her was tenuous, that she was far less devoted to their liaison than he, Dan Willoughby played his hole card often. He sprung for trips to Mexico—Hermosillo, Cancun, Cabo San Lucas, Puerto Vallarta—and Los Angeles, Seattle and San Francisco. He bought memberships to a health club, where they flaunted their affair by nuzzling and kissing between reps with free weights. Yesenia gave him a snapshot of herself—signed on the back "your future wife"—and he tacked it to his office wall where it could be viewed by other A.E.I. employees. With another couple, they took in the Phoenix Grand Prix and posed, kissing, for a photograph, which Yesenia framed and displayed in her apartment.

Willoughby pursued her with such intensity that he began neglecting his work, which did not go unnoticed at A.E.I. More and more often, he would get up from his desk in the middle of the afternoon, duck into the restroom, emerge wrapped in the scent of Brut and announce, "I'm going to Digital."

His affair with Yesenia had become office lore and on those occasions when he slipped out early, no one believed he was calling on Digital Equipment. It became something of an office joke, then an office tradition. Whenever employees decided to trash an afternoon, they would head toward the door, loudly announcing, "I'm going to Digital."

More uncharacteristically, he began neglecting his children, who had been the anchor in the roiling water of his past few years. As his marriage disintegrated, as his wife became more prosperous and more absent from the nest, he had huddled his children around him, fortifying himself with their adoration.

"Who's the king?" he would ask them, and bask in their playful rejoinder: "You are, Dad."

"Mommy will be gone again this week," he would tell them. "We can do fine without her. We can take care of ourselves, can't we?"

They never disagreed.

Nothing in his life had been able to wedge itself between him and his children. Except Yesenia.

He skipped Hayden's sixth birthday party to frolic with her in Cabo San Lucas, bringing back photographs of the two of them—himself tanned and muscular, Yesenia bursting out of a revealing swimsuit—astride a "WaveRunner," an aquatic motorcycle.

Jack Mulkins called early in March 1990 to tell Yesenia that he and Charlie were coming to visit. Shortly after they were married, she and Jack had gone to Mexico and adopted Charlie. She cared about the child but had no inclination to care for him. She was happy to cede custody to her husband when they split up.

Despite being past the normal child-rearing years—he had a son by a previous marriage who was only two years younger than Yesenia—he made a good home for Charlie, saw to it that he attended school and participated in sports. Yesenia was always welcome to visit and, whenever possible, Jack took Charlie to visit her.

"Okay," Yesenia said. "I'll tell Danny you're coming. We can go to dinner."

In her occasional phone calls to Oregon, she had told her husband about her current flame, about his money and the clothes he bought her and the trips they took. Mulkins carried no torch for her—getting shed of her was one of his happier days—and therefore had no objection to meeting her boyfriend. In truth, he was eager to do so. Maybe he could let the poor bastard know what he had gotten himself into.

Yesenia opened the door and found two solemn uniformed police officers.

"Yesenia Patino?"

"Yes."

"We have a warrant for your arrest."

"What for?"

"Failure to appear in court on a shoplifting charge. You'll have to come with us."

"I have an appointment at the dentist," she said.

"Lock your door and come with us."

She called Dan from the police station. He left his office near the airport and drove to the Mesa jail, posted a $500 bond and drove her to her dental appointment. While he waited to take her home, he called Richard Fuller and arranged for him to represent her on the criminal charge.

Nothing about her deterred him.

Leaving her apartment that day, he said, "I'll see you tomorrow night. We'll take Jack to the Rusty Pelican."

After he left, Yesenia placed a phone call and arranged for a friend to pick her up that evening, a male friend. She wasn't going to let something like being arrested spoil her day. Or her night.

Chapter Twenty-two

Slipping his arm around Yesenia, Dan looked across the table at her husband and said, "I'm in love with her. I want to marry her some day."

Jack Mulkins nodded. "Well, when that time comes, Yesenia and I should obtain a divorce," he said.

"Would that be a problem?" Dan asked, still a little uncertain about Jack's feelings toward his wife.

"Not at all," Jack said. "I'll do it the minute you ask me to."

Dan grinned and nodded a silent thank you.

Considering that one was Yesenia's husband and the other her lover, and considering their contrasting personalities and backgrounds, the two men hit it off remarkably well. Mulkins, a few years older than Willoughby, had the pale skin of someone sequestered in a land of short summers, and the easygoing manner of someone resigned to living out his years on the path of least resistance. Willoughby had the hearty, burnished look that comes from the beach, the desert, the gymnasium, and rather than coasting into his winter years, he was as coiled as a soldier entering battle for the first time. He seemed to form an immediate trust of Mulkins, and while that confidence was not altogether mutual, they were eminently forthright with each other.

For her part, Yesenia was a cameo player in this scene, but her role defined the two men. When she talked to Jack, one would have thought they were distant relatives. When she talked to Dan, one would have known they were in heat. She talked little, however, and mostly surveyed the restaurant while the men got acquainted.

After a drink, she broke free from Dan's clutches to go to the restroom.

"We'll get together and talk privately," Danny said to Mulkins as she walked away. "I'd like to find out a little more about this lady I'm involved with and find out where she's coming from.

"Sure," Mulkins said. Now was a good enough time for him.

"I really love her, but the problem I'm having is keeping her occupied until we can get married. She can't spend a day at home. She has to be out somewhere all the time . . . in a bar or talking to someone or playing pool or shopping. She can't just sit. She can't stay at home."

"You think you're telling me something?" Mulkins was sardonic, maybe even a bit spiteful.

"What do you think of her, Jack?"

Mulkins gazed off across the room, wondering how to answer.

"I mean, can she be trusted?" Dan pressed.

After a few more seconds of study, Mulkins responded in a flat, wry monotone, "She is a habitual, chronic, pathological liar."

Willoughby was dumbfounded. He was anticipating a critical appraisal, but nothing so acerbic and abrupt. He had caught her in lies, suspected she was seeing other men, observed her short attention span and plumbed her shallowness, but hearing her summed up so bluntly by her husband floored him.

"Would anything . . . I mean, would she ever stop lying?" he sputtered.

"I don't think so," Mulkins said.

Yesenia returned to the table and Dan changed the subject. "You know, Jack, I'm married to a real bitch," he said. "I've got to get away from her. There's no romance in our marriage, no nothing."

"Why don't you divorce her?"

"I'd like to tomorrow, but I can't. I'd like to come out of my marriage with something."

From Yesenia, Mulkins was aware of Trish's business and the money it took in. He couldn't see the problem. He was living fine on a retired fireman's pay; Willoughby surely made more than that.

"You've got a good job, a new car," Mulkins told him. "She's got her own income, so she can't get anything from you. Why can't you leave? How much money do you need?"

"I need my children," Willoughby snapped. "If I divorce her, I would lose my children. I can't do that."

Yesenia appeared to be ignoring the conversation.

Mulkins said, "You can work out a visitation arrangement. The courts aren't going to cut them out of your life."

"*She* will," Dan said. "She's got enough on me to put me away for the rest of my life, and she'd do it."

As he rambled on, Mulkins became convinced that he really would not consider divorcing his wife. They were deep in their cups now, and Mulkins felt that the conversation was becoming farcical.

"Sounds like a dilemma to me," he said, hoping the subject would then change.

"I'll figure it out," Willoughby said. "Maybe I'll take her to Mexico and get rid of her."

"Yeah," Mulkins laughed, "that's what I'd do."

* * *

Trish entered through the side door off the driveway, slouched through the den and dropped her tote bag, stuffed with papers, onto her desk.

"Is something wrong?" Thera asked. For the first time since before they had sipped the elixir of Matol and plunged headlong into the business, Thera was worried about her daughter's health. More days than not lately she came to work looking haggard and hollow-eyed.

"No, I'm just tired," she said. "I didn't get much sleep last night."

"Maybe you should see a doctor."

"I'll be all right. I think I'll just go back to the bedroom and lie down for a while."

Watching her approach the bedroom, Sterling went to the office and asked his wife if Trish was ill.

"She says she's just tired."

Thera was certain of the reason for her daughter's frequent sleepless nights. She had heard the fights on the telephone, had seen Dan's surliness toward his wife. Moreover, she had begun to notice in their children the classic signs of an antagonistic household. They, too, were becoming brusque, even combative. She had seen Hayden strike his sister and vice versa—something they had never done until recently. Their personalities were changing, turning resentful and sullen.

Their mother was working long hours and their father was home far less than what they were accustomed to, so they were more and more in the care of Janie Clepp, Thera and Trish's trusted assistant. An abrupt change of routine is enough to tip children off balance; endlessly dueling parents is far worse.

After Trish had slept a couple of hours and returned to the office only slightly refreshed, Thera broached the topic of disorder in the Willoughby house.

"Trish, is there a problem with Danny?"

"I just don't know how to deal with him anymore. He's so

belligerent toward me. He explodes over everything I do. He's changed.''

Everyone in the family had noticed the change, though not to the extent that Trish had. After his mother died two years before, Dan gradually began to behave as though he were free of some unseen mooring that had held him in check. On a weekend visit from California, Val had been shocked when Dan came home on an adrenaline high, prancing around the house and waving his arms as he described how he had punched a coworker that afternoon. *My God,* Val thought, *he's nearly fifty and bragging about some schoolyard scuffle.* It was also after his mother's death that Dan turned to weightlifting to forestall the onslaught of the years. The physical change in him was striking enough that Thera guessed that he was complementing his workouts with chemical boosters, substances that worked on the brain as well as the body. To her and her husband and sons, however, the changes in Dan were not alarming; men tormented by middle age had behaved worse.

''Why don't you talk to your bishop?'' she asked her daughter.

''I did, Mom. He didn't take me seriously. He thinks it's just a temporary thing . . . that our marriage is strong and we'll work it out. He's probably right.''

A couple of days later she made an appointment with a marriage counselor, and went alone. Her husband took his mistress to the horse races.

Along with frequent visits and telephone conversations with her after their separation, Mulkins had continued to support his wife in a minor fashion—she remained on his health insurance policy at a cost of $150 a month. He did not dislike her. Rather, he had come to understand her nature and to accept it, but not live with it. She was not, he believed, an evil person, just one without inhibition or moral constraints.

A few weeks after that first meeting with Willoughby, Mulkins and his son returned to Arizona to spend some time at their place on the Verde River in the Coconino National Forest 125 miles north of Phoenix. In part because he wanted to reciprocate for their previous hospitality, but mostly because he was concerned about the direction their affair was taking, he invited Dan and Yesenia to meet him at a Chinese restaurant in Cottonwood.

They tossed down several drinks before ordering dinner, and as the alcohol took effect, Mulkins began to sense that their relationship had, in fact, shifted—to what he wasn't sure—and accelerated. Yesenia, it was obvious, was impatient with Willoughby's languor in leaving his wife. She wanted a ring, a diamond ring, even if she had to marry to get it. *Poor bastard.* The toll of an unhappy marriage and the demands of an impatient mistress showed on Willoughby's face and in his posture. Unlike the self-assured and prancing colt he had met earlier, Mulkins now detected a tension, a whiff of desperation.

Willoughby dwelled on his marriage, his misery, his wife.

"Maybe if I took her to the Grand Canyon," he mumbled, swirling the liquor in his glass before gulping it down, "she would fall in."

"Are you serious?" Mulkins asked.

Willoughby did not reply immediately, just stared into the distance. "I think I'll take her to Mexico," he said at last. "I think anything can be accomplished in Mexico."

Suddenly, Mulkins was deeply uncomfortable with the conversation, apprehensive that if Willoughby were serious, he might be attempting to involve him in his scheme. He tried, with only modest success, to get through dinner with no more discussion of Willoughby's wife.

Willoughby rambled about his family, how his children had met Yesenia but he had them on his side, had them trained not to tell their mother anything that was going on. They were completely loyal to him . . . he thought. He was sure of the younger children, but Marsha was different. He was not one hundred percent certain of her.

As dinner wound down, they talked about Yesenia. Dan agreed to remove the last financial burden she posed to Mulkins by paying for her health insurance. He wrote a check for $150 to cover that month's premium and promised to send a check each month until he could obtain a separate policy for her. Shouldn't take long. She would need a physical exam, but, because of her youth, there was no reason to anticipate problems.

Mulkins awoke with the bad taste of the previous night's conversation stuck like peanut butter to his tongue. The surreal texture of the evening, Willoughby and Yesenia pawing each other one moment and making blasé references to murder the next, encroached on his sleep. He had not taken the talk of disposing of Trish seriously, but—who knows?—maybe the man was capable of doing something stupid and making Yesenia a part of it.

He called early, before she could begin her daily outing.

"I'm concerned by the way he talks about his wife," he told her."

"Why?" she asked with eerie nonchalance.

"I'm afraid he's going to do something to her."

"So?"

"How would he do it?" he asked, still hoping this was some kind of joke.

"He's going to San Francisco to talk to the Don," she said. "Some people in the Mafia owe him. He spent a year in jail to keep the heat off of somebody."

"Could you be a part of something like that?"

"Yes, I can," she said.

Mulkins thought he knew her, but now he was aghast.

"How could you do that? How could you even think about it?"

"For the money," she said. "He a millionaire."

Her brashness infuriated him. She was taunting him the way

she taunted Willoughby for not leaving his wife, the way she taunted all men.

"I don't believe you would do something like that," he said, "and I don't want to hear any more about it."

He hung up and sat brooding for a long time. *This isn't funny anymore. This is very serious.* Should he tell someone, the police or the FBI? Mulkins realized then that he was, in some small way, frightened of Willoughby. Although he did not entirely believe it, he had no reason to doubt that Dan Willoughby had friends in the Mafia. It was more likely, he felt, that Willoughby made the boast to impress Yesenia, perhaps to intimidate and control her. He couldn't be certain. Suppose it was true. Suppose Willoughby had friends who would happily retaliate against a disabled fireman with a big mouth?

He considered calling Trish Willoughby, just a short anonymous call to alert her to her husband's frame of mind. She could deal with it as she saw fit, and he would be off the hook. But maybe not. Unless Willoughby had been talking to others about getting rid of his wife—and how likely was that?—he would know who made the call.

For now, he would let it slide. It was all too absurd anyway. *Yesenia may have only a molecule or two of conscience, but she is no killer,* he told himself. Willoughby was just a guy trying to hang onto his youth through a young mistress. The fires would abate. He would awake some morning weary of her callow perversity, her insatiable appetites. She would first exhaust him and then repulse him, and he would slither back to the solace and saneness of his old life. Women such as Yesenia do not stay around long. The demands of their maintenance become burdensome and they are scuttled, or they become bored and find another sucker. Yesenia wasn't capable of loving Willoughby or anybody else, he believed. Anybody except Yesenia.

Chapter Twenty-three

May in Arizona is full-blown summer and the staunch sun worshipers, defiant of ultraviolet wrinkles and melanoma, are already radiantly bronzed. For teenagers, especially, laying out is almost a religious discipline in which degrees of piety are measured by levels and lines of pigmentation.

At sixteen, Marsha Willoughby had such things on her mind.

"I can't have a bikini," she groused as Hayden and Thera splashed in the pool a few feet away. Her father was across the pool, perusing a sheaf of Spanish lesson papers.

"Why not?" Yesenia asked her.

"My mom won't let me."

Her swimsuit was a standard, modest and proper one-piece, the kind worn by overweight mothers or girls with nothing to flaunt. She studied Yesenia's garb, a modified one-piece, but as revealing as a bikini, cut low in the front and down the sides, with a French arc up the thighs, leaving liberal dermis to catch the rays.

"Well, if I was your mother you could have a bikini," Yesenia said. Primed by the young girl's pouting response, she added, "If I was your mom, we'd have a good time. We'd go out and do things."

She wanted Marsha to like her, wanted her as an ally in what she now saw as a tug-of-war for Dan Willoughby. He despised his wife, but it wasn't clear that Yesenia was winning the battle.

Because of the years of adversity she had endured before being adopted by the Willoughbys, Marsha was a guarded young woman. She held her emotions and her thoughts in close check, one moment seeming to go with the flow, following whatever course her chaperons charted, and the next moment reverting to her own compass and heading. In bringing her here, Dan Willoughby had demonstrated a stunning trust in her discretion. Yesenia had no reason to question his judgment.

"I need to go see my Spanish teacher," Willoughby had announced to his children earlier that afternoon. "Come on, you can swim while we're there."

He gathered up his Spanish language lesson papers, loaded his children into the Jag and drove less than a mile to Yesenia's new digs in the Windemere Apartments in Gilbert, where Gilbert Road intersects with the Superstition Freeway, just around the corner from the church where he taught Sunday school and performed baptisms. He had moved her here two months earlier, in part to upgrade her lifestyle and in part to place her closer to him.

The woman Marsha knew only as Victoria was effusive upon their arrival. She offered them soft drinks and invited Marsha to use her bedroom to change into her swimsuit. While changing, Marsha noticed familiar clothing hanging in the woman's closet, clothing that belonged to her father. In the bedroom, she also saw photographs of her father and this woman embracing and kissing at the Phoenix Grand Prix.

She said nothing to her hostess or to her father, but she would never again believe their cover story, that Victoria was

only his Spanish teacher. They adjourned to the pool to bask
in the sun for a couple of hours.

Perhaps because there were no repercussions from that meeting, or perhaps because he was desperate to reassure Yesenia
that he was extracting himself from his marriage, Willoughby
thrust his mistress and his children together again a few days
later, while Trish was away on business.

Taking them to a movie was less noteworthy than the brazen
way he assembled them. He picked Yesenia up at her apartment,
drove her to his house—risking exposure to the neighbors—
and invited her inside while the children prepared for the outing.
His willingness to parade his affair so openly was either a crass
statement of his fundamental arrogance or a pitiable cry of
desperation. It was the conduct of a man begging to be caught,
begging to be flogged back to reason—or that of a man twisted
by profound delusions of his own invincibility.

The gynecologist who examined Yesenia for the insurance
company found little of note. Except for a few missing pieces
of female equipment—a hysterectomy some years earlier, she
told him—everything was normal. While more usual for someone older than Yesenia, a hysterectomy wasn't grounds for
failing a physical. She was sound and healthy, perfectly insur-
able.

With her own policy in force, she could now sever the last
financial tie to her husband. But she was restless for more. She
wanted the quick divorce Jack Mulkins had promised her, and
she wanted a token of Dan's love. A diamond would do nicely.

She turned the screws mostly by reminding Willoughby that
there were other cabbages in the patch. When he left her apartment at night, she often dressed up and hit the streets—and
took little care to conceal it from him. He sent her baskets of
fruit and the flower truck continued to be dispatched to her
apartment once or twice a week.

"Same rules for both or no rules at all," one card read. If

he thought he could compel loyalty from her by threatening infidelities of his own, Willoughby had hoodwinked himself. Yesenia didn't care whom he screwed. She wanted a ring.

On June 13, 1990, the Willoughbys kept an appointment with Dr. Newt Randall, the psychologist that Trish had been seeing for several months. Dan had accompanied her to a couple of counseling sessions but had shown little interest in marriage therapy. Randall found him to be a poor candidate for it. To the doctor's trained eye and ear, Willoughby was both emotionally inaccessible and utterly insensitive to his wife's feelings.

He had long since come to the conclusion that the union was beyond salvage and that it was only a matter of time until Trish recognized that for herself. For now, though, she was adamantly unwilling to concede that likely denouement. Her marriage had been sealed in the LDS Church, rendering it eternal, endowing it with a life and legitimacy beyond death. Other factors fortified her: Her mother's marriage had seen its storms and endured them because Thera had refused to capitulate to the angry gales, and Trish, after all, was her mother's daughter, the blood of her blood. She also believed that where children were involved, the battle was well worth fighting. She was forty-one years old and had too much invested in this life to allow her husband's midlife crisis to demolish it.

While he admired her fortitude, Randall did not share her faith that willpower alone could precipitate a happy ending. Her husband had already disconnected from her—if, in fact, he had ever been connected.

Anger from the early morning argument stuck in her gut and lingered there throughout the day. It was about Yesenia. Trish had no direct knowledge of the affair, but Yesenia had begun calling the Willoughby house as though she were a friend of the family. Sometimes Trish answered, sometimes Marsha, and they dutifully handed the phone to Dan.

"My Spanish teacher," he would explain after hanging up from a short, hushed conversation.

His interest in his family had been dwindling and he spent too much time with his Spanish teacher, Trish felt. That morning, her anger boiled over. Frazzled from another sleepless night, frazzled from marriage counseling sessions that were going nowhere, frazzled from her husband's attempts to align their children against her, frazzled from the intrusion of this Mexican tutor into their lives, Trish vented her frustrations in heated language and Dan responded in kind.

Marsha departed for school with their angry words ringing in her ears. When she returned home that afternoon, her mother was still bristling and unable to keep inside herself things the two of them had never discussed with each other.

"That woman is more than just his Spanish teacher," she fumed.

"I think so too," Marsha said.

She told her mother about the times Yesenia had been to their house while she was away, and she told her about the visit to Yesenia's apartment and the photographs she saw there.

"My wife is going to be coming to see you," Dan panted into the phone. There was an apprehension in his voice that Yesenia had never heard before. "Marsha told her about the pictures. You just deny everything. Remember, you're just my Spanish teacher."

"Okay."

Yesenia hung around the house all morning and prepared for the meeting. She carefully hid anything that would have suggested Dan's presence here, and she placed a picture of herself and Abel Ramon on a table beside the sofa. When her expected caller failed to appear, she changed into a swimsuit, went to the pool and was lounging there when she saw the slender, well-dressed blonde walking up the pathway toward her apartment. She had never met Dan's wife, had never even seen a picture of her, but she knew immediately that the blonde was Mrs. Willoughby. She left her lounger, draped a towel over her shoulder and approached the woman.

"Hi. I'm Yesenia."

Trish glared at her for a second. "I know who you are and I know you've been sleeping with my husband," she said, loudly enough that others around the pool turned to look.

"Wait a minute," Yesenia said, feigning shock at the accusation. "Let's go inside and talk about this."

Entering the apartment first, she pushed the door back and said, "Come in."

Trish let her eyes rove over the contents of the small apartment. Neat but nothing fancy.

"I know what's going on," she said, looking Yesenia in the eye again.

"No, no," Yesenia said. "That's not right. I'm not . . . I'm not interested in your husband. All I am is his Spanish teacher."

Reaching for the picture of Abel Ramon on the end table, she said, "This is the person I'm in love with. I can't see me going out with your husband. I'm not interested."

She was a master of mendacity, maybe better than Dan. Pathological. Compulsive. Unfettered by conscience. Untainted by guilt. Her guilelessness took some of the edge off Trish's fury.

"Well, I want to tell you something," she said. "My husband has all kinds of problems . . . he's not himself right now."

Yesenia frowned just as little, as if to say, *Poor guy, but what's it got to do with me?*

"He's not good for you," Trish continued, some of the sting returning to her voice.

"But, I'm just . . ."

"I want you to stop seeing him."

". . . helping with his Spanish lessons."

"I want you to stop seeing him for any reason."

"Sure," Yesenia said. When that appeared to settle the conflict, she asked, "Would you take me shopping?"

Trish slumped a little, disarmed by Yesenia's manner as much as her words. She did not act like a woman confronting her lover's wife. *Take her shopping?* "Where do you want to go?" she inquired .

"Fiesta Mall," Yesenia said. "If you could give me a ride and drop me off there, I would appreciate it."

"I'll take you." It was an opportunity to keep the conversation going, to try to crack this tart's facade, or, if nothing else, give her some insights into Dan Willoughby.

Turning onto the freeway and heading westbound, Trish said, "You know that car Danny's driving?"

"The Jaguar?"

"Yes. I bought it for him."

"Really?" Yesenia was surprised.

"Really." There was a reason for the disclosure. Trish wanted her to know that Dan lived well on her money, not his. A woman like this would have no use for a man of limited means, a man on an allowance.

Yesenia studied Trish Willoughby as they drove toward the mall. *Nice lady,* she thought. *Not like the bitch Danny is always talking about.*

"Thanks a lot for the ride," she said when the Mercury Marquis pulled to a stop at the mall.

Still unsure what to make of her passenger, Trish nodded and forced a faint smile. "Remember what I told you," she said.

"Sure," Yesenia rejoined cheerfully. "I'll remember."

Dan left the envelope on the kitchen table, where his wife and daughter Marsha could not overlook it. They opened it and read it together.

"I allowed an innocent and open relationship (business only) to be misunderstood. If you had asked, you might have seen that I was not as guilty as you both assumed I was," the letter began. "Yesenia was only my Spanish teacher. That is the truth."

Dan explained how important to his business it was for him to learn the specialized Spanish vocabulary Yesenia was fluent in, but "If I had known that relationship would cause these problems, I would never have entered into it." He promised Yesenia would not be in contact with the family again, and reiterated his openness and honesty had prevented him from thinking anything bad could have come from his actions. He continued, "I hope, however, in the future that we all try to see the good in people and not what we might perceive as bad. No one likes to be accused of something when they are innocent."

Willoughby then professed his love for them all, writing, "I've literally sacrificed my body so that my family and Mom's business could get started so we all could improve our lifestyle." He closed by reminding them he had "paid a heavy price," but had done it all "for the love of my family."

After writing that letter, Dan picked Yesenia up at her apartment and drove to Metro Center in Phoenix, to a place called Gold Art Creations. There they browsed and haggled and considered options before deciding on a $3,800 half-carat, pear-cut diamond in a solitaire Tiffany setting—Yesenia's *engagement* ring.

The next week, he moved her out of Windemere to a new apartment in the Green Tree complex in Chandler. Farther from him, farther from his wife.

Victim Patricia Willoughby, 42, was known to everyone as "Trish."
(*photo courtesy Thera Huish*)

Trish, 3½, was the fourth of
Thera and Sterling Huish's five
children and the only girl.
(photo courtesy Thera Huish)

Trish Huish dropped out of her
Bountiful, Utah high school
in her senior year.
(photo courtesy Thera Huish)

Wanderlust took Trish Huish
to California miles away
from her family.
(photo courtesy Thera Huish)

By 21, Trish Huish was involved
in her first failed marriage.
(photo courtesy Thera Huish)

Trish and second husband Dan Willoughby relax in June 1988.
(*photo courtesy Thera Huish*)

Dan and Trish Willoughby two years before she was murdered.
(*photo courtesy Thera Huish*)

The Huish family in May 1989. Back row: Dan and Trish Willoughby, Val and Diana Huish, Cara and Nick Huish, Arlene and Bob Huish. Front row: Thera Huish, newlyweds Rick and Millie Huish, Sterling Huish. *(photo courtesy Thera Huish)*

Thera Huish (left) and her daughter Trish were successful business partners. *(photo courtesy Thera Huish)*

Willoughby told his family Yesenia Patino, a married woman,
was only teaching him Spanish.
(*photo courtesy Arizona Attorney General's Office*)

Patino and Willoughby on the beach at Cancun.
(*photo courtesy Arizona Attorney General's Office*)

Yesenia Patino. *(photo courtesy Arizona Attorney General's Office)*

Yesenia Patino. *(photo courtesy Arizona Attorney General's Office)*

Yesenia Patino. *(photo courtesy Arizona Attorney General's Office)*

Police at the rented Rocky Point home in Mexico where the murder occurred. (*photo courtesy Arizona Attorney General's Office*)

Fingerprints on bottle linked Yesenia Patino, 34, to the murder scene. (*photo courtesy Arizona Attorney General's Office*)

$6,000⁰⁰

DOLARES DE HALLAZGO

Alias: Yesenia Guzman, Alfredo Patino, Yesenia Derascon, Victoria Mielke, Victoria Willoughby
Edad: 35 anos de edad
Sexo: Fememino
Raza: Latina
Height: 1.70
Weight: 61 kilos

¿Ha visto a esta persona?

Si le ha visto, $6,000⁰⁰ dolares de hallazgo puede ser suyo!

Yesenia tiene un delito de mayor quantía pendiente sobre un cargo de un robo en Los Estados Unidos. Tambien se le requiere en relación a un homicidio que ocurrió el 23 de febrero 1991, en la ciudad de Puerto Peñasco de México. (PUNTO DE SABER) En 1980 Yesenia cumplió el cambio de sexo (masculino a femenino) Entonces ella tambien pudiera estar vistiéndose y actuando como un hombre.

ZERO IN ON CRIME
WITH
SILENT WITNESS

620 West Washington, Phoenix, Arizona 85033

Thousands of copies of the Huish family's flyer offering a reward for information on Yesenia Patino were distributed.
(*photo courtesy Thera Huish*)

Patino at the police station in the tourist port city of Mazatlan,
Mexico.   (*photo courtesy Arizona Attorney General's Office*)

Alfredo G. Patino was arrested for shoplifting in Oregon in 1977. (*photo courtesy Arizona Attorney General's Office*)

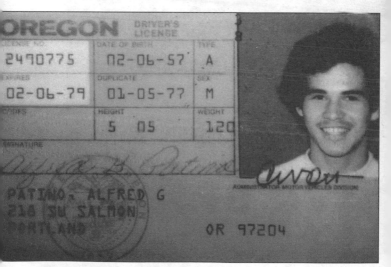

Police found a driver's license for Alfred Patino in Yesenia Patino's purse. (*photo courtesy Arizona Attorney General's Office*)

Patino, several years before the 1982 trip to Trinidad, Colorado to undergo a sex change operation. (*photo courtesy Arizona Attorney General's Office*)

Willoughby was arrested for the murder of his wife on December 9, 1991. (*photo courtesy Gilbert, AZ Police Department*)

Yesenia Patino on
the stand testifying.
(*photo courtesy*
Phoenix Newspapers, Inc.)

Thera and Sterling Huish after hearing the verdict.
(*photo courtesy* Phoenix Newspapers, Inc.)

Lieutenant Joe Ruet.
(*photo courtesy Gilbert, AZ Police Department*)

Kay Lines, investigator for the Attorney General.

Debbie Schwartz, Lines's partner in the investigation.

Chapter Twenty-four

Dan Willoughby ducked into the restroom, washed up, splashed on cologne and was headed for the door when Phil Cantrelli, spoiling for a confrontation, stopped him.

Their friendship had deteriorated to the point that not only did they not hang out together anymore, they could barely work together. Willoughby flaunted his affair with Yesenia in a way that grated on Cantrelli. He was tired of lying for Willoughby when Trish called the office looking for him. He was tired of listening to his lies, tired of watching him manipulate the other A.E.I. employees and tired of having to take up the slack as Willoughby shirked his work to spend time with his mistress.

Willoughby had hired a new saleswoman from Minneapolis. She had quit her job there and was in the process of moving, but Willoughby had not done the necessary paperwork to bring her on board at A.E.I. Though it was not his responsibility, Cantrelli had seen to the matter and, in the process, realized he was thoroughly fed up with his former pal and skirt-chasing rival.

"Going to Digital, I guess," he said before Dan could get out the door.

Willoughby turned, smiling, but his face quickly turned crimson as Cantrelli dressed him down in decibels their coworkers could not ignore. Willoughby stepped close to him, close enough that they were virtually nose to nose, and curled his hands into fists. Hours in the gym had thickened his arms and shoulders into fighting heft, but Cantrelli continued the provocation.

"Hit me, Dan. Goddammit, hit me."

The muscles in Willoughby's neck and jaw strained against the skin.

"Go ahead," Cantrelli taunted. "You know what, Dan? I won't hit you back, but I know who's going to hit you. And I'm going to stand here and watch him beat the shit out of you."

It was a bluff, but it worked. Cursing, Willoughby stepped back, turned and bolted out the door.

Friday the Thirteenth. If there was a heavy heart at A.E.I. it might have belonged to Tina Roush. She had remained Dan's friend, even as nearly everyone else in the shop had grown to detest him. He had hired her, tutored her, helped her through personal problems. She had seen nothing, not even his affair with Yesenia, that would turn her against him.

His moodiness, testiness, arrogance, trickery and, at times, meanness had thoroughly alienated the others, who were hoping for the worst when Rob Chandler showed up at the office that day. Something definitely was up. He was the regional manager from Los Angeles, and while such visits were not unusual, this one—unannounced—reeked of trouble. When Chandler insisted on a private meeting with Willoughby, the others, silently hoping for the worst, waited anxiously for the reason for the tête-à-tête to reveal itself.

After Chandler left, Willoughby began cleaning out his desk.

He had been fired, a victim once again of loose ethics and, this time, a more serious transgression. He had been caught forging routing slips again, but of more immediate concern to his superiors, there were serious problems with his expense accounts. Some had been grossly padded to cover the cost of Yesenia accompanying him on business trips, and some were falsified to cover travel that did not relate to business.

Before leaving the office, he wrote a check for $6,000 to reimburse the company—a fact discovered by the other employees when a secretary found a photostat of the check, which he inadvertently left in the copy machine.

For several months, while he was jetting around the hemisphere for week-long or long-weekend trysts with Yesenia in California or in one of Mexico's exotic coastal resorts, Dan had frequently discussed a possible career move with his wife. He wanted out of the air freight business. It was too stressful, he said, too demanding of his time. He was always keyed up, he said. Trapped. Drained. Burned out.

"I could get out and help you with the Matol business," he told her. "I could spend more time with the kids and take some of that pressure off you."

Trish was not averse to the idea. Though she had her suspicions about the ubiquitous Spanish teacher, she also believed it possible that some of her husband's erratic and deleterious behavior was due to job tensions. She took no position on the matter other than to tell him the decision was entirely his.

Therefore, she was not surprised that Friday, July 13, 1990, when he announced, "I quit. I'm not working for A.E.I. anymore."

"What happened?" she asked.

"My people were getting screwed around . . . not getting enough money," he said. "I stood up for them . . . really got into it with the regional manager. I told him I was tired of my people getting stiffed, and I told him to stuff it."

Trish didn't care, at least not about the loss of income. T&T Distributors, with only three employees, was now bringing in an average of $40,000 a month. They talked at length, calmly for a change. Dan told her he had some ideas for developing a business that would involve trade with Mexico. Because he had supported Trish during the years she struggled to find her niche, he reasoned, there was no shame in her paying the bills while he searched for his. He could attend to the children more and even take a little time to work out the kinks from years of job stress.

He sketched a scenario—not of loss, but of gain, of a new beginning—to which his wife hopefully subscribed. Relieved that the issue had been settled, they spent the evening packing and departed the next morning for a seven-day family vacation in Mazatlan.

Yesenia left the same day for Portland to visit her husband and son.

"He might just be dangling you along," Mulkins said.

"No," Yesenia shot back. "He's madly in love with me."

Still fearful that Willoughby might take drastic steps to dissolve his marriage by means other than divorce, Mulkins wanted to discourage his wife from continuing the affair.

"Maybe so," Mulkins said. "But I don't think he's going to leave his wife. Why don't you just find somebody else?"

"He'll leave her," she insisted. "But I'm getting tired of waiting."

"Do you love him?"

"No. I don't even like his lovemaking. I'm sick and tired of it."

"But you want to marry him."

"Yes . . . for the money," she said. "I want enough money to get Abel out of jail and live with him in Mexico."

"I think you should get away from him."

"I'm going to marry him," she said firmly.

Struggling to stifle his anger, Mulkins told her it was insane for her to remain involved with Willoughby if he were seriously plotting to do harm to his wife.

She was not a person who elicited pity, but along with his anger at her foolishness and immaturity, her husband felt something close to compassion. She had grown up poor, lived a hard life on the streets, learned selfishness as a survival tool. Now she was knocking at the door of her biggest opportunity, her grandest score. But to realize it, she had to endure a man she did not love, a man whose lovemaking bored her, a man who scared her just a little. If her lover could kill his wife, he could do the same to her. *Poor Yesenia.* The hook had been set.

"Sometimes Dan frightens me," she acknowledged reluctantly, suggesting that she may have felt there was no safe exit for her.

"You mean the Mafia stuff?" Mulkins asked.

"Yeah."

"What happened in San Francisco? He was going to see some people there."

"They didn't want anything to do with it," she said. "They told him it was not within their camp, you know? They take care of business things, but when it comes to family situations, you better take care of it yourself."

Mulkins snorted, a sharp exhale of relief. Just as a different picture of Yesenia had formed in his mind when she professed a willingness to participate in "getting rid" of Trish Willoughby, a new impression of Dan Willoughby was now taking form: a blowhard, all talk and no walk.

If Yesenia feared her lover, it could not be discerned from her actions. Theirs had always been a tempestuous affair, beginning with his suspicions of her infidelities and her impatience with the pace of his separation from his wife. Each wanted to possess the other, but for different reasons, and neither was capable of making the relationship whole. So the storm never slept. At a baseball game that summer, an argument became so heated that Yesenia broke one of Dan's teeth with a punch to the mouth. At a mall, he had to restrain her from punching a woman who spoke to him.

He sent flowers with notes imploring loyalty. "Remember, same rules for both or no rules at all." For Yesenia, that was no choice at all. She would do what she damn well pleased. No rules for Yesenia.

She nagged him to break free of his marriage even as she antagonized him with her own promiscuity. The pressures weighed heavily on Willoughby. Though unemployed now and free to spend his days in Yesenia's bed, or pump iron with her at Gold's Gym or brown beside her at the Golden Glo Tanning Salon or linger over long lunches at Keegan's or the Rusty Pelican, it was not enough. He could not monitor every minute of her day, and he was positive that when he was not around, another man was.

His behavior became more erratic, his temper more mercurial, a development that did not go unnoticed by his in-laws.

Before leaving town to accompany Trish on a business trip, he gave Nick a $10,000 check to invest in some stock for him when the market opened the next day. Early the next morning, Nick discovered that the bank would not cash the check because Dan's signature did not match the one on file. When Trish had opened the joint account, it turned out, Dan had not been present, so she had signed his name.

Frantic, Nick called his sister's house, hoping to catch them before they left town.

"Dan," he said. "The bank won't cash your check. The signatures don't match."

"Goddammit," Dan exploded. "You goddamn bastard. I can't believe you're not competent to handle this shit."

"Wait a minute—"

"Here I am getting ready to go on a goddamn trip and I have to spend this fuckin' time with you."

"Listen," Nick tried to interrupt. "I'm doing this for you and I don't—"

"Just forget the goddamn thing," Dan ranted. "I'll take care of it myself."

When they returned from their trip, Nick went to Trish's office and took her aside, where their mother could not hear.

"I don't know what your husband's on," he said, "but if he ever talks to me like that again, I will never have another thing to do with him."

Trish apologized, but she and her brother both knew that there was little she could do. Dan was beyond her control, possibly beyond his own control.

Only a few weeks after promising Trish and Marsha in writing that the Spanish teacher would never be exposed to the Willoughby family again, Dan returned to her apartment with Thera and Hayden. Jack Mulkins was there with his son Charlie, and they were moving furniture to a U-Haul trailer.

"What's going on?" Willoughby demanded.

"This is stuff that belonged to Jack and me," Yesenia said. "I don't want it anymore. I want some new furniture."

"I'm taking it to my place in Cottonwood," Mulkins said.

"Okay, take it," Willoughby said. "Whatever you want."

The children were talking quietly on one side of the small room. Dan took Yesenia by the arm and led her to the other side. Mulkins picked up an end table and was about to carry it through the door when Willoughby erupted.

"How many times do I have to tell you," he yelled, "that if I'm going to trust you to be the mother of my children that you have to stop this fooling around?"

Mulkins stopped in his tracks. The children looked at their father.

"Go outside and wait for me," he instructed them.

The party had been going for a while when Dan arrived. Yesenia had invited her mother, her three brothers and assorted other relatives. After leaving home in Oregon, she had not maintained close contact with her family. After they drifted south and found work in Arizona, she slowly moved back into their circle and established a modest rapport with them. Her brothers had managed to climb a little up the economic ladder from the migrant farm worker rung they were born on, but only a little. They were still laborers, but less itinerant than their parents had been.

Yesenia seemed to have done much better for herself. She had clothes and money, and the apartment was furnished with new furniture, compliments of her sugar daddy. She was fond of boasting that she would be rich as soon as he dumped his wife and married her.

Dan opened a beer and struck up a conversation with Antonio, the brother he knew best because he was the closest to Yesenia. Since moving from Indio a few months earlier, Tony talked with his sister by telephone nearly every day and was becoming a fixture in her apartment. Dan befriended him as well—in his usual way, extending favors and money and impressing him with his connections.

Tony was always willing to accept his benevolence, but this night he was testy and obviously unimpressed with Willoughby's talk about his plans for Yesenia and himself. He had heard it too many times. Now it triggered in him an uncharacteristic surliness, a temptation to deflate Willoughby's bombast.

"Yesenia is never going to marry you," Tony said. The volume in the small apartment had been rising steadily along with the alcohol consumption, but Tony spoke above the din.

"You're full of shit," Willoughby said. "What do you know about anything."

"She won't marry you," Tony said, a little louder.

Willoughby shoved him and Tony shoved back. Fists were thrown and the others tried to break up the scuffle. A neighbor dialed 911.

"It was wild," an excited Yesenia said, recounting the ruckus over the phone to Jack Mulkins the next morning. "The police came and everything."

After that, Willoughby seemed driven to prove to everyone, to Jack Mulkins, to the family of Yesenia Patino, perhaps most of all to himself, that he was man enough to take what he wanted.

Chapter Twenty-five

Except for the one visit to Yesenia's apartment, Trish Willoughby made no particular effort to keep tabs on her husband. Despite his protestations and Yesenia's convincing manner, she believed there was more to their association than linguistic tutoring. She was willing to forgive his dalliance to preserve her marriage, and she had taken on faith the promise he made in the letter to her and Marsha.

Although Dan still used her frequent business travel as a weapon against her in his war for the hearts and minds of the children, the daily discord between them abated a little. Dan had even begun to hang around their office a little, calling on Janie Clepp, Thera and Trish's assistant, to type letters for him or to mail packages through T&T's postage permit.

Thera disliked having him around. He was surly to her and contemptuous of Trish. Except for oblique references to a Mexican deal he was working on, he never discussed the packages he was mailing to Texas and Colorado or the phone calls he was making to gymnasiums and health clubs in those states. Thera was suspicious of his activities. She had long believed he was taking illegal steroids. The hours he spent lifting weights could not, by itself, account for the bulk he had added to his body. Fifty-year-old men can certainly respond to exercise without chemical aid, but as swiftly and as utterly as her son-in-law? Her knowledge of those drugs was limited, but she had read that in addition to the muscular enhancement, there were deleterious side effects—both physical and mental. Anabolic and androgenetic steroids, synthetic derivatives of testosterone, can hasten muscular development and, in some cases, fortify the libido, but they also can heighten hostility and aggression. The demand by athletes and bodybuilders had created a $400 million black market, and Thera had no doubt that Dan Willoughby was using her business to grab a piece of that action.

By using T&T Distributors as a shipping point, Dan had made his business her business, but she did not voice her concerns to her daughter. Trish was struggling enough to cope with an inscrutable husband; for her mother to tread into the fray could only exacerbate the ordeal.

She did, however, make known her feelings that Dan's presence in the office was disruptive. He distracted Trish. He peeved Thera. He took up too much of Janie Clepp's time. If in fact he was bootlegging steroids, the profits were not going into the Willoughby family general fund. From all appearances, Trish had become his sole source of support.

"You can't just spend all your time hanging out," Trish insisted when her frustrations boiled over.

"I stay busy with the kids," he argued. "Who do you think gets them off to school when you're away and picks them up after school? Who cooks their dinner when you're working late?"

"And you've got all day to play," she said, "or hang around our office disrupting us."

"I'm trying to put some deals together," he said. "It takes time, Trish."

"You could get involved with Matol," she said. "You could be making money tomorrow."

"I know, I know. Remember, I told you I might be able to open some markets in Mexico."

"Danny," she said, "I've told you that Matol has no license to sell in Mexico. Why don't you forget about that and do something here? It wouldn't even be a full-time job."

He resented being a kept man, resented the fact that he had been fired from his last three jobs and was, in all probability, unemployable in the air freight business. He resented being dressed down by a prosperous and successful wife, resented the corner he had painted himself into. If he neglected Yesenia, he would lose her; if he continued to live by the sweat of Trish's brow, she could jerk his chain at will. He was squeezed into a narrow corridor between his two lives, jostling to buy time on both sides.

"I'll give it some thought," he said. "I've been thinking about the business lately, anyway."

"What about it?"

"I think you should incorporate."

"Why?"

"Well, there are some legal issues, maybe some tax advantages involved."

"The partnership is working fine," she said.

"Yeah, of course, but Sterling and I should have our names on the business . . . you know, just in case . . . for everybody's protection."

She was still determined to ride out the bumps in her marriage, but until she had a clear indication of where things were headed, Trish had no intention of giving her husband even partial legal control of her business.

"I'll talk to Mom about it," she said.

* * *

Dan and Yesenia had something to show her, so Tina Roush agreed to meet them for lunch at the Rusty Pelican, one of Willoughby's favorite haunts, early in September. She had socialized with them a few times. She was with them at Keegan's Pub in Scottsdale six weeks earlier when Yesenia delivered her ultimatum to Dan—"You have one month to give me a ring"—but mostly had tracked their relationship through frequent meetings and phone conversations with her ex-boss.

No sooner had she pulled her chair up to the table than Willoughby, beaming, lifted Yesenia's left hand to display the stone on her finger.

"Danny gave it to me," Yesenia said, as effusive and euphoric as a lottery winner. "We're engaged."

"Congratulations," Tina said, with faint mockery that flew under the radar of Yesenia's callow brain. If the irony of a married man becoming engaged to a married woman could escape her, there was no danger of insulting her with voice inflection.

Dan put his arm around Yesenia and hugged her. She kissed him on the cheek.

"How are things at the shop?" Dan asked.

"Same, I guess," Tina said.

"Phil still hitting on you?"

She scowled. "Yeah and it's getting worse. He bugs me at the office and calls me at home at night."

"Probably hard for him to believe that any woman would reject him."

"He's started making threats," Tina said.

"What kind of threats."

"My job. He's dropped hints that if I don't have sex with him, he could get me fired."

"Sounds like a lawsuit. Has anyone else heard him say that?"

"Nah. He did leave a message on my answering machine . . . something to that effect."

"Save that tape. You may need it."

* * *

Trish had not burdened her parents with her marital problems. Beyond an awareness that something was amiss and that she was seeing a counselor, they had remained largely in the dark about intimate matters of her household. They had no clue that Dan Willoughby was involved with another woman, or even that Trish harbored such suspicions.

That day, however, she returned to the office from a business meeting in downtown Phoenix in such a distraught state that the topic was all but unavoidable.

"I've been chasing my husband," she told her mother, and then related the details:

En route back to Mesa, she spotted her husband's car merging onto the Superstition Freeway near the Rusty Pelican restaurant. Engrossed in conversation with his companion, Dan failed to notice his wife close behind him until she announced herself with a blast from the Merc's horn. She signaled for him to pull over and he ignored her.

She jerked the car into the left lane and accelerated, pulling even with the Jaguar.

"Pull over," she shouted, waving her right arm like an angry traffic cop.

Shielded from her by his tinted windows, Dan pretended not to see or hear her. Yesenia Patino slumped down in the passenger seat in a fruitless attempt to conceal herself.

"Dammit, pull over," she yelled with another long blast of the horn.

Willoughby sped up, passed the car in front of her, changed lanes and tried to lose himself in the flow of traffic. Trish stayed with him. She grabbed her cellular phone and dialed his number.

"Yeah," he answered, apparently not expecting the voice he would hear.

"Stop that car, Dan Willoughby," Trish said.

"I can't talk right now," he said.

"I thought you weren't going to have any more to do with

that woman." She was several car lengths behind him and exceeding the speed limit.

"We'll have to talk later," he said, goosing the Jag toward an exit ramp.

Trish followed, but caught a red light on the access road and lost him.

"Who was the woman?" Thera asked.

"I don't know ... it's his ... he says she is his Spanish teacher. He spends too much time with her."

That was as close as Trish would come to an insinuation of infidelity, and Thera did not press further. If there was more to be told, Trish would pick the time to tell it.

It had worked before, so Dan stuck with his story, stuck to his posture of ignorance and innocence.

"What were you doing with her?" Trish demanded when they were at home that evening.

"I was just giving her a ride," Dan stammered. "I had to pick up some Spanish papers from her and she wanted a lift to the mall. That's all."

"You told me you weren't going to see her again," Trish said.

"I told you the family would not be exposed to her again," he said. "But she can be a lot of help to me, Trish. You know how hard I've been working on those Mexico deals and I need her help with the language."

"Why didn't you stop and talk to me?"

"She was scared. She didn't want to be the cause of a fight between us. She was terrified. She didn't know what you would do."

Her patience was nearly exhausted. "I don't know how much more of this I can take, Danny," she sighed. "You spend money like there's no tomorrow. I never know where you are during the day. You think I'm swallowing this crap about a Spanish tutor. I've just about had enough."

Willoughby suddenly became the wounded party.

"It's all so innocent," he sulked. "I don't know why you

can't have a little trust in me. I'm trying to do what's best for all of us.''

For the next couple of weeks, the mother and daughter were absorbed in their business and nothing more was said about the highway chase or the other woman. Trish still came to work tired too often and sometimes seemed to slide through the day lost in her own thoughts, but she rarely complained.

Because her mood appeared to be no different that late September day as they were driving toward Phoenix for a meeting with a group of Matol distributors, Thera was unprepared for her daughter's abrupt request.

"Mom, I want you to promise me something," she said, without facing her mother.

"Sure, honey."

"If anything ever happens to me, promise you'll take care of my children."

Thera took her eyes off the road and stared at her daughter for as long as safety would permit.

"Trish, nothing is going to happen to you," she said.

"Just promise me that," Trish said, brushing aside her mother's assurances. "And another thing, if anything happens to me, you have to make sure you never give Danny any money to live in my house with some bimbo."

"You're talking silly."

"Promise me."

"Okay. I promise."

Chapter Twenty-six

Incorporate. Neither partner was keen on the idea, but as T&T Distributors grew, both recognized that some arrangement beyond a joint proprietorship might be desirable. In fact, the business was only an informal joint venture. T&T Distributors had been registered as a sole proprietorship by Thera Huish and she had "gifted" a one-half interest to her daughter with no formal documentation. With the company at its present size, perhaps a different structure was now warranted.

They had already taken one important step toward guaranteeing the security of the business—dual $250,000 life insurance policies to protect each partner against the death of the other. That amount had seemed adequate at the time, when the business was just taking off, but now neither partner had a solid feel for the value of T&T.

They balked at Dan Willoughby's persistent demands that they incorporate—neither understood fully the implications of such a move—but his badgering at least raised an issue they felt was worthy of consideration: insuring the long-term well-being of the business and gaining maximum tax advantage along the way. For that, they needed expert advice and were willing to listen—even to the expert Dan selected.

"I'd like for both of you to go with me," he said, appearing unexpectedly at their office in mid-October.

"Go where?" Trish asked.

"I've made an appointment with a lawyer. I want him to explain incorporation to you."

Reluctantly, they agreed. They were not certain that incorporating was not in their best interest—provided it was done a certain way—and, besides, no harm could come from hearing the lawyer's advice.

When they arrived at Richard Fuller's office, though, Dan took charge, and it was obvious that he already had worked out the details. He asked Fuller to explain the advantages of a buy-sell agreement—a compact which states that if one partner chose to leave the business, her half would be purchased by the other, or in the event of a partner's death, it would be purchased from the surviving spouse. The agreement would be funded—the terms guaranteed—by insurance policies on the lives of the partners.

Dan made a hard sell for such an agreement as a companion document to articles of incorporation, to which his name would be prominently attached. He orchestrated the meeting, instructed Fuller in the details, assured his wife and mother-in-law that this was in their best interests.

Fuller filled in the blanks, and they left with a portion of the documents that would need to be executed.

"Here," Dan said, thrusting the papers into his wife's hand as they walked to his car. "I want you to get this taken care of."

Thera bit down on her lip and held her tongue, but Trish could no longer constrain herself. She paused on the sidewalk and stiffened.

"Dan Willoughby, you will never have your name on anything that Mother and I have built," she said through taut lips.

"We built this. You have never done a thing. It is our business and it stays our business."

Her daughter's vehemence astonished Thera. She had never heard Trish, who always tried to keep her marital problems private, lash out at Dan with such force and finality. She could only guess at the dimensions of the fault line that lay beneath her daughter's normally tranquil surface, but she was certain of one thing: Dan Willoughby would never get his name or his hands on T&T.

"I just think . . ." Willoughby started to explain.

"We've got to get back to work," Trish snapped.

Willoughby, looking sheepish and a little silly, shrugged and walked behind the two women to the Jaguar.

Tony had hung around the apartment too long. Night fell and he was worried about driving home in the old pickup truck with the broken headlight. With his record of driving while intoxicated and several unpaid traffic tickets to his credit, he was reluctant to confront the police again.

"Can I leave it here and pick it up tomorrow?" he asked Yesenia.

Before she could answer, Dan interceded. "Yeah, leave it here. I'll get it fixed for you."

Tony thanked him and added, "I don't have any money right now, Dan."

"Don't worry about it. You can pay me when you can."

The next morning, Dan drove the truck to a garage and paid $83.04 to replace a dimmer switch and fix a short in the headlamp.

He liked having Tony owe him.

The incorporation papers prepared by Dan's lawyer were gathering dust on Thera's desk. While she and Trish had been partially sold on the notion of incorporating, they were content to move slowly.

Believing he would prevail, Willoughby had ceased to badger them about it and reverted to a strategy of charm. Early in November, he telephoned the offices of T&T Distributors and spoke with his mother-in-law.

"Thera, I need to know what Trish's travel schedule is for February," he said.

"Well, I'll have to check. It may not all be decided yet. Why do you want to know now?"

"I want to give my family a special Christmas present. A trip to Mexico. I want to book a condo in Rocky Point."

Thera scowled. Trish did not like Mexico, but it did not seem prudent to argue the point with Dan.

"I'll try to figure out what her schedule is," she said.

"Let me know as soon as possible," he said. "I'd like to take them on Valentine's Day."

This time, Tony had bigger problems than a broken headlight. He had been stopped by the police and cited for speeding and driving on a suspended license. His first thought was to call Yesenia and ask for Dan Willoughby's phone number.

"I've . . . uh . . . got these . . . uh . . . citations," Tony stammered when he finally reached Dan.

"Go over to Yesenia's tomorrow and I'll meet you there," Dan told him. "We'll take care of it."

When they met the next morning, Tony handed him the traffic tickets.

"I've got a good lawyer," Dan said.

Tony knew Willoughby would pay the attorney and would not ask for reimbursement.

"I'll do you a favor for the money, Dan," Tony said, not wanting to appear a complete parasite.

Willoughby smiled. "I do have a favor you can do for me."

"What is it, man?"
"I'll tell you later."

Duke Boggs flipped on the porch light, opened the door and found Dan Willoughby, a strained expression etched on his face, facing him through the glass storm door. He had not seen a lot of his neighbor lately and Boggs was curious about how his life of leisure was going.

Through either a long streak of good luck or pure adroitness on his part, Willoughby had managed to keep his personal life concealed from his neighbors and members of his church. He had been fired from three jobs for ethical lapses and dishonesty, but word had not reached the Houston Ward of the LDS Church in Gilbert. He escorted Yesenia to restaurants and bars and health clubs, bought jewelry for her, kept doctor and dental appointments with her, sent flowers to her weekly, attended sporting events and dances with her, roamed the malls with her—all without ever being spotted by, or arousing suspicion among, anyone from the other side of his life.

For all Boggs knew, Dan Willoughby was a contented househusband. He pushed open the door and invited Willoughby inside and asked him to sit down. He quickly sensed there was something unusual about this visit. Willoughby tried to make small talk, which turned to babble in slurred words.

"Dan, are you drunk?" Boggs asked him. It did not seem likely. From all appearances, Willoughby was still the devoted family man, still the faithful Sunday school teacher.

Willoughby straightened himself a little and tried to speak more clearly. "Of course not," he said. "I've been . . . I'm taking medication."

Boggs was a devout Mormon, loyal to the church doctrine that renounced alcohol, among other earthly temptations. Seeing the strange look in Willoughby's eyes, hearing the speech that was nearly incoherent, he feared that Willoughby was becoming worldly and told him so, not in accusatory tones, but in the Mormon spirit of looking after a brother. Defensive, but not defiantly so, Willoughby insisted that he was not drinking and that his friend should lay his concerns to rest.

The reason for the visit was still unclear as Boggs escorted him to the door.

As he stepped outside, Willoughby turned to face him, a sadness weighing on his brow.

"Duke," he said, "will you always be my friend?"

"Sure Dan," he said. "Of course, I'll be your friend."

Willoughby nodded and turned toward home. Boggs stood at the door and watched to make sure he reached his house safely. Afterwards, he talked for a long time with his wife about the change that seemed to be coming over Dan. Since they knew nothing of any difficulty he might be experiencing, they didn't know what kind of help to offer him.

But they knew what to do for themselves. A few days after that visit, they withdrew their daughter from Willoughby's Sunday school class.

None of her threats or demands had made any difference. Dan had declined to get involved in the Matol business. He spent money like the Prince of Brunei and breezed through his days with no apparent obligations or responsibilities. He saw that the children were fed, dressed and off to school each morning and was usually there when they came home in the afternoon, but as far as Trish could tell, he did little that was productive or worthwhile in between.

Occasionally, he still came to her office to ask Janie Clepp to type letters or to ship a package. Thera resented both activities, but resented even more his inimical attitude toward her and Trish. In sum, he had become an aggravation neither woman could bear any longer.

"Why don't you make him do something?" Thera asked her daughter.

Trish, busy writing checks for her monthly household bills,

sighed. "I can't make him do anything. I just don't want to provoke him. I don't know what he would do."

Her fear of him was becoming a disturbing subtext to these conversations.

"He needs something to do," Thera said. "Why don't you make him pay the bills. Let him take over the checkbook . . ."

Suddenly, Trish seemed lost in thought.

For all practical purposes, she and Dan had ceased to be husband and wife, and she had no doubt that the Spanish teacher was the wedge between them. She was making the payments on his car and, because he no longer had an income, was also paying for all his other indulgences—including, she was sure, his dalliance with Yesenia Patino.

Dan could not easily conceal his expenditures. Because Trish paid the bills, she had a monthly log of his considerable credit card charges. The health club dues, the tanning salon visits, the manicures and the restaurant tabs were bad enough, but the hotel bills and plane tickets and tickets to ball games and department store purchases and all the other trappings of the idle life were infuriating.

Finally, she took a monumental step, which required only a few telephone calls. That evening, she informed her husband of what she had done.

"I've taken your name off all my credit cards," she said.

Willoughby was stunned. Without plastic, he would be unable to feed the large goat that his mistress had become. She expected things of him—rent, furniture, clothing, jewelry, flowers, nights on the town, weeks on the beach. Cut off his plastic and Trish might as well cut off his penis.

"This kind of spending has got to stop," Trish told him, "and you have got to straighten up. If you don't, Dan Willoughby, I'm going to divorce you."

The mountain had erupted and rained hot ash down upon him. The waters were rising to his chin. The gravy train was off the rails. Either his anger dissipated or he faked it marvelously. With humility and contrition, he pleaded for patience, vowed to purge his demons and get control of his life again.

Trish, hopeful once more, swallowed his promise, and not entirely because she believed he would keep it. She did not deem herself blameless in the mess their lives had become. Her work schedule and long business trips had its own disruptive impact on the family. They both would have to make concessions.

At work a few days later, she told Janie Clepp about cutting off Dan's credit cards.

"I don't want him to have a lot of money," she said. "He would be out of control. I'm tired of paying for his habits and his hobbies."

With his cash flow contained, she believed, he could be steered back into the marital fold.

"When the holidays are over," Trish said, "we're going to get back on a regular schedule, back to our old family routine."

Janie hoped that her boss's optimism was not misplaced. She was fond of Trish, just as she was fond of Dan.

Chapter Twenty-seven

With a pen and note pad in hand, Deborah Fife leaned back in her chair, pressed the "play" button on her answering machine and jotted down the string of names and numbers that had been left in her absence. It was the day before Thanksgiving, nearly noon, and she was eager to get a head start on the holidays. When the machine fell silent, she laid the notebook aside; she would return the calls on Monday.

For three years, she had been the manager of Rita's Mexican Vacations, a small agency in downtown Phoenix that specialized in finding beachfront condos for vacationers. Many of the Americans who owned condos in Mexico rented them out when they were not in use, and Rita's was a kind of time-share matchmaker. Rather than being a regular walk-in travel agency, most of its business was conducted by phone and mail.

After the weekend, she dialed the number Dan Willoughby had left.

"I'm looking for a nice, private beach condo in the Rocky Point area where I can spend some time with my family," he told her.

"There are some nice facilities closer in, where you can enjoy the beach and still have the conveniences of being in town," she told him.

"No, I want something very quiet and very remote," he insisted.

Leafing through her files on Rocky Point, she mentioned a development called Las Conchas. "It's a couple of miles from town and there's nothing out there except the houses and a small museum."

"What about telephones?"

"There are none in that area."

"That sounds good."

She explained that she had a packet of general information about houses and the town, along with maps and material that might be helpful. "I can mail it out this afternoon," she said.

"No, I'd like to come by and pick it up in person," Willoughby said. "I work at the airport, in shipping, and I'm going to be out moving around this afternoon anyway."

Willoughby was waiting at her office when she arrived before nine o'clock the next morning. They went over the maps and the descriptions of the available properties, along with rules pertaining to each unit. Renters have to take their own linens and blankets and soap, along with food, water and firewood. Nights in February are chilly on the Gulf of California.

"You have to go prepared," she said. "There's nothing out there."

He seemed extremely impatient.

"I'm going down this morning to check them out," he said. "I have to go to Gila Bend on business. Might as well drop on down to Rocky Point."

Willoughby had told Fife that he was taking his family to Rocky Point as a special gift, particularly a gift to his wife. In that case, Las Conchas struck her as an odd choice. *If my husband were taking me someplace,* she thought, *I would rather go to a nice hotel, where he could take me dancing and to dinner.*

She handed him brochures on some of the newer hotels in Rocky Point.

"These are not as expensive as the private houses," she said, thinking he might want to reconsider. "You wouldn't have to take any supplies with you. And you'd be right on the beach."

"I think the private house is better," he said. "We have three children. We need the room."

He left in a hurry. Trish was traveling on business again and he had things to do before she returned. He drove back to Gilbert, put his Jag in the shop for minor repairs and, driving Trish's Mercury, picked up Yesenia and lit out for Puerto Penasco.

"I want to make an appointment to have some pictures taken," the woman on the phone had said. She sounded young and had a Spanish accent.

"When would you like?"

"Thursday."

"About two o'clock?"

"Okay."

"What's your name?"

"Yesenia Willoughby."

Michael Pitts wrote the name in his appointment book. It rang a dim bell.

The couple arrived at the Pioneer Photography Studios in Mesa with two sets of clothes apiece, one casual and one slightly more formal. Yesenia's hair was thick, dark and billowing, Dan's was razor-cut and streaked with silver. Dan was tanned and trim, but with a slight, middle-age sag about the jowls and chin. Yesenia was coquettish and impish at once, but there was also a coarseness about her, a texture that low-cut blouses and diamond rings could not cloak. Pitts had never seen her before.

The man looked familiar. Willoughby. Oh, yeah. A little more than a year before he had met with two women in a park beside a small pond to photograph them for the cover of a company magazine. Matol Botanical International. Huish and Willoughby. He had also photographed them playing golf with their husbands.

When the session was done, they discussed photo packages and prices. Willoughby specifically wanted a large portrait— a thirty-inch by twenty-four-inch print, along with an assortment of smaller ones. Money was not an issue. These, after all, were his engagement pictures.

Deborah Fife had given Willoughby information on two Las Conchas residences. The large one, owned by Jim and Barbara Grubb, seemed to her to be the least desirable for the simple reason that it was farther inland, set off by itself to the side of the beach area. The unit owned by Charles and Sue Salem was closer to the beach and the water.

"I want the Grubbs' house," Willoughby told her by telephone after he returned from Rocky Point.

"Did you check them both out?" she asked.

"Yeah. I like this one because it's quieter, a little more remote. And it's larger. Will you find out if it's available on Valentine's Day weekend?"

"Sure."

When they talked a couple of days later, Fife informed him that the owners would be using the house that weekend. "What are your other choices?" she asked.

"The weekend before or after."

She called him back the same day. He could have the house on February 22 and 23.

"You can send a deposit to secure the rental and pay the balance later," she advised him, "or send a check for the full amount."

"I want to pay in cash." he said. "I just don't want any

record of it in my checkbook. It's going to be a surprise for my wife."

"Well, you could send a cashier's check."

"I want to pay cash," he said firmly.

"Then you'll have to bring it by in person."

Fife was growing impatient with him. He was making this transaction more difficult than it needed to be. Normally, her clients received their information by mail, booked their units by telephone and mailed in their payments. At the appropriate time, she mailed the keys to the beach houses to them, and when they returned, they mailed the keys back to her. No hassle.

When he came by to make his cash payment, Willoughby asked for the keys to the house.

"I can't give you a key now," she told him. "You're not going until February and there are other renters going before then. I'll mail them to you the week before your trip."

"No, I'll come back and pick them up," he said. "I'll need two keys."

"I can only give you one," she said, tiring of his demands. Two keys. Nobody ever asked for two keys.

She gathered up a sheaf of papers—brochures, fliers, photographs and the like—and handed them to him, along with his rental contract. While he waited, she typed another list for him, a compendium of things to see and do in the Las Conchas area.

When she was finished, he pointed out the first item: *Visit CEDO Museum and see the whale skeleton. It's a few blocks from the house, to the left, up on the hill. Tours and lectures on Tuesdays and Saturdays at 4:00 p.m.* CEDO was an acronym for Centro de Estudios de Desiertos y Oceanos (Center for the Study of Deserts and Oceans). Housed in a Moroccan-style building on a dune looking down on the residences of Las Conchas, CEDO was not just a museum, but a field station for research, a wet laboratory and a small reference library. It's centerpiece exhibit was a fifty-five-foot fin whale skeleton.

"Your kids might enjoy this place," she said. "It's just a few blocks from the house."

Sales was her forte, not company management. She was an ace at knocking on doors, dialing cold calls, talking up her product, recruiting distributors, building downline channels, moving merchandise. But with no formal business education to inform her and no experience to guide her, Thera Huish was bewildered by the arcane jungle of company organization.

Their partnership consisted of a simple system of dividing the labor and the profits: She worked the field, Trish handled the books and the ordering and shipping; each month, they paid their expenses and split what was left. Fifty-fifty. No fancy formulas. But the business had grown dramatically, and for all she knew, it would continue to grow.

The buy-sell agreement had a certain appeal, but it was not clear to her that the $250,000 insurance policies she and Trish had purchased—each naming the other as beneficiary—were adequate to fund such an arrangement.

Recognizing that she needed professional advice—and not just from Dan Willoughby's attorney—Thera contacted the First Capital Life Insurance Company and arranged to meet with two agents, Phil Guthrie and Bob Yerken, to do an assessment of value of T&T Distributors. Calculating that the company was worth $2.5 million, the agents recommended that each partner purchase additional life insurance policies of $750,000.

Trish's policy was issued early in December by Transamerica Occidental Life. Thera's was delayed by problems in scheduling her physical examination and by the busy Christmas season that was nibbling at her time.

Richard Fuller continued to send documents for her signature and she continued to let them pile up on her desk. He had made a convincing argument for incorporating—not only were there tax advantages, but it could provide them with a legal shield against personal responsibility for any financial obligations of the corporation—and so two weeks before Christmas, the corporation was formed. They named it Emerging, Inc., and its sole purpose would be to collect from Matol monies owed to T&T Distributors. Dan Willoughby's name did not appear on the articles of incorporation. That entity would be controlled by mother and daughter.

Beside getting the other benefits of a corporation, Thera believed the incorporation accomplished two other things: It formalized Trish's stake in the business and put another layer between it and any community property claims Dan might bring in the event of a divorce.

Dan apparently believed the opposite. Since Trish had no documents of ownership in T&T Distributors—her share had been a gift from her mother—it might be difficult for him to establish a community property interest. The corporation was a more binding definition of her legal ownership and, therefore, his ownership.

At any rate, he now focused on bringing about the execution of a buy-sell agreement, which would force Thera to purchase half the business from him if Trish should die. He made regular inquiries about its status and pressured the partners to move forward on it. They were in no rush.

"We'll get around to it eventually," Thera told him, without revealing her reservations, which arose mostly from a lack of knowledge about such things.

"We have got to get this done," he persisted.

"Don't worry about it," Trish said "It isn't that important."

"It is important," Dan said.

He oozed an urgency that made Thera realize that her resistance was in inverse proportion to his assertiveness. For fourteen years, he had been like a son to her, and in the span of one contentious year he had all but obliterated the bond.

"Well, I don't have paperwork on it," Thera said, "and I really don't know very much about it."

"I'll go down and get the paperwork for you."

He returned shortly with a stack of forms printed out of

Richard Fuller's computer. Each was a variation of the standard buy-sell contract.

"Richard said you can choose any one of these you want and just put in the figures," he said.

Unceremoniously, she tossed the papers on her desk and said, "I'll look them over when I have time."

Her son-in-law was clearly exasperated by her show of indifference. She liked that, liked inflicting discomfort on him for a change.

In naming her mother as the beneficiary of both her insurance policies, Trish had made it clear that in the event of her death, she did not want Dan to have the money, did not want him to live in idle luxury, not in her house, not with some bimbo.

In their first meeting, Richard Fuller had explained Arizona's community property laws and the ways assets are allocated in divorce settlements or after the death of a spouse. The legal fine points were confusing, but Thera did not ask the questions that were racing through her mind. Did community property mean that Dan had an inalienable right to everything that was Trish's? If they divorced, could he claim his share of the business his wife had built? If his wife died, would Thera be obligated to pay him a million dollars or more for Trish's half of the business? Would a buy-sell agreement cement his claim on his wife's estate, including the insurance settlements? Was there a way to protect her own interest and honor Trish's intentions.

Thera didn't know, but she knew who to ask.

But it could wait until after Christmas.

Chapter Twenty-eight

Two days before Christmas, Yesenia Patino boarded a plane for Boise, Idaho, to spend the holidays with her estranged husband and son. She still cared for Charlie; it had been her idea to adopt him, and when she separated from her husband she was the first to acknowledge that he would be better off living with his father.

And she remained fond of Jack. Theirs had been a curious liaison from the beginning, but he had made a huge difference in her life and he certainly was not to blame for their separation. She simply wasn't wife material, and it was her promiscuity that doomed their union. The parting was amicable and Jack Mulkins morphed back into the paternal role that had brought them together in the first place. "If you ever get into trouble, I'll be your last resort. You can depend on me for sanctuary," he had told her.

Jack and Charlie were staying in Jack's motor home in LaGrande, a small town in eastern Oregon near the Umatilla National Forest, and he was not displeased when she called and asked if she could spend Christmas with him. He would have to drive to Boise to pick her up and then they would drive to his home in Portland. A lot of miles, but Jack had things on his mind that he wanted to discuss with her. It would be worth the effort.

It had been a few months since he last spoke with Dan Willoughby, and he had tried to assure himself that Willoughby's talk of getting rid of his wife had been just that—talk. Still, he could not put it completely out of his mind. Yesenia called occasionally, but their conversations were brief and he learned little, except that she and Dan were still involved and Dan was still promising marriage and still dragging his feet.

On the drive across Oregon, Yesenia was spirited and flighty as usual, but when Mulkins broached the subject of her affair with Willoughby, she was, for a change, almost taciturn. He reminded her that she had committed bigamy by marrying Abel Ramon while she was still married to him and cautioned her against repeating that mistake.

"Just give me some time to dissolve our marriage before you marry Dan," he said. "We won't have to go to court or anything. We'll just get a lawyer, fill out some forms and that'll be it."

She nodded and said, "When we decide to get married, we'll do that."

"Are we getting any closer to this?" Jack asked.

She didn't answer right away.

"In February, I'll be a millionaire," was her response, after reflecting for a moment.

Obliqueness was not one of Yesenia's more overt traits, and that she should employ it now was disquieting. He wanted to know where she was headed, and at the same time didn't want to know. He was feeling his way along the precipice of a black hole, curious about its contents and equally frightened by them.

"So, he's going to get a divorce from his wife?" he asked.

She looked at him for a second.

"I can't tell you," she said. "Matter of fact, I'm not sure I can trust you anymore."

* * *

If the conversation didn't exactly disillusion Debra Martz, it certainly did nothing to hoist her holiday spirit. Dan Willoughby, a philanderer?

She had known him for a couple of years, from her days as a personal trainer at the Pegasus Fitness Center. He had been a member there and they occasionally talked and became casual friends. On her birthdays or other special occasions, Dan would leave a generous gift for her—fifty, sometimes a hundred dollars. When she went to work part time for the Golden Glo Tanning Salon, he became a regular there also. She did not know a lot about him, only that he was pleasant and generous and was married and had children.

What Linda Levine was telling her now was at odds with every impression she had of him.

"Dan Willoughby asked me to have a drink with him tomorrow," Linda said. Tomorrow was Christmas Eve, when men with families tend to be preoccupied with home.

"You know he's married and has three kids?" Martz said. Linda was a habitual flirt, but Martz did not think she would knowingly take up with a married man.

"He told me his wife died in a car wreck two years ago," Levine said.

Willoughby's phone number was on his membership form, so Martz fished it out of the files and called him. Something was screwy. She knew Willoughby better than Linda did and he had never hinted at this tragedy. She confronted him with what she had just heard.

"Yeah, she did die in a car wreck two years ago," he said. There was a convincing poignancy in his tone.

"You never told me about that."

"Well, I didn't want to burden you, you or anybody else, with it."

She wasn't sure what to believe and neither was Linda Levine, who opted out of the drink date anyway.

*   *   *

Thera and Sterling arrived at the Willoughby house with arms full of packages early on Christmas morning and the entire family gathered by the tree. Wrapping paper, toys, clothing and other items covered the floor as the children tore into their presents and the adults, with less alacrity, opened theirs.

When all the others had been opened, Dan brought forth the *special* gift he had withheld until the last, and he did so with a flourish.

"This is for my family," he announced, handing the box to the children for them to open at their mother's knee. It contained brochures on Rocky Point, a photograph of the beach house and a few Mexican trinkets.

The first thing Thera Huish noticed was that Dan was taking far more delight than his family in this gift of a two-day Mexican vacation in a remote beach house on the outskirts of a sleepy village that offered little excitement beyond a small museum of whale bones. No white-knuckle rides. No theme parks. No chorus lines. Just sun, of which there was plenty in Arizona, and water, of which there was plenty in their own backyard pool.

Still, the children were passably pleased, but Thera sensed that Trish's perfunctory "thank you" was counterfeit. She didn't even like the country and Dan knew it. If he wanted to take his wife somewhere for a couple of days of solitude, it wasn't necessary to travel all the way to Rocky Point; the Arizona deserts teemed with isolation. Still, the gesture struck her as no more than a continuation of the selfishness her son-in-law had displayed for the past several months. He liked Mexico and therefore, by God, that's where he would spend this mini-vacation.

And there was an upside to it. His pleasure at bestowing this prize upon his family had lifted his spirits and transformed his personality from the malevolent creature he had become back to the Dan of old. He was nice to Trish, even affectionate. He was nice to everyone.

January 1991 arrived with a calm the partners in T&T Distributors had not felt in months, a harmony precipitated by the change in Dan Willoughby's attitude. At regular intervals, he brought up the issue of the buy-sell agreement, and while relentless, he was not overbearing. A nudge here, a reminder there.

He even began to exhibit a serious interest in the Matol business. Three weeks after Christmas, he and Sterling accompanied their wives on a four-day company convention in Anaheim, California. Before leaving, Dan arranged for the four of them to meet in Southern California with Alicia Chelette, the wife of an old friend and colleague from his air freight days. Abe Chelette now ran his own trucking company and divided his time between residences in Phoenix and Los Angeles.

Alicia was interested in becoming a Matol distributor, he assured them, and so they agreed to meet with her at their hotel before returning to Phoenix. Trish did most of the talking, explaining the product and the opportunities in multilevel marketing. Alicia signed up on the spot.

With one enlistee in the bag, Dan seemed energized. Shortly after that, he told Thera he was going back to Los Angeles to work with Alicia on expanding the business there.

"You don't have to pay my airfare," he said, "somebody else is taking care of it. I'll be gone three or four days."

They had talked little in the previous few months and she was pleased by his newfound enthusiasm. "Good," she said, "and good luck."

He and Thera departed about the same time—he for Los Angeles, she for a training seminar in Lancaster, California. At the airport awaiting her flight back to Phoenix a couple of days later, she decided to call Trish and brief her on the results of her trip. Dan answered the phone.

"Oh," Thera said. "You're already back from your trip?"

"Yes, and I'm so excited," he said. "Everything's in place and this is really going to go now. I've got twelve or fifteen people who are going to join the business. It's great, Thera. Everything's in place and I'm really going to work this business now."

She nearly swayed from the shock.

"That is very good to hear, Danny," she said. "I mean, I hope you've gotten your life together so you can start doing something."

"I have, Thera. Believe me, everything has changed."

Hanging up the phone, she felt buoyant, as though she had popped to the surface after being underwater too long. Nothing made her happier than the thought of seeing her daughter happy again, of seeing her grandchildren happy again. They had suffered as much as anyone from the antipathy that had invaded their house, and Thera let herself believe that at long last their ordeal was coming to an end.

She did not know that Dan Willoughby had not been in Los Angeles. He had made another trip to Rocky Point with Yesenia Patino.

"Danny is pushing us for this buy-sell agreement, and I really don't understand it," Thera said.

Terry Greenman of Beneficial Life Insurance Co. had sold the dual $250,000 policies to Thera and Trish a year earlier, so he knew a little about their business and their financial objectives.

"Would you like me to assist you?" he asked.

"I feel like we need some help," she said.

"Good. I'll come by your office, pick up the paperwork and evaluate it. I can probably come up with a few ideas for you."

After studying the sole proprietorship papers, the articles of incorporation for Emerging, Inc., and the estimates of their company's value, Greenman suggested that the business be placed in a trust administered by a trustee and controlled by

Thera and Trish. There would be no need for a buy-sell agreement.

"I know a lawyer who handles these things," he said.

Charles Mattich agreed to come by their office on a Saturday in mid-February. Dan insisted on attending the meeting.

Mattich presented them a complex, densely worded trust indenture, but explained that it amounted to a simple transfer of shares from Emerging, Inc., to the trust, which they decided to name Synergy Group. If one partner died, the shares automatically would be assigned to the other.

As the creator of the trust, Mattich would appoint a trustee to administer it, and an accountant would see to the books.

Willoughby became angry. It was not an easy document for a non-lawyer to comprehend, but one aspect was clear.

"I don't want my money handled by some trustee," he snapped.

"Wait a minute, Danny," Trish said. "This is not your money. This is mine and Mother's. You have nothing to do with it."

The argument continued for a few minutes until Dan announced that he had another appointment. Standing to leave, he said, "I don't want anything done with this until I give my approval."

When he was gone, Thera instructed Mattich to prepare the paperwork and proceed with the trust.

"It will take two or three weeks," he said. "I have to go to San Diego, but my staff can work it on while I'm gone."

Mother and daughter agreed to say nothing to Dan until the trust was a done deal.

With that out of the way, Trish turned her attention to preparing for the trip to Rocky Point. Nick had agreed to the loan of his van for the weekend. Trish's Mercury Marquis was hardly large enough for a family of five and the supplies they would need for the trip to Rocky point, and Dan's Jag was even smaller.

"Nick," Trish pleaded with him. "Would you please get that door handle fixed before we leave. I don't want Danny to have anything to grumble about. It doesn't take much to make him mad these days."

Three days after their meeting, Charles Mattich telephoned with good news. "I don't know why it happened so quickly, but the trust is finished. It's completed. It just needs to be signed and notarized."

"We'll be here in the morning, if you want to come by," Thera said.

They sat at the kitchen table and placed their signatures on a simple, one-page instrument:

MINUTES
These Minutes and Resolutions have been
Presented to and Voted Upon by the Board of
Trustees
of
SYNERGY GROUP
CHARLES MATTICH, Creator of the Business
Trust Organization, does hereby cause this Trust
Indenture and Declaration to be executed on the
Twenty First day of February, 1991, and ack-
nowledges signing hereof to be a voluntary act and
deed.

Still unsure of the full legal consequences of the arrangement, Thera joined her daughter in signing the document. At the very least, she felt, it would protect Trish's interest in the business should she divorce Dan, an eventuality that seemed more and more likely.

She resolved not to tell Dan about the trust. Trish could

reveal it to him if she chose. Something told her she would not.

On Thursday night, the family gathered at Trish's house for a going-away party. The Willoughbys would leave early the next morning for their special vacation in Mexico.

Nick had seen to the repair of the door handle and had delivered the van to them that morning. Dan spent most of the day packing it with the items the instruction sheet from Rita's Mexican Vacations had indicated they would need—linens, a few pieces of firewood, food. Lots of food.

"I don't know why Danny is packing all this food," Trish moaned to her mother. "We're only going to be gone two days."

Chapter Twenty-nine

Antonio Patino was baffled by the favor Dan asked.

"You're going to take me to Mexico," his sister told him just after Valentine's Day.

That was Dan's favor? That's what he wanted in exchange for having fixed his pickup and providing a lawyer to fight a stack of traffic tickets? Tony had expected something a little more demanding.

"Why am I taking you to Mexico?" he asked his sister, reminding her that his driver's license had been suspended.

"To pick up some money. Some people in California owe Danny some money and we're going to pick it up."

"How much money?"

"About $20,000."

Later, Dan and Yesenia came by his house and reiterated the request. Dan told him some Italian brothers from California owed him money and were going to meet him in Rocky Point to make the payment.

"Why there? Why in Rocky Point?" Antonio asked.

"It's neutral ground," Willoughby replied.

Antonio dropped the questioning. He owed the man a favor and this seemed easy enough.

"You need to be on the beach by three o'clock Saturday," Willoughby said. "Yesenia knows the place."

Yesenia called early Saturday morning to be sure he was awake and on schedule. They would need to leave by eight. Half an hour later, she called again to prod him along.

He picked her up in the silver-gray 1964 Chevrolet truck Dan had generously repaired and they took the standard route everyone in Phoenix followed to Puerto Penasco—west on the interstate, south to Gila Bend, where they stopped for gas, on to Ajo and the Organ Pipe Cactus National Monument, through the Lukeville border crossing and south to the shore.

They arrived at one-thirty and killed time on the beach near Manny's Place, the restaurant Dan had designated. Bored, Antonio went for a long walk, and when he returned to the restaurant, Willoughby was there. After half an hour and a couple of beers, Willoughby checked his watch and said, "I have to be going."

He had parked farther down the beach road, so Tony and Yesenia dropped him off at the van and then, with Yesenia driving, headed into town. She stopped the truck in front of the police station and instructed him to wait in the park across the street. She would return shortly with the money. As she sped away, Antonio was still wondering what he was contributing to this episode.

He bought an ice cream bar from a nearby vendor, sat on a bench and waited. Twenty-five minutes passed before the truck roared up the street and skidded to a stop. "Let's go," Yesenia yelled.

She looked different. She was wearing sunglasses and a black beret that Tony had not seen before.

"Did you get the money?" he asked.

"Yes," she said, racing back toward the empty highway.

A few miles outside of town, she pulled to the side of the road and told Tony to drive.

When they were back on the highway, she rolled down the

window and tossed the hat out, saying, "I don't need this no more."

As they approached the border crossing, Yesenia said, "I'll do the talking."

Antonio probably wished he had handled the border guard.

"Where are you going?" the guard asked.

Yesenia and Tony could have produced their green cards, which granted them legal residence in the United States. Instead, Yesenia pointed straight ahead and said something which the guard understood to be, "Over there."

Thinking they were Mexican citizens merely crossing the border to shop—a common occurrence—she waved them through. When they continued past the store, the guard quickly notified the park rangers at the Organ Pipe Cactus National Monument station. Ten miles into Arizona, Tony and Yesenia were stopped and taken back to the border, where they were searched and questioned. They were carrying nothing suspicious. Even the two rings—a large diamond and another made of pearl drops—tripped no alarms. The curio shops in Mexico abound with such trinkets.

Yesenia protested that the border guard had misunderstood her, that she had said they were going to Phoenix. After an hour, the guards were satisfied that there had been a misunderstanding and allowed them to go on their way.

In Ajo, they stopped for gas, and Tony called his wife to tell her they were on their way home but would arrive late. It was after ten-thirty when he dropped Yesenia at her apartment and drove away, still mystified by the whole day and by his sister's peculiar demeanor. Yesenia liked money. She was obsessed by it. But on the long drive back from Mexico, she never once showed him the $20,000 she had picked up for Dan. She never even mentioned it.

She had been giddy, chattering faster than Tony could monitor and urging him to drive faster. He didn't question her about what had occurred after she dropped him at the park in Puerto

Penasco. There were some things about Yesenia he was afraid to know.

Alone in her apartment, Yesenia was too revved to sleep. She held the rings in her hand, fondled them, slipped them on and off her fingers. She drank beer and paced the floor with her hand bearing the rings held up to her face.

She had to talk to somebody. She wanted somebody to know she was rich.

Struggling to shake the sleep from his brain, Mulkins picked up the phone and said, "Hello."

"I'm a millionaire," Yesenia shrieked. "I got a carat."

It was one o'clock in the morning and Mulkins had been in bed for a couple of hours. Having his sleep cut short left him unfocused and his head throbbing.

"What are you talking about?" he said.

"I got a carat," she shrieked.

"Well, carrots are pretty common," he groused, hoping the sarcasm would calm her down.

"Danny gave me a carat diamond ring," she shouted. "It's going to be my wedding ring."

"Slow down a minute . . ."

"I'm a millionaire," she said again. "I'm a millionaire."

"What the hell is going on down there?"

"Danny gave me a diamond . . . and . . . he's going to take my mother to Hawaii."

She was spitting out words like a Gatling gun, which did not surprise Mulkins. Since her Christmas visit, Yesenia had called only a few times, and the conversations were brief and inconsequential. Usually, she sounded drunk and erratic and babbling. On February 9, three days after her birthday, she had called early in the evening but again was erratic and high-strung, giggling about the flowers Dan had sent for her birthday and the note that said, *Querida, mi amore, felice cumplianos—su futuro esposo, Daniel.* (My love, happy birthday—your future spouse, Daniel.) Mulkins had ended the conversation after six minutes. After that the calls stopped. Until now.

And now he couldn't slow her down. His brain cleared a little, enough for him to realize that in her present state—whatever it was and whatever it had been induced by—conversation was futile.

He suggested they talk in the morning, hung up the phone and went back to bed.

An hour later, the phone rang again and again Mulkins stumbled through the fog of stupor to the telephone.

"I'm a millionaire," Yesenia squealed. "I got a carat. Danny gave me a carat."

He tried to interrupt. *Dammit, we just had this conversation. Call tomorrow when you're sober. Do you know what time it is?*

He held the phone away from his ear and let her carry on until she started to run out of steam. "We'll talk tomorrow," he said, and dropped the phone into its cradle.

Chapter Thirty

Like just about everyone else in the Phoenix area who read the newspapers or watched television, Debra Martz knew about the murder of Trish Willoughby. It had been less than two months since a doleful Dan Willoughby had told her that his wife had died in an automobile accident, and she had believed him—sort of. Reading about the murder had vindicated that kernel of doubt she had harbored. Men lie, and for sex men lie big.

Why he would be calling her now, so soon after his wife's murder, was a mystery, but not for long.

"I guess you've been reading the papers," he said. She could hear traffic noise in the background and assumed he was calling from a pay phone.

"Yeah," she said.

"Well, now you know I'm a liar."

Still confounded by the reasons for the conversation, her reply was another terse, "Yeah."

"I would appreciate it if you would keep that under your hat."

* * *

The request was highly unusual. In fact, in all the time Patrick Simmonds had managed the Bowers Worldwide Travel Service in Tempe, this was the first time it had been made of him.

"I'd like for all my records to be taken out of your computers," Dan Willoughby said.

Each time the agency made travel arrangements for a customer, the computers generated an invoice containing the customer's name, the date, form of payment, airline ticket number, passenger names, destination, itinerary and price.

Bowers Worldwide had forty-two separate invoices charged to Dan Willoughby—travel for Willoughby and his wife, the Willoughby family, Willoughby and Yesenia Patino.

Simmonds also had read the newspapers.

"There's nothing to take out of the computers," he told Willoughby, putting a swift end to the conversation. What he did not tell him was that all of the company's records were on microfiche and there was no way to eliminate them.

Tina Roush was still his friend, which was more than he could say about Phil Cantrelli. She would understand the spot he was in, the suspicion he was under, the possibility that the cops would falsely charge him with Trish's murder. Tina would be sympathetic.

Not so with Phil. Phil hated him. Phil threatened to have him beaten up. Phil had heard him ruminate about knocking off his wife.

"I want you to do something for me," he said.

"If I can," Tina said, talking to him from her phone at Air Express International. In spite of everything she had read and heard in the past few days, Tina was still loyal to her old boss. She did not for a moment believe he had anything to do with his wife's death.

"You know the answering machine tape . . . Phil threatening you to have sex with him?"

"Yeah."

"Call him up and tell him that if he shoots off his mouth to the police, you're going to give that tape to his wife."

"I don't still have the tape," she said.

"He won't know that."

"I don't know . . ."

"Look, the cops have talked to me and I know they are going to make me a suspect. If they find out about Yesenia, they're going to think this is some sort of twisted love triangle."

Tina did not promise that she would deliver the threat to Phil Cantrelli, but left the matter dangling.

He signed off with another request. "If anybody calls, tell them I'm a wonderful person and a good family man, okay?"

"Okay."

"If the police call, tell them the same thing."

"Okay."

Jim Parker returned from lunch on Wednesday, February 27, and found a note his secretary had left on his desk: Dan Willoughby Called—Urgent.

It had been a while since he had talked to the Willoughbys. Five years earlier, when Dan was prospering in the air freight business and Trish was struggling along in multilevel marketing, they had asked him to evaluate their finances and future needs and recommend a life insurance plan. Their family was growing—they had recently adopted a son—and because both supplied income, Parker suggested a combination of policies, life and term, that resulted in Dan's coverage amounting to $200,000 and Trish's totalling $150,000.

There had been no change in the coverage for five years, so he assumed that Willoughby wanted to talk about an adjustment. He returned the call.

"Dan, how are things going?" he asked.

Willoughby realized that Parker had not been reading the newspapers. "Trish was murdered last Saturday in Mexico," he said.

He launched into the story of taking the kids to the museum and returning to find Trish near death. "I got her to the car and rushed her to the hospital as fast as I could," he said. "It was too late. There was nothing that could be done for her."

Parker offered condolences and volunteered to meet whenever Dan was ready to discuss filing an insurance claim.

"The funeral is tomorrow," Willoughby said, "and the viewing is tonight at the Houston Ward church."

"I'll be there," Parker said.

Cherie Erickson answered the phone at A.E.I. It was Frank Ortiz calling from El Paso. He wanted to talk to Steve Tanabe.

She handed the phone to her boss and could tell from his expression that this was no ordinary business call. Frank worked for an air freight forwarding company on the Texas–Mexico border that had formed a joint venture with A.E.I. a few years earlier.

Although she could hear only one half of the conversation, she knew it concerned Dan Willoughby, who occasionally visited El Paso in his capacity as district manager for A.E.I.

After hanging up the phone, Steve leaned on his desk and said, "He wanted to know if it was true that Trish Willoughby had been murdered. You're not going to believe this, but he said the last time Dan was in El Paso, he had asked him if he knew of any Mexican hit men. Frank thought it was a joke and told him no."

Tanabe was shaken by the call, but composed enough to look up the number and dial the Gilbert Police Department.

On February 28, Detective Patrick McNabb stopped by to take a statement from Tanabe and Erickson. Most of the other

A.E.I. employees were away from the office attending Trish Willoughby's funeral.

Yesenia partied that rainy day of the funeral, got down and rowdy at Guedo's, a restaurant-bar in Chandler that she and Dan had frequented together over the previous several months.

She was drinking hard and flashing money. Miguel Terrazas, the bartender, knew her from previous visits and she was not his favorite customer. She tipped big, but otherwise was a nuisance. When she was drunk, she was loud and profane and offensive to others in the bar.

By ten o'clock, she was more boisterous and obnoxious than usual. He served her a drink and she handed him a fifty-dollar bill and told him to keep the change. Then she swore at him and Terrazas decided she could stuff the tip.

"I don't want your money," he said, ripping the fifty in half and tossing it back at her.

Yesenia tottered to a pay phone near the restrooms, dialed 911 and requested that the emergency operator dispatch an officer forthwith. "Somebody made a rude comment to me," she said.

The operator informed her that fell somewhere below the bar of exigency.

Yesenia called back, got the same response, and called again. Finally, the police showed up, but not to enforce fancied statutes against impudence.

"Do not use the emergency line again," the cop admonished her.

As soon as he left, she dialed 911 once more. It would be the last time. The officer returned and informed her that she was in violation of laws prohibiting misuse of a telephone. It was only a misdemeanor and could have been handled with a ticket, but her raucous intoxication was an aggravating circumstance. She was placed under arrest and booked into the Chandler city jail.

Dan Willoughby's plate had been full since his return from Mexico, and his contacts with Yesenia had been nominal. He was busy with his children, busy fending off his mother-in-law, busy trying to erase some of the paper trail that would tie him to Yesenia, busy playing the bereaved widower to his neighbors, busy going through the motions of making funeral arrangements.

After the funeral, he busied himself stripping his house of Trish's memories, removing photographs, knickknacks and bric-a-brac, all the things that whispered her name, and stowing them in cartons he would offer to her family, or simply discard.

It was well past eleven o'clock when the phone rang. The younger children were already asleep and he told Marsha he would return soon.

Yesenia was still drunk when he posted her bail and drove her home. She was beginning to make him nervous. She was definitely becoming a problem.

PART FOUR
The Reckoning

Chapter Thirty-one

Friday, March 1, 1991

Kay Lines was immersed in an old murder case when he received a telephone call he could have lived happily without.

"Mr. Lines," the voice on the line said, "this is Patrick McNabb at the Gilbert Police Department."

"Yes?"

"We've got a case here and I smell a rat."

Lines had been reading the newspapers and had a pretty good idea what was coming.

"It's the woman who was murdered in Mexico . . . Patricia Willoughby. You probably know about it."

"A little." Her funeral had been held just yesterday.

"This looks like more than we can handle," the detective said. "It reaches to Mexico, Texas, who knows where else. We don't have the resources to work a case like this, not by ourselves."

"You think the husband had something to do with it?" Lines asked. It was a natural assumption.

"Well, we've been getting some interesting phone calls," McNabb said.

Before he joined the state attorney general's staff as a special investigator, Lines spent twenty years as a deputy sheriff in Maricopa County. He had worked more than thirty-five murder cases—five of which resulted in death penalties—and he had come to prefer the quieter, more routine life of probing fraud and corruption for the attorney general. When a murder case came along now, it was likely to be an older one lacking the immediacy that made such investigations tedious, frustrating and exhausting.

He was, in fact, up to his boot tops in such a murder, one that had bedeviled Arizona for fifteen years—the killing of *Arizona Republic* reporter Don Bolles, who was deep into an investigation of organized crime in the state. Among the subjects of Bolles's articles was Kemper Marley, a land and liquor magnate with friends in high political places. He also, it appeared, had friends in low criminal places.

Bolles had leaned hard on Marley, who moved in and out of politically appointed positions despite the shady air that trailed him wherever he went. For nine years, Bolles reported such things as a grand theft at the highway commission when Marley was there, nepotism at the fair board when Marley was there, and finally the problem with Marley's appointment to the state racing commission.

Marley was forced to resign after Bolles exposed the fact that he had a liquor contract with the track monopoly, a blatant conflict of interest. Don Bolles was killed six weeks later. Lured to the Hotel Clarendon by a caller who promised juicy information on Marley, Bolles waited in the restaurant but the informant didn't show up. Instead, he was outside attaching a homemade bomb to the underside of Bolles's car. The reporter returned to the car and was preparing to drive away when six sticks of dynamite exploded beneath him.

A street thug named John Harvey Adamson later admitted planting the bomb and fingered two other men: Phoenix contrac-

tor and Marley protege Max Dunlop, who arranged the killing
at Marley's request, and James Robison, a plumber who built
the bomb. In 1977, after Adamson had cut a deal for a twenty-
year sentence in exchange for his testimony, Dunlop and Robison were sent to death row. Three years later, though, their
convictions were overturned on a technicality.

Ten years passed before the charges against them were
refiled. This time, the prosecution would be handled by the
attorney general's office, and Lines was assigned to help reas-
semble the case. Looking at the documents spread across his
desk, he felt more than a casual interest in seeing Dunlop and
Robison back behind bars. He had not known Don Bolles
personally, but he had respect for anyone willing to take on
the business and political corruption that pervaded the state.

The case being offered to him now had the distinct odor of
a heartache. It was a fresh case and clearly fell within the
jurisdiction of the local authorities. It would be handled by the
attorney general only if the county attorney, for one reason
or another—personal, political or legal—couldn't or wouldn't
prosecute it. In that case, the AG could assume jurisdiction.
Lines knew of no such circumstances in the Willoughby murder.

"Why don't you contact the sheriff's office?" he suggested,
speaking softly, almost in a whisper, his tone more like that of
a country preacher—he was in fact a stake president in the
Mormon Church— than a career cop.

"We did and they don't want any part of it," McNabb said.
"We also called the county attorney. One of his investigators
came out and talked to us, but they won't take it either. Will
you take it? We'll be the assisting agency. We'll give you all
the help we can."

Lines leaned forward on his desk and tried to recall what he
had read about the case. News reports had been skimpy. Family
vacation in Puerto Penasco. Woman killed by intruder. Possible
robbery. Husband says Mexican police have suspects. Mexican
police refuse to comment.

He considered the obstacles the case presented, the biggest

of which was venue. Arizona might be able to claim jurisdiction, but there could be problems getting witnesses subpoenaed from Mexico, problems communicating with the police there—Lines spoke limited Spanish—and the investigation would likely entail extensive and expensive travel.

"If we don't get your help," the detective sighed, "this one is never going to be solved."

Staring at the files on his desk, Lines realized that, with or without him, the killers of Don Bolles were going back to prison. They had been caught fifteen years before and, although the state's justice had been long delayed, it was now all but a certainty.

Trish Willoughby's murderer might have been a Mexican burglar or it might have been her husband. The truth was not likely to be found by the authorities in Rocky Point. The methods and technologies of Mexican law enforcement, he knew, were fifty years behind those of the United States. And in some areas of the country, the local police were inclined not to involve themselves too much in crimes committed by one American against another. In the death of Trish Willoughby, Lines knew, somebody did in fact stand a very good chance of getting away with murder.

McNabb waited for his answer.

"I'll talk to the people down here and get back to you," Lines said.

Grant Woods had been in office less than two months, not enough time for Lines to have a solid feel for how he would run the attorney general's office, how he would allocate its resources, how he would draw his battle lines and, more importantly, how he would calculate his political risks.

Maybe he won't want this case, he thought. Beyond the demand it would place on the budget and staff, the case had risks for a young officeholder with political ambitions. It was entirely possible that he could jump feet first into a high-profile case and end up with nothing but mud between his toes.

But from what he knew about the new AG and from what he had observed in the early days of the administration, Lines suspected that he would soon be on the trail of Trish Willoughby's murderer.

Woods was only thirty-six years old when he was elected in a campaign—typical of Arizona's—rife with smear and loathing. His opponent in the Republican primary charged that Woods and his father had business ties with a gangster named Mario Renda (a charge that evaporated under close scrutiny) and the name calling got worse when he went up against a Democrat in the general election.

In news accounts of the campaign, his friends described him as "kick ass" and fully up to the brawls of state politics. On the wall of his office, he kept the framed words of a popular Paul Simon song about a scarred and bruised prizefighter who can't hang up his gloves.

Clearly, he had grit and intensity, but he also possessed contradictions—a complex political compass that would drive his fellow Republicans to distraction. One of his earliest heroes was Robert Kennedy, and he shared many of the late senator's passions, particularly for civil rights and the plight of the disadvantaged, and he openly chided the Republican Party's record in those areas, did so even while mingling with Democrats.

"I'm happy to attend Democratic Party functions," he said at a fund-raiser for a Democratic candidate for governor. "It's nice to see Hispanics in the room who aren't serving chips."

That crack brought howls of outrage from Republicans, including Woods's old friend, Sen. John McCain, who demanded that he apologize to Hispanic GOP activists.

Replied Woods: "If the Republican Hispanics active in the party were offended, then I apologize to both of them."

Of a Republican state senator, he once said, "We were feeling more hopeful about Tom Patterson when we heard his favorite book was *Roots*. Unfortunately, he read it from back to front and believes it ends with Kunta Kinte.''

In most ways, in dress and manner and audacity, he was an unlikely Republican. He grooved on Jimmy Buffett, considered Kris Kristofferson one of the great American poets and the sixties one of the great American decades. He also possessed a dramatic flair that would, in time, lead him into local theatrical productions and his own radio show.

More to the point of his style as attorney general, Woods had brought to the office a group of aggressive young lawyers spoiling to take on the world. They would not be reactive prosecutors; they would go after the business.

As much as he wanted to forgo this particular case, Special Agent Lines started brushing up on his Spanish.

Chapter Thirty-two

Sgt. Joe Ruet wasn't sure what it would take to convince the state investigator that this was a murder worthy of the attorney general's attention. All he really had that Friday was evidence of an extramarital affair, the vague phone call about Mexican hit men and a gut feeling that festered like a raw ulcer.

When Kay Lines arrived at the police station, Ruet introduced himself, shook hands and escorted him into an office where he had placed the Willoughby murder file, embryonic as it was, on a desk. Lines was mostly passive as Ruet went over each of the phone calls his department had received and outlined the results of their initial interviews.

From Noreen Robinson, a floral designer at Plaza Flowers on South Dobson in Mesa, they had obtained the name Yesenia Patino. Robinson had supplied them with a large stack of sales slips and copies of the notes Willoughby had written, or dictated by phone, to accompany them.

Willoughby had aroused her curiosity long before she read about the murder.

"I guess we were ... I was nosy," she told the cops. "I knew he had been sending flowers to this lady (Yesenia) and to his wife, too."

Sometimes the orders were placed simultaneously, one delivery to Trish and another to Yesenia. It would have been a difficult pattern for any florist, nosy or not, to overlook.

Lines said nothing, but, like Ruet, he knew this was not the stuff of murder conspiracy.

From an officer at the M & I Thunderbird Bank, they learned of Willoughby's checking account on which Yesenia wrote checks. From a health club owner, they learned that Willoughby and Patino had purchased dual memberships. The list went on, but still pointed to nothing more than an errant husband with a young mistress. The tip that Willoughby had inquired about Mexican hit men was tantalizing, but Ruet had been unable to follow up on it.

After exhausting his list of leads, Ruet searched Lines's face for clues to his interest in the case, but came up empty. Lines had a reputation for a quick mind and a keen ear, but all Ruet could see was a stolid, somewhat somber visage, like that of a guy at the end of a long line at the DMV.

"I think we should talk to Dan Willoughby," Lines said.

Ruet liked that. No nibbling at the edges. Cut to the chase. See what the rascal has to say for himself.

Based on what he had seen so far, Lines had no intentions of grilling Willoughby. In fact, he had no compelling reason to suspect him of anything, except cheating on his wife. He would listen to his story, take his measure and proceed from there.

Dan Willoughby must have known that sooner or later the cops would come calling, and he apparently had braced himself well for this moment.

He opened the door and, with gravity appropriate for a new widower, invited the investigators inside. Ruet was in uniform.

Lines, as usual, wore less intimidating attire: boots, jeans and a western shirt. After introductions, Lines said, "We'd like to talk about your wife's murder. Could you come down to the police station with us."

"Sure," Willoughby said, appearing eager to see an investigation finally get underway.

En route to the station in Lines's car, neither officer spoke of the murder. If Dan Willoughby was not involved, they had no reason to put pressure on him. If he was involved, it would serve their purpose to let him baste in the silence.

At the station, Lines gestured to a chair and Willoughby obediently sat down. Lines pulled up another chair to sit facing him. Ruet, behind his desk, turned on a tape recorder but let his colleague ask the questions.

For most of an hour, Willoughby recounted the fatal weekend at Rocky Point, essentially the same story he had recounted for his in-laws: the visit to the museum, returning to find Trish near death, rushing to the Red Cross station for help, the American doctor who assisted. It appeared to be a burglary, he said, because the contents of his wife's purse were strewn around the room and her wedding ring, worth $10,000, was missing, as was the $400 she had been carrying in her purse.

At times, his voice broke and he paused to compose himself.

When he got around to the black Toyota pickup with the three Indians, Willoughby fleshed out the story from previous tellings. Not only had the police informed him that a Toyota truck was seen parked near his beach house, not only was one individual seen walking from the truck to the house, but the guard at the Las Conchas gatehouse had actually talked to the truck's occupants "about some tools that had been left at a job site" there. That established the presence of the three Indians beyond a mere intangible sighting. That gave them faces and voices, and it gave Lines a witness who could either confirm or confute a key part of Willoughby's story.

"Were you familiar with Rocky Point?" Lines asked.

"Not really. I hadn't been there in a long time . . . and I had never been to that particular area . . . Las Conchas."

Lines registered zero reaction to each of Willoughby's answers, and his voice was a placid, reassuring monotone as he shifted the discussion away from the murder.

"Were you happily married?" he asked.

"Oh, yeah," Willoughby answered without hesitation. "My marriage was great. In fact, I've been more happily married since I quit my job."

"Why did you do that?"

"It was a very stressful job. I was in knots all the time. Trish and I had talked about it. We had a mutual agreement that when she began making a certain amount of money, I would quit and spend more time with my family. Last summer, her business was bringing in twenty thousand, thirty thousand a month and, by golly, I quit."

"Mr. Willoughby, I have to ask you some unpleasant questions. I'm sure you know that."

"Of course, I understand."

"You've told us your marriage was great . . ."

"Absolutely."

"Have you ever had any affairs . . . been involved with any other women."

"Not at all. Nothing like that." Again, he appeared to be overcome by emotion and tears ran down his face.

Lines, still as stoic as a tree trunk, nodded slightly.

"Is there anything you could add to what we've talked about that might help us?" Lines asked.

"You know, when something like that happens, you search your mind, you wonder who, who it is that could have . . . who you could have made so mad that they would do something like this," Willoughby said. "I've searched my mind for my enemies and her enemies. I can't come up with anything."

"Well, if you think of anything, get in touch with us."

"I certainly will," Willoughby said. "And I'd like to ask you to do something for me."

"Sure," Lines said.

"Just find the bastard that did this."

"You have my promise, Mr. Willoughby," Lines said. "You have my promise."

After dropping him at his house, Lines and Ruet drove toward the high school that Marsha attended.

"He just screwed himself," Lines said.

Ruet grinned. The AG's investigator was hooked.

"He could have said he was having marital problems and was involved with another woman and that might have been the end of it," Lines said. "Until he lied, there wasn't much to go on, you know."

Picking Marsha up at school, they took her to the police station and heard her version of the weekend. It, too, did not deviate from what she had been telling her uncles and grandparents. Her father had herded the children into the van and returned to the house to get his passport. After ten or fifteen minutes had passed, she tried to go back inside to get a Granola bar, but the front door was locked. Her father came out, tucking in his shirt, and prohibited her from entering because she might disturb her mother's sleep.

How long had her father been inside the house with the door locked? Lines asked.

She could not recall exactly. "Quite a while," she answered at one point. When the question was posed again, she said "a long time."

Lines took Marsha home and drove back to his office in downtown Phoenix. There wasn't much more he could do north of the border. Ruet and McNabb could run down the leads in Gilbert and Mesa and Chandler, but the real mystery was in Mexico. It had been a week since the murder and for all Lines knew, the crime scene had already been corrupted, if not demolished. Since he had no authority in Mexico, he also would need an invitation to go poking around in Puerto Penasco.

With the help of a Spanish-speaking investigator on the AG's staff, he contacted the Sonoran State Judicial Police, who acknowledged that they were out of their depths with this case—the Rocky Point police department did not even possess a fingerprint kit—and were eager for outside help. The crime scene had been carefully preserved, they assured him, and the house had been under constant guard since the night of the crime.

"We will be there Monday," Lines told the Rocky Point police chief.

He was able to move swiftly partly because the attorney general had taken a strong interest in the case, but also because Gov. Fife Symington had agreed to make available any Department of Public Safety criminologists that might be required. Lines also would have access to the governor's airplane and his pilot.

Having to bail Yesenia out of jail on the night of his wife's funeral had spooked Dan Willoughby, and the arrival of the police at his door the next day only added to his edginess. It was just a matter of time before the cops connected him to Yesenia, and he did not want them questioning her right now.

Rather than being appeased by the opportunity now to become his wife, his mistress was as unbridled as a mustang. In fact, she was near delirious with her new jewelry and visions of the money she believed was forthcoming. After trying to talk with her on Saturday, Willoughby wanted her out of sight and out of mind. He told her she was going to have to leave town. Soon. The next day.

He called Jack Mulkins and told him, "She'll be coming to Portland to stay with you for a while."

"What's wrong, Dan?"

"I can't control her any longer," he said, carefully neglecting any mention of his wife's death.

"Why not?"

"I'm having a lot of difficulty with my family and I can't keep an eye on her."

"What's she doing?"

"Oh, she's fooling around and all kinds of stuff. I think she would be better off if she stayed with you for a while."

Mulkins had no idea what was happening in Arizona. He only knew that Yesenia had been calling him at all hours and, in drunken slurs, babbling about being a millionaire. He suddenly felt a little queasy about the whole situation.

"I don't know that I want her up here," he told Willoughby.

"If she was with you, she'd have to behave," Willoughby pleaded. "Things are getting out of hand and I can't deal with her right now."

In his gut, he knew that Dan and Yesenia were not leveling with him. Dan would not send Yesenia back to him to correct her behavioral problems. His impulse was to tell them to solve their own problems and stop bugging him.

But he had promised Yesenia that he would be her shelter of last resort if the need ever arose. Reluctantly, he agreed to put her up for a while.

On Sunday morning, Yesenia dressed, packed a small bag for the trip, and called Jack.

"You were just here for Christmas," Mulkins said, put off by the abrupt imposition, "and now you want to come back. How long are you planning on staying?"

"A couple of months."

"Months? I thought you didn't even like being here."

"Now I want to be there," she said, ignoring his subtle effort of dissuasion.

She explained that she would spend Sunday night at the Airport Hilton in Phoenix—that was Willoughby's idea; he wanted her out of her apartment immediately—and catch a plane to Portland the next morning. She gave him her flight number and arrival time.

Then, in the cryptic fashion that had become her norm, she

added, ''While I'm there, I'm going to be going by the name Victoria.''

That was the name she had used during their marriage. Why she was reverting to it now was unclear to him, but he didn't bother to ask.

The Gilbert police were proceeding cautiously. They had known about Yesenia for several days, but all they knew was that she was Dan Willoughby's girlfriend. They could have picked her up at any time for questioning, but about what? The flowers she had received? The joint checking account? Lines had cautioned them to keep an eye on her but not to arrest her.

On Sunday evening, while Lines was packing to leave for his trip to Mexico, Patrick McNabb answered the phone at police headquarters and the caller identified herself as Mary Maxon, manager of the Green Tree Apartments in Chandler.

In the six months or so that Yesenia had lived there, she and Mary had become casual acquaintances and Mary had seen Dan Willoughby visiting her apartment. A few weeks earlier, not long before Trish's murder, she had given Yesenia a ride to the bank and Yesenia told her she had just returned from Mexico. ''My honey took me to Rocky Point,'' she said.

After the murder, the police had stopped by to make inquiries about Yesenia, so Mary Maxon was not completely in the dark about their suspicions. When the pickup truck pulled up to Yesenia's apartment that afternoon and three men began loading it with the contents of her apartment, Mary called the cops.

''Yesenia Patino is skipping out,'' she said.

Chapter Thirty-three

Sunday, March 3

Antonio had seen little of his sister in the week after their trip to Mexico. Before, they had talked on the telephone almost daily, sometimes several times a day, but for the past few days she seemed to have slid off the side of the planet. Fine with him.

Ruben had come to his house on Monday with a copy of the *Mesa Tribune* and showed him the story about Mrs. Willoughby's death. Maybe it had something to do with Yesenia. Maybe it had something to do with the Italian brothers from San Francisco and the money they owed Dan Willoughby. He knew virtually nothing. Above all, he didn't know if he had allowed himself to become involved in something criminal by driving Yesenia to Mexico.

After a week, he had begun to think that whatever had happened in Rocky Point would blow over, that he was in no danger—from the Mafia or the police or anybody else. But when Yesenia called on Sunday morning, the dread rushed through him like a brushfire.

She wanted her brothers to help her move out of her apartment, to take her furniture someplace and store it, sell it, give it away, just get rid of it.

"I'm going away for two or three years," she said. "Maybe to Europe or someplace far away."

She told him she had been arrested on Friday night, that Dan had bailed her out and demanded that she leave town.

Tony rounded up his brothers, Ruben and Albert, and they went to her apartment to get her things. She took Tony aside and said, "If the police ever ask you about going to Rocky Point, you tell them we went there Friday to party with some friends and came back Saturday. Tell them we were hanging out on the beach with Juan, Maria, Jose and Hector. Okay?"

"Okay." He was still confused, and Dan Willoughby did nothing to clarify things.

Arriving to retrieve the clothes he had left in her apartment, Dan was reticent and anxious.

"I'm sorry it had to happen this way . . . that Yesenia has to leave," he said. He then talked privately with Yesenia for a few minutes, tossed his clothes in the Jaguar and left. Yesenia called a taxi, leaving her brothers in the dark.

Patrick McNabb, dressed in plain clothes and driving an unmarked car, cruised through the gates of the Green Tree Apartments, slowed as he passed the office and tennis courts and spotted, to his left, three Hispanic men loading furniture and boxes into an old pickup truck. He turned down another drive and parked on the other side of a sloping expanse of lawn and killed the engine. He had a broad, clear view of Yesenia's apartment.

Now and then, one of the men made a trip to a nearby dumpster to discard bags and boxes of trash. They appeared to be in no particular hurry.

"There are three guys here," McNabb told Ruet by car phone. "They're cleaning out the apartment."

"What about the woman?"

"No sign of her. She could be inside."

"Don't let them leave the grounds," Ruet said.

"I don't think I should try to stop them," McNabb said, almost apologetically, "I don't have my weapon."

"Dammit, Pat, you went on stakeout without a gun?"

"I was in a hurry."

"Just sit tight. I'll be right there."

En route to the apartment, Ruet called Lines and briefed him on the developments, including the uncertainty of the woman's presence.

"If she's there, go ahead and pick her up," Lines said. "Try to find something to hold her on."

No one had a clear idea of what involvement, if any, Yesenia Patino might have had in the death of Trish Willoughby, but because she was involved with Dan Willoughby, they wanted her available for questioning. More than likely, she knew plenty.

Ruet got to the apartment just before the three men finished their task. He linked up with McNabb and they watched one of the men lock the apartment, get into the truck with the other two and drive away. As it turned onto Elizabeth Circle, they fell in behind and remained close as it motored slowly through the streets of Chandler.

Ruet placed another call to Lines.

"They're leaving with the furniture," he said. "The woman's not around."

"Just follow them and they'll probably lead you to her," Lines said.

After a few miles, Ruet became apprehensive about that eventuality. He didn't know who the three men were. They could just be three guys who bought Yesenia's furniture before she hit the road.

On the phone again, Lines suggested a strategy.

"Stop them on the pretense that you're investigating a burglary," he said. "See what they have to say."

McNabb pulled beside the truck and Ruet, in uniform, signaled to the driver to pull over. The truck promptly pulled to the curb. The two cops approached it warily and the three occupants, tense and frightened as they produced identification, slumped with relief when they learned it was a burglary investigation.

"Oh, no," said the one named Ruben. "This stuff belongs to our sister. We're just moving it for her."

"Where is she?" Ruet asked. "We'd like to verify that."

"She's at the airport . . . at the hotel. She's taking a trip."

"Which hotel?"

"The Hilton."

Kay Lines was ready to turn in. Although it was just past nine thirty, he would be leaving for Mexico early in the morning with a team from the Department of Public Safety, and he anticipated that they would put in a long day in Rocky Point.

But Ruet's call was too good to pass up.

"I'll meet you there," he said, and was en route to the Hilton Hotel in a few minutes.

The two officers were in the lobby when he arrived. Together, they identified themselves to the desk clerk and promptly learned that Yesenia Patino had not checked in, but a thirtyish Hispanic woman had registered under the name of Victoria McDonald.

As they waited for the elevator, Lines asked the two cops, "Do you have anything to hold her on?"

Ruet shook his head. "We don't have anything, but Mesa's got an old shoplifting warrant, but that will only hold her until somebody bails her out."

They rode up to the fourth floor, exited to the right and found the room number the desk clerk had given them. McNabb rapped on the door.

"Hi," the young woman said, displaying only fleeting alarm at finding three badge-toting men in the hallway.

"Yesenia Patino?" McNabb asked.

"Yeah," she said, flashing a smile that erased that first brief flicker of concern.

"May we come in?"

She opened the door wider and stepped back. In a white blouse and pastel orange skirt, she was every bit the dish they might have expected in a young woman who had torn an affluent, older, upright, churchgoing man away from his family. Nice legs, firm butt, adequate breasts and a sassy walk.

They informed her that she was wanted by the Mesa police for failing to appear in court on a shoplifting charge, and they asked if she would answer a few questions. She assented.

"Your brothers told us you're taking a trip."

"Uh huh."

"Where are you going?"

"To Oregon, to visit my husband and son."

"Do you know Dan Willoughby?" McNabb asked.

"Oh, yeah, I know Danny." she said.

"Is he your boyfriend?"

"Oh, no. I'm his Spanish teacher."

She did not appear ruffled by the questioning.

"Have you ever been to Rocky Point, down in Sonora?"

"Yeah, my brother and I went a week ago."

"February 23?"

"Yeah. My brother, Antonio, and I went down there to party on the beach with some friends."

She and Antonio had driven down on Friday, spent the night on the beach with four friends named Juan, Maria, Hector and Jose—she couldn't recall their last names—and returned Saturday evening, she said.

"Did you see Dan Willoughby in Rocky Point?"

"No."

"Did you know he was there?"

"I knew he was in Mexico, but I didn't know if it was Rocky Point or Nogales."

"Do you know Dan Willoughby's wife, Patricia?"

"Yeah, I met her once. She's a nice lady."

Looking around the room, Ruet realized that she had no luggage—only a large beige purse, one hardly large enough to carry a change of clothes. He asked if he could inspect the bag.

"Sure." Her ready compliance was disarming. She obviously lied about the extent of her relationship with Dan Willoughby, but otherwise she did not behave like a woman with a lot to hide. No jitters. No sweat.

Emptying the contents of the bag onto the bed, Ruet found, among the more mundane items, two expensive-looking rings, a phony passport and an old Oregon driver's license issued to Alfred G. Patino in 1977. It revealed that Alfred was born February 6, 1957. Height: five foot five. Weight: 120 pounds. He bore an eerie resemblance to Yesenia.

"Who is Alfred Patino?"

"Oh, that was me," Yesenia said without hesitation.

The three investigators looked at each other, then at the woman, then at each other again.

"That was you?" McNabb said, not sure his circuits were processing the data properly.

"Yeah," Yesenia said. "That was me before I had . . . well, before I had the . . . corrective surgery."

Chapter Thirty-four

They met in 1980, in a bar in Portland, on a night when clouds rolled in from the Pacific, clipped the peaks of the Coast Ranges and spilled their cargo onto the streets of the city. The bar was warm and dry and convivial, and though they were starkly different in every respect, the two men struck up a conversation.

Jack Mulkins had time on his hands, a disability income, a soft heart and a life spent mostly alone.

Alfredo Patino had a ready smile, a gregarious personality, a tragic history and a scar wider than a ship channel on his psyche.

At first, they spoke the standard barroom banter, but eventually Alfredo confided that he was about to be kicked out of his apartment. Mulkins felt a pang of sympathy. He had a son not much older than this young man, and perhaps from his years as a fireman and paramedic, years spent steeped in human hurt and adversity, he also had compassion for the wretched. Alfredo, small, almost frail looking, did not strike him as a street survivor.

"Well, if you need a place to stay I could put you up at my house for a while," Mulkins told him. "My son lives with me, but we have plenty of room."

Alfredo accepted the offer and moved in with Mulkins a few days later. To his son and his friends, Mulkins introduced Al, as he called him, as his roommate. His feelings toward the young man were awkward. Mulkins was not homosexual, but he enjoyed the company of the younger man, who, with barely enough facial hair to shade his upper lip, hardly looked his twenty-three years. The pitch of his voice was prepubescent and he walked with a nuance of grace. Perhaps his blithe spirit and unstudied inhibition emitted a whiff of sensuality that the older man perceived in some distant detector—a fringe memory of femininity sloshing around out where old molecules of the senses go to die.

Alfredo had hinted at problems in his past, but it never seemed to Mulkins that he was carrying overly burdensome baggage. Most of the time, there was no sadness in his eyes, no strain to his smile, no wounds in his posture. But occasionally, some lost scrap of ache seeped into his mood. That happened not long after he moved into Mulkins's house. He opened a liter of rum, drank it straight, make oblique references to suicide, and passed out. Jack, who had been trained as an emergency medical technician, stayed up all night keeping an eye on him.

One evening a few weeks later, Jack's son was away and they were at home alone.

"I've got a surprise for you," Al said, leaping to his feet and disappearing into the bedroom. He emerged a few minutes later wearing a dress and high-heeled shoes.

As much as he was taken aback, Mulkins was just plain taken. Alfredo, so attired, was as alluring as most of the women who frequented the bars where Mulkins often whiled away an evening. With a little makeup and a hairstyle, he could easily pass for the other gender, which he had in fact been doing since he was a teenager.

* * *

Not bad looking, Detective Al Imig thought as the woman came into view and approached the undercover officer who had accompanied him to make this bust. She was wearing a short skirt, matching shoes, a little too much makeup and about the right amount of inexpensive jewelry for a prostitute working the streets of Woodburn, Oregon, a small town north of Salem on the interstate route to Portland.

Someone at a local business reported that a woman was soliciting sex on the sidewalk, so the vice cops rolled. One was fitted with a wire and dressed in civilian clothes. Imig observed from a nearby car.

The woman approached the undercover officer and offered to perform oral sex for a modest sum.

"You're busted," the cop said, hoisting his badge.

The woman started to walk away, and when the cop grabbed her, her wig fell off and she came clean. Not she, he. Among the other fake items in Alfredo Patino's costume were water balloons tucked into his bra

Pretty convincing woman, Imig thought. *Damn convincing woman.*

After letting the sight of him as a woman soak in, Yesenia sat down beside Mulkins and introduced the fiend that had followed him since childhood. He was a woman inside, a male by genetic accident. It tormented him in ways he could not explain to anyone, especially to his parents. When he was a teenager, he tried to commit suicide, and his mother had committed him to a mental institution. When he was released, he separated himself from his family and took to the streets. He survived by dressing as a woman and hanging out at straight bars, selling oral sex to men who had no idea he was a male. All the while, he brooded about suicide and fantasized about becoming a woman.

From the doctors at the state mental hospital, he learned

about sexual reassignment—and about the enormous cost of such surgery.

Mulkins took in every detail and before long what had begun as a friendship between two men looking across the generational divide began to evolve into something else.

Sex change surgery became central to their conversations, and eventually they contacted Dr. Jeffrey Hyde, a Portland psychiatrist with experience in gender identification problems. After a few sessions, he determined that Alfredo was a good candidate for sex reassignment. He prescribed daily doses of estrogen, told Alfredo to begin dressing as a woman, living as a woman. As the counseling proceeded and the superficial transformation progressed, Al and Jack began dating, presenting themselves, in restaurants, dance halls, movies and elsewhere, as a heterosexual couple.

Alfredo acquired a birth certificate in the name of Victoria Yvonne McDonald. Jack Mulkins got a marriage license, the legality of which was suspect, since Oregon did not permit same-sex marriages. But to Mulkins, the marriage would accelerate Alfredo's psychological conversion to womanhood. The two men were wed in 1981.

When Dr. Hyde deemed the time appropriate, he referred Mr. and Mrs. Mulkins to a surgeon.

Trinidad, Colorado, 193 miles south of Denver in the foothills of the Rocky Mountains, wasn't exactly on the main road to anywhere, but it had a couple of assets that appealed to Stanley Biber, a young surgeon fresh out of the U.S. Army. One lure was the scenery—the twin Spanish Peaks that rose up 13,000 feet to the west, the 9,500-foot tabletop Fisher's Peak to the east and the Purgatoire River slicing between. The other attraction was the town's dearth of doctors.

For someone who had grown up in the relative metropolis of Des Moines, Iowa, this place was faraway and bordering on desolation, a former way station on the Santa Fe Trail and a once-prosperous coal mining hub that had seen the pits play out and the population depart for new digs. The interstate highway connecting Denver and Albuquerque was far in the future, and therefore few transits passed through Trinidad and even fewer stayed for long.

But, because the town needed doctors, Stanley Biber could build a practice quickly, and if he succeeded, it would enable him to indulge his other passions: farming and ranching. Land was cheap and plentiful, and since his boyhood in Iowa, Biber had harbored an affinity for the soil and the crops and animals it could nourish. His parents, Orthodox Jews, had wanted him to be a rabbi, but he was determined to be a farmer. He had been captivated by the aroma of the feed stores and the way the earth breathed life as it soaked up a spring rain. At Drake University, as often happens when the schemes of childhood confront the world's grander options, that agrarian aspiration was put aside, diverted by the lure of the liberal arts.

A serious interest in medicine began to emerge during those years, and Biber later discovered, at the University of Iowa School of Medicine, that he had both a passion and a faculty for that field. Degree in hand, he left the Midwest for an internship and surgical residency in the Panama Canal Zone. When war broke out in Korea, he went there to run a field hospital: A MASH doctor and all that implied—long hours bent over soldiers whose limbs had been blown off by land mines, whose torsos had been ripped open by grenades, whose bodies were mangled by rockets and rifle fire and shrapnel. He once passed out after performing thirty-six abdominal surgeries without a break, but the war endowed him with a special perspective on surgery. The human body is amazingly resilient, recuperative, restorative. Limbs can be reattached; organs can be bypassed, substituted or abandoned; tissue is the clay of the potter surgeon.

While he was being processed out of the Army at Fort Carson, Colorado, in 1954, he heard from a friend that Trinidad needed a surgeon. After one reconnaissance visit, he hauled his belongings to town and hung out his shingle.

In the years that he ran a general practice—he was the town's only surgeon—he became acquainted with a social worker who sometimes brought her clients to him for treatment.

One afternoon in 1969, she showed up at his office alone, tentatively took a chair by his desk but then got directly to the purpose of her visit.

"Can you do my surgery?" she asked.

"What kind of surgery?" he asked.

"I'm a transsexual," she said.

"What is that?" Biber replied.

He truly did not know. In his fifteen years in Trinidad, his time had been spent cutting away cancerous body parts, reattaching severed fingers, repairing defective hearts, the standard menu of human misery. In those days, sex-change operations were still far outside the medical mainstream, in part because many surgeons would have no part of them. Transsexuality, the common medical wisdom had it, was a psychiatric problem, an affliction that required treating the mind and not the genitals.

His patient was a man who had been living as a woman and wanted, finally, to become one completely. Over the next few weeks, Biber scoured medical books and journals to acquaint himself with the subject, and in the process located a doctor at Johns Hopkins University in Baltimore, who offered to send him a few rudimentary, hand-drawn sketches of the procedure.

To Biber, it looked remarkably similar to prostate surgery. With the audacity that is often characteristic of young surgeons, Biber agreed to perform the operation. He was not entirely satisfied with the results—"It looked awful," he would later acknowledge—but the patient was pleased and Trinidad was on its way to being known as the Sex Change Capital of the World, a designation many in the town at first resented but later embraced when Biber's practice provided an economic bonanza.

As his reputation spread by word-of-mouth and the traffic through his clinic quickened, Biber refined his technique to the point that he would eventually boast, ''I can fool their gynecologists.''

It is done in a procedure of deceptive simplicity.

With the patient anesthetized, feet secured by stirrups in the manner of a woman undergoing a pelvic examination, Biber methodically, as if by rote, removes the testicles and the pulpy inner tissue of the penis and, using his fingers, sculpts a vaginal cavity. The inverted penis skin is stretched around a plastic form and inserted into the cavity to form the lining of the new vagina. An incision is made for the urethral opening and a realistic labia is created by tucking excess tissue along both sides of the opening. In a mere three hours or less, the patient's gender is reassigned.

By the time Alfredo Patino came to see him in October of 1982, Biber was sixty-eight years old and had performed nearly three thousand sex changes, all but two hundred or so being male-to-female. He had developed an elaborate screening process that required the patient to spend a year of dressing as the target gender and undergoing intense psychological or psychiatric counseling and hormonal therapy. After all that, he made the final decision based on a personal interview. Often, he would confide, his decision came from the gut as much as the head.

He had become an institution, a surgical icon, but he hardly looked the part. He had fulfilled his childhood aspiration by becoming a weekend rancher and farmer, and he usually came to his office looking as though he had just left the animal pens. Wearing a cowboy hat, a down or sheepskin jacket, boots and jeans, he arrived in a pickup truck to an office that was just as unpretentious. A visiting journalist once wrote that the linoleum-floored office upstairs in a bank building might have been ''decorated by the Salvation Army.''

But from these unpretentious surroundings, he turned out what would be known as Biber's Girls.

With her period of psychiatric counseling, estrogen therapy and lifestyle modification complete, and with the report from Dr. Hyde in hand, Alfredo Patino knocked on his door. Biber needed only a brief interview with him to conclude that he was, indeed, a solid candidate for the surgery.

Maybe too solid.

In all—the surgery, the counseling, the drugs, the breast augmentation—Alfredo's conversion to Victoria had cost Jack Mulkins a little more than $30,000, and it took only a few months for him to learn what his money had bought.

Dr. Biber declared Victoria's operation one of his best and instructed her not to engage in sexual intercourse for three months, the time it would take for her new female sex organ to heal. She complied, but during that time, her husband discovered that the surgery had done nothing to dampen her promiscuity. In fact, it seemed to liberate the last of her inhibitions. She was unable to resist the call of the night, the siren song of Portland street life.

By the time the surgical healing period had elapsed and Victoria was free to test her new equipment, it would not be with her husband, but with a young man she met on one of her neon forays. From a transvestite prostitute, Alfredo had merely transfigured into a transsexual prostitute.

She and her husband had normal sexual relations, but it was not enough for Victoria, who needed a string of partners to quench her thirsts. She made little effort to conceal her outside trysts from her husband. She came and went as she pleased, and Mulkins could only plead and scold, both to no avail.

Mulkins owned a motor coach, which he had purchased after taking disability retirement from the fire department, and he decided to put it to use in his quest to extract his wife from her licentious lifestyle. On the road, perhaps, she would be constrained.

They lived and traveled in the coach for weeks or months

at a stretch, roaming the Pacific coast, the Rockies and the desert southwest. At times, it seemed to work, but each time Mulkins found it was only a temporary fix. Wherever they went, Victoria found men to feed her cravings, which may have been emotional as much as physical. She was forever restless, unceasingly incorrigible.

After a few years, she wanted a child, so Mulkins accommodated her. They went to Mexico, to Guaymas, Sonora, where they found six-year-old Charlie and paid an attorney in Hermosillo $250 to prepare the adoption papers. They set up housekeeping in San Carlos, but motherhood did not domesticate her either.

They left Mexico after Victoria was raped—or alleged she was—by a group of *federales,* federal policemen.

Passing through Phoenix on the way north, Victoria made the decision to bail out. Jack cramped her style. Charlie was a burden. She wanted to be wild and unfettered, and Mulkins, worn down by her ways, was ready to turn her loose.

He would take Charlie to Cottonwood, settle down for a while, find a part-time job and enroll the boy in public school, where he could learn English.

Victoria got off the coach in Phoenix and quickly shed the oppressive life of marriage and motherhood and the staid, dreary Anglo name she had adopted. Victoria McDonald Mulkins ceased to exist.

She was now Yesenia Patino. Unshackled.

Chapter Thirty-five

From the Hilton Hotel, Ruet and McNabb drove Yesenia to the Mesa police station, where she was booked on the old shoplifting warrant and placed in a cell. McNabb, who would accompany Lines to Mexico the next morning, went home to get a few hours' sleep.

Ruet went back to Gilbert to confer with Chief Fred Dees, who had been alerted to Yesenia's arrest and had come to the police station for a full briefing. After listening to Ruet's account of the night's events, Dees folded his arms, lowered his head and said, in the manner of a messenger delivering bad news, "It may be time for a dumpster dive."

Ruet groaned. It was nearly midnight and he was exhausted. But he recognized that it was a savvy suggestion, or, in this case, a direct order. Yesenia, sticking firmly to her story that she was only Willoughby's Spanish tutor, had told them little. Maybe in cleaning out her apartment, the Patino brothers had discarded something of value, something that would begin to fill in the puzzle. Rummaging around in trash bins is not glamorous police work, but garbage is often revealing.

"I'll get another officer to help you," Dees said. "A patrol-
man will meet you there."

To Ruet's good fortune, the trash hunt was made easier by
the fact that none of the other residents of the Green Tree
Apartments had utilized the dumpster since the Patino boys.
The boxes and bags they had deposited there were intact at the
top of the heap. Ruet retrieved them, made a cursory inspection
to verify that the refuse came from Yesenia's apartment and
loaded them into the trunk of his car.

At the police station, he hauled the bags into his office and
began to sort through them. The dumpster had yielded a bumper
harvest. No smoking gun, Ruet thought, but one with the barrel
still warm. Maybe. It all depended on what the investigators
found in Rocky Point.

Before leaving her apartment the previous day, Yesenia had
discarded a rich lode of materials that confirmed much of what
Ruet already knew, and added a wealth of new details. He had
a Southwest Airlines frequent flyer card, photographs, receipts
from a photography studio, florist cards, canceled checks, a
pair of black boots stained with what could be blood, and a
Day Runner appointment book crammed with appointments,
names, dates that she had traveled with Willoughby—including
the two trips they made to Rocky Point in the weeks before
the murder—and other scribblings that could be important.

Now he wanted to talk to her again, wanted her in his custody.
He drove back to the Mesa PD and explained that their shoplifting suspect might have important information about a murder.
She was released to him. He placed her in his own jail to be
held, uncharged, for questioning the next day. He locked the
dumpster trash in the evidence room, called it a night and
headed home for some much-needed sleep.

Believing that Yesenia was snugly ensconced in the Hilton
Hotel and would leave Phoenix on schedule the next morning,

Dan Willoughby called Jack Mulkins and announced, "She's on her way."

His voice exuded relief. Yesenia was out of his hair and he had more important business to attend to. He had a meeting on Monday with Jim Parker of IDS Financial Services to begin processing his claim to the $150,000 policy on Trish's life.

At two-thirty Monday morning, he learned things were not moving so smoothly.

"Will you accept a collect call from Yesenia Patino?" the operator asked.

What now? "Yes . . . I'll accept it."

"Danny, I'm in jail . . . in Mesa."

"What have you done now?"

"Oh, nothing. It's that shoplifting thing."

Unperturbed, she explained about the visit she had received at the hotel, but, knowing the phone could be tapped, he cut her short and thought for a moment about how to handle the situation.

There wasn't much he could do. It would be imprudent to rush to the Mesa PD to bail her out. To involve his lawyer, as he had often done in the past, would also be foolish. He needed to put distance between himself and Yesenia, but for the moment, he could only wait and see how the string played out.

"Look, you'll have to sit tight for now. I can't do anything until tomorrow."

Dan Willoughby's day had been thoroughly spoiled before it even started. After arising early and bracing himself with a few cups of coffee, he called Jack Mulkins again.

"She's not coming," he said.

Disgusted by the disarray in Phoenix, Mulkins snarled, "Why not, Dan? What the hell is going on?"

"She's been arrested for shoplifting and she's in jail."

"Are you going to bail her out?"

"I'm going to do what I can."

He lied. Involving himself with Yesenia at this point still seemed like a bad idea. He would tend to his insurance claim and worry about her later.

Joe Ruet was stumped.

He had Yesenia in jail and a bundle of evidence that would surely excite Lines and McNabb, but there was nothing in his possession—as far as he knew at that point—to connect her to a murder. Even if there was something incriminating among Yesenia's refuse, he could do nothing until Lines and the criminologists returned from Mexico. In urging him to find a reason to hold her, Lines had, in fact, specifically instructed him not to charge her with anything related to Trish Willoughby's death. That would start the judicial clock ticking, and they would have to bring her to trial or release her in ninety days. More importantly, it could also send Dan Willoughby into hiding.

The best he could do was hold her for twenty-four hours for questioning.

No such luck. In one of those inscrutable, bureaucratic, paper-shuffling, miscommunication screw-ups, Yesenia was back on the streets by Monday afternoon.

It happened just before the end of the day shift, before Ruet checked in for his nightly tour of duty. Someone noticed that a female prisoner was being held without charge and, thinking she had been there since three o'clock the previous day instead of three that morning, set her free.

Confused by the jumbled occurrences of the previous twenty-four hours and elated to be so abruptly released, Yesenia left the police station without her beige bag, without even bothering to inquire about it.

With no money for bus fare, not even a quarter to make a telephone call, she left on foot, stopping at a television repair shop a few blocks away and persuading the owner to let her use his phone.

Marsha answered.

"I'm sorry about what has happened," Marsha said.

"That's okay, I'm all right," Yesenia said. "Can I talk to Danny?"

"He's busy," Marsha said. "He's talking to some insurance guys."

"Okay, I'll call later."

Again, she set out on foot, not sure where to go or how to get there. At an intersection a mile from the police station, she spotted Harold Grimes, an old trick of hers, a businessman she sacked out with when Dan wasn't around, and flagged him down. She asked if he would drive her to Antonio's house.

En route, she called Dan again from Grimes's car phone.

"I got out of jail," she said, thinking he would be pleased. Instead, he was cold and contentious.

"You've got to get out of here," he said. "Get the hell out of the country . . . go to Mexico."

"I don't have any money to go anywhere," she said.

"Get your brother . . . your mother . . . to help you. Just leave."

Her mother was at Tony's house when she arrived a little before five o'clock.

Herminia Delfina Patino had been fretting over her daughter since reading about the murder of the Willoughby woman a week before and even more so since learning that Yesenia was leaving town in a hurry and might not return for months or years.

"I thought I would never see you again," she said when Yesenia walked in. She was visibly shaken and Yesenia tried to calm her.

"Everything is fine," she said. "But I don't need to be in the States anymore. They are going to question me more about the murder. I had nothing to do with it and I don't want to be questioned. I need to go to Mexico."

Her mother nodded. She and Tony would scrape together

whatever money they could and drive her to Nogales, a bustling border town sixty-two miles south of Tucson. There, she could cross into Mexico. After that, she would be on her own. That prospect did not cause the family particular concern. Yesenia, like Alfredo, was a skilled survivor.

Chapter Thirty-six

Monday, March 4

Although he had no idea what the crime scene in Rocky Point would yield, Kay Lines felt better knowing that Dan Willoughby's mistress was in custody. She had left the Hilton Hotel with Ruet and McNabb, who could no doubt find some reason to hold her until he returned from Mexico. She was carrying a phony passport, for one thing. Also, there was the outstanding warrant from Mesa. He only needed a day or two, just long enough to scour the beach house and get statements from the medics, the Rocky Point police and the security guards at Las Conchas.

On Monday morning, he drove to a private hangar at the airport where the governor's twin-engine King Air was waiting. Also waiting was the crew that had been assigned to this portion of the investigation: Det. Patrick McNabb of the Gilbert PD; Department of Public Safety criminologists Carey Chapman, Benita Harwood and Mike Eyring; Martin Marquez, the DPS's liaison with Mexico; Steve Mitchell, the assistant attorney gen-

eral who would prosecute the case if one could be made, and
Ben Loretto, the pilot.

The flight took a little more than an hour, and the Rocky
Point police were waiting to drive Lines's crew to Las Conchas
and the house where Trish Willoughby had been bludgeoned
and stabbed.

Like others in the resort development, the house rested on
a fluttering blanket of sand. Its bleached white stucco walls
were topped by curls of red tile, and the front portico, facing
the sea, was covered by a flat roof supported by columns and
arches. As promised, the interior had been untouched since the
night of the murder. Seals had been placed across the front and
back doors and a police officer stood guard.

The Americans were briefed and then allowed to enter. Chapman, whose primary responsibility was to search for latent
fingerprints, proceeded first to the master bedroom, pausing at
the door to look for blood splatters on the floor—evidence
he did not want to disturb with footprints. Seeing none, he
approached the bloodstained bed, took photographs of the scene
and then dusted the room.

From there, he moved to the living room, the other bedroom,
the rear entry and the kitchen, which was still cluttered from
its last use. A teakettle was on one burner of the stove and a
newspaper had been tossed carelessly on another. A trash can
lined with a black plastic bag was overflowing. Dishes were
in the sink, and an empty, two-liter Coke bottle was on a counter
nearby. Chapman worked quickly, lifting prints from a variety
of surfaces, carefully tagging and cataloging them.

Lines, too, looked over the house, looking mostly for a murder weapon. The criminologists had already removed three
table knives found beside the bed, but another weapon had
been used, something heavy enough to crush the victim's head
into pulp. In a closet, he found a hammer and a crowbar, but
both were covered with dust. They had not been used in a long
time.

He examined the front-door-locking mechanism and determined that it would not automatically lock from the inside. The latching device would have to be pushed forward and then twisted to secure the door. At his request, the caretaker removed the mechanism. It was important evidence.

Next, he went outside to talk to the police officers and a group of witnesses who had been assembled for him. With Marquez serving as translator, he questioned them about the night of February 23, any contact they had with the victim or her family, anything they saw and heard.

They shed little light on what might have occurred inside the house, but they put a serious dent in Willoughby's story. The police had never had any other suspects, they informed him, and no one at Las Conchas knew anything about three Indians in a black Toyota pickup truck. No one had seen a Toyota truck parked near the beach house and no one had seen a man walking toward the back door.

When Joe Ruet came on shift Monday afternoon and discovered that Yesenia Patino had been released, he was furious and heartsick. He put out a bulletin for her arrest and recruited another detective to help him check out her known haunts. They went back to the apartment she had abandoned, stopped by the Chandler bar where she was arrested for making bogus emergency calls and any other place they could glean from her Day Runner appointment book, which doubled as a sketchy diary. Nothing. They checked the airlines for anyone traveling under the name Yesenia Patino or Victoria Patino or Victoria Mulkins. Nothing.

They visited the addresses of the brothers who had hauled her furniture. No one was at home. She probably had not gone far, Ruet believed, because she had left her money behind in her beige purse and she had no car.

Since the dumpster evidence indicated that he was her primary means of support, their best bet was to keep an eye on Willoughby. In a jam, no doubt, she would run to him.

* * *

When the crime scene had been thoroughly scoured and charted, the criminologists bagged up the bloody linen from the bedroom and dismantled the bed to cart it back to Phoenix. They had a generous cache of evidence. Now they would have to see what it added up to.

After renting rooms for the night, the Arizona investigators mapped out the remaining work to be done in Rocky Point. While Lines and McNabb interviewed witnesses, the criminologists would begin processing the evidence, particularly the fingerprints.

Before leaving Phoenix, Lines had obtained the print cards of Dan and Patricia Willoughby, Yesenia Patino and Antonio Patino. He expected to find the Willoughbys' prints. If others were present that could not be identified, they could quickly compare them to Yesenia's and Antonio's, thereby ruling them out in short order or giving them some serious explaining to do.

In a village as small as Rocky Point, Lines was able to cover a lot of ground in a hurry. He went back to Las Conchas and, from a variety of angles, photographed the house and those surrounding it, including the CEDO museum on a dune behind the development. He measured distances between the houses, distances from the Willoughby house to the museum, from the house to the Las Conchas gatehouse and to the Red Cross station. Then he sketched the entire layout in his notebook.

He talked to the medical technicians who had transported Trish to the hospital that night and to the doctors who tried to save her life. He interviewed police officials and the judge who had helped Willoughby with the legal process of removing his wife's body from Mexico. From the medical examiner, he obtained a copy of the autopsy that was performed in Rocky Point. From the Hotel Del Mar registration records, he learned that Willoughby and Yesenia Patino had stayed there on two occasions, once a few weeks before the murder and the other on the weekend preceding it—records that refuted Willoughby's claim that he had not been to Rocky Point *in a long time* before taking his family there that fatal weekend.

Meanwhile, McNabb talked by phone with Det. Todd Baty, who had been assigned to help with the case when it became obvious that the investigation would be far-flung and more complex than anything the department had handled.

Baty had interviewed Dr. Harold Lowry by telephone and had learned that on the night of the murder, Willoughby had been less than distressed by the assault on his wife. In fact, the doctor had described his actions as "bizarre." His wife was dying in a hospital a few miles away, but Willoughby had remained at the beach, chatting with the neighbors.

Baty's best find that day, however, came in a call to the U.S. Customs Services station at the Lukeville border crossing. Computer records revealed that Tony and Yesenia had entered the United States before six o'clock on the Saturday evening that Trish was killed. Of greater interest to the investigators, those records showed that the brother and sister had not crossed into Mexico on Friday, as they claimed, but at noon on Saturday. Yesenia's story of going to Rocky Point to party with four friends was bogus.

Though he had been working on the case for five days, Lines had no delusions about where the trail was leading. Willoughby had lied about the state of his marriage, lied about his relationship with Yesenia Patino, lied about the events of Saturday, February 23, lied about three Indians in a Toyota pickup. Yesenia's story, too, was rife with falsehood. So he could document that they were liars. Proving that they were conspirators in a murder was another matter.

He had a motive but no murder weapon, no witnesses, no evidence, as yet, to confute Willoughby's alibi that he was far from the house visiting a museum with his children when his wife was assaulted. Maybe he had hired a hit man to do his dirty work, but if that were the case, how did Yesenia figure into the scheme? Maybe Tony was paid to kill Trish, but why would Yesenia accompany her brother to Mexico and risk incriminating herself?

If Willoughby killed his wife, or arranged for her death, it was a scheme of monumental stupidity—except in one respect, the choice of a remote Mexican village as the venue. With the primitive police methods and technology of Rocky Point, with the international border and jurisdictional divisions to impede an investigation, all the ends might never meet up, all the dots never neatly connect.

Lines presumed that if Willoughby and Patino had schemed to kill Trish, a conspiracy charge could be made in a short time. Certainly the complicity would have been hatched in Arizona, and Willoughby, so far, had not demonstrated a flair for covering his tracks.

There remained, however, substantial blank spots in the obvious picture Lines was beginning to form in his mind. One hole was the missing murder weapon. Another was the murder itself. Who was in the house and exactly what happened. Trish's head had been wrapped in a towel, crushed with a heavy instrument and then pierced with a table knife. It was a particularly macabre measure of overkill, considering that, as the Mexican medical examiner noted, there were no defensive wounds on her hands and arms. If she were rendered unconscious before the blows were struck, as it appeared, what necessitated both a ferocious bludgeoning and a knife to the brain?

There was a surrealism, a sickness, about this crime and the detective's suppositions that repulsed him as certainly as it fascinated him: the Christmas gift of death. Using the children as an alibi and letting them discover their dying mother. Arranging for his mistress to be present at the finale. The flirtation with the Mexican judge while cutting the red tape that held his dead wife in Rocky Point.

All of that presumed, of course, that Dan Willoughby was

guilty of murder. All Lines knew for certain was that he was guilty of being a lying, unhappily married lecher.

If there had been a conspiracy between Willoughby and Patino, he needed something to break the seal, a wedge to slip between them. Conspiracies usually fail because of the near impossibility of keeping them hitched up. Someone spooks or gets drunk or gets angry and blabs and the seam starts to unravel. A cop has only to find the right pressure point.

Carey Chapman was grinning like a Cheshire cat when Lines arrived back at the motel early Tuesday afternoon.

He had spent the previous evening and all of that morning sorting through the latent fingerprints he had lifted from the beach. With the aid of his field fingerprint kit, which allows for preliminary identification, he had made a whopping find.

"Two prints belong to Yesenia Patino," he said. "One from the back door and one from a plastic Coke bottle in the kitchen."

That didn't make their whole case, but now Lines knew where to squeeze.

He placed a call to the Gilbert police station, got Joe Ruet on the line and said, "We've got two of Yesenia's fingerprints in the house. Hang on to her until we get back."

"Too late," Ruet said. "She's already gone."

Chapter Thirty-seven

Now the investigation was a divided highway, one lane the hunt for the elusive Yesenia Patino and the other the pursuit of Dan Willoughby. Both suspects had told stories that were full of holes. Patino's alibi was shot and Willoughby's was as slender as fishing line. But, so far, nothing added up to a murder charge. Unless Yesenia surfaced soon, this job was going to be as arduous as Kay Lines had initially imagined.

If she had not been released, Yesenia would probably already have been charged and Lines would have been back on the Don Bolles case. Instead, he faced the prospect of sloshing around in this swamp indefinitely. It was a swamp in more ways than one, gurgling with enough sleaze and muck to gag a wart hog, and Yesenia Patino was his ticket out.

His gut told him that she was in Mexico, and to find her would require a measure of cooperation south of the border that he was not sure he could rely on. The authorities in Sonora had been helpful—the governor even sent two emissaries to Rocky Point to help snip through Mexico's storied red tape—but Yesenia, if she had a double-digit IQ, certainly was not in

Sonora. She could be anywhere else, though, and Lines would have to cultivate contacts in several Mexican states and prod them to stay alert for her.

Along with that, there was a mountain of work to be scaled in Arizona: telephone records to gather and numbers to track down, bank records to analyze, the lives of Dan and Trish Willoughby and Yesenia Patino to reconstruct, dozens of individuals to interview and innumerable leads to follow up.

The Gilbert Police Department had made three detectives available, but Lines still needed someone from his own staff to help string together all the evidence.

He recruited Debbie Schwartz, an unlikely investigator, but one for whom he had great respect. She had begun her working life as an English instructor at Arizona State University, but, unhappy with the low pay, quit to become a cop, a calling not known for elevated salaries, but more remunerative nonetheless than the classroom. She signed on with the Scottsdale PD, went through the academy and worked her way up from patrol to detective in six years. In 1980, she joined the attorney general's staff as a special agent.

Like Lines, she had a well-earned reputation for thoroughness and tenacity. She was a quick study, a skillful interviewer and a demon for details, and she took her work seriously. He filled her in on what he and the Gilbert cops had learned so far, and they began to compile a list of people who might have helpful information. Schwartz would start with the Willoughbys' neighbors and Dan Willoughby's former coworkers in the air freight business. Lines would circle closer to the core. He wasn't yet ready to squeeze Willoughby, but he would feel him out, toss out some rope and see if Willoughby entangled himself in it.

"Where is she, Dan?"

Jack Mulkins was out of patience and pissed off. He had heard nothing from Phoenix since Willoughby's call on Monday informing him that Yesenia would not be coming to Portland.

Now, three days later, Willoughby was on the phone again, the phone Mulkins had wired to a tape recorder.

"I don't know where she is. I don't give a damn."

"I know you know where she is," Mulkins insisted. "How do I know she's not layin' out in the desert someplace."

"Jack, she got out of jail and where she went from there I don't know. She wasn't anything to me, Jack. Our relationship was purely platonic."

"That's a damn lie," Mulkins said. "Have you forgotten everything you told me? We talked about me divorcing Yesenia when you were ready to marry her."

"Look, my wife has been murdered and I'm very upset and I'm trying to pull my life together. My mother-in-law is trying to implicate me in the murder and take my kids away. I don't want anything more to do with Yesenia."

Mulkins couldn't be sure that the story about his wife's murder wasn't just another of Willoughby's tall tales. He had read nothing about it in the newspapers, but there was no reason why the Oregon papers would have an interest in a murder that happened so far away. Even if it were true, he was too angry now to be delicate about it.

"Yeah, and I know what you were planning to do. Remember? You told me you were going to take her to Mexico and she wouldn't come back?"

"I can't talk on the phone about this," Willoughby snapped.

"I want to know where Yesenia is," Mulkins said. "I'm going to give you one week. If you don't find out where she is, I'm going to turn it over to the police, to the missing persons bureau."

"You stay out of it," Willoughby said, his voice turning icy. "You'll be better off if you do. You're involved in it too."

"Involved in what?"

"Well, you could be pulled into it. If you call the police, they'll tap your phones. You'll have cops following you around, knocking on your door. They'll make your life miserable."

"I'll give you one week to find Yesenia," Mulkins said.

After they hung up, Mulkins thought about his possible involvement in a murder plot—if, in fact, Willoughby's wife had been killed. He had heard Willoughby make references to such a scheme but he had kept quiet, partly out of fear and partly out of disbelief. Willoughby had always seemed to be filled with hot air rather than evil, but maybe he was deranged enough to kill his wife.

He dialed directory assistance and got the number for the *Phoenix Gazette.* An editor named Jeff Unger answered at the city desk.

"I'm trying to confirm that a Mrs. Willoughby has been murdered," Mulkins said.

"That is true," Unger said.

"Can you fax me a copy of the story?" Mulkins said.

"Sure," Unger said. "Give me the number."

Mulkins read the article over and over. If Willoughby had murdered his wife, he might also have murdered Yesenia. Early the next morning, he called Willoughby and again demanded to know where Yesenia was.

Willoughby erupted. "You can't call me at this number," he shouted.

"I've got to know where she is, Dan."

"Well, we can't talk about it now. This line may be tapped."

"We're going to talk about it."

Willoughby gave him another phone number and said, "That's my friend Duke Boggs's number. You can call me there."

Mulkins hung up, brooded for a while and then dialed the number Dan had given him. Boggs answered and laid the phone down, and within thirty seconds Dan was on the line. The conversation was protracted and contentious but, in the end, Mulkins learned nothing.

Fed up with Willoughby's evasiveness and his threats, he slammed down the phone and quickly picked it up again. His next call was to someone whose name he had gleaned from

the Phoenix newspaper article: Sgt. Joe Ruet of the Gilbert
Police Department.

Nick Huish felt a small rush of adrenaline at being invited
to the police station. Ever since the investigators returned from
the crime scene in Mexico, he had waited for some report on
what they had found, if anything. But no information had been
forthcoming.

He was determined that the investigation of his sister's murder was not going to die from lack of interest or taper down
to the vanishing point and be consigned to the graveyard of
unsolved cases. He did not know the investigators well, and
therefore had no measure of their devotion to the case, but he
was prepared to prod them—and their political bosses—by any
means at his disposal. He made notes of things that might help
them—names of Dan's friends, neighbors, business associates,
episodes of his brother-in-law's erratic behavior. It occurred to
him that he did not really know Dan very well, and possibly
no one else did either, but a lot of people knew him a little,
and collectively they might round out a portrait of a killer.

Early on, he made frequent contact with the Gilbert police
and offered them tips and leads they might pursue. He could
be a valuable resource, but the detectives were a little wary of
him. He was as aggressive as a hungry wolf and more than
willing to assist the investigation, but if he turned into the
proverbial loose cannon the investigation could be harmed.
Still, they needed all the cooperation they could get from the
family—not just information, but, possibly, assistance in playing the line on which they hoped to hook Willoughby. Nick
was impassioned and tireless and he seemed to possess keen
instincts about this case.

In his first meeting with Patrick McNabb, Nick had startled
the detective by asking, "What can I do to find the he, she or
it who is involved in this."

It? The cops had told no one that Yesenia Patino was a

transsexual. To their knowledge, even Dan Willoughby didn't know.

"Why did you use that word . . . *it?*" McNabb asked.

Nick shrugged. "I don't know," he said. "Just an expression. Why?"

"Before this is over, that word will leave an indelible mark on your brain."

"Why?"

Wondering if he had said too much already, McNabb replied, "You'll see," and changed the conversation. It was one piece of information the investigators did not want leaked to the press, and Nick had already demonstrated a tendency to contact the newspapers and stoke the embers of the story to keep it alive. His greatest fear was that the story would slip to the back pages—or out of the paper altogether—and the interest of the authorities would wane as quickly. Conversely, the cops feared that too much publicity, too much leaked information, could jeopardize the investigation. It would not serve their purpose for anyone—particularly potential suspects—to know how much they knew. The victim's brother could be helpful to them, but only if he could be managed.

Entering the police station, his heart rate accelerated. Something good must be up. He asked for Sergeant Ruet and was directed to a room down a short hallway, where three men were waiting.

"Do you recognize any of this stuff?" Kay Lines asked, spreading some of the contents of Yesenia's oversized purse on the desk in Joe Ruet's office.

"What is all this stuff?" Nick wanted to know.

"Just tell us if you recognize it," Lines said.

Nick sorted through the clutter and spotted Trish's wedding ring, then the pearl ring Thera had purchased for her.

"That's my sister's ring," Nick said. "Where did you get it?"

"Are you sure? One hundred percent unequivocally sure

that this is your sister's ring?'' Lines asked, ignoring Nick's question.

"I'm ninety-nine percent sure," Nick sighed.

"That's not good enough. Is there anyone else in your family who can identify it?"

"Yes. My mom. She gave Trish that ring."

Thera Huish gathered her purse, fished for her car keys and hurried out the door. Like her son, she interpreted the summons to the Gilbert police station as a positive sign. Like her son, she also was impatient to learn how the investigation was progressing.

In the ten days since her daughter's funeral, she had heard little of an official nature. She knew from the newspapers that the attorney general's office was involved, but she feared that because Trish was murdered in Mexico the hunt for the killer might, for one legal technicality or another, flounder.

A couple of days after Trish was buried, Val and Bob had returned to California with their wives, and the house seemed large and empty again. Sterling was there, of course, and Nick talked with her daily about their suspicions of Dan, but much of the time she felt alone with her own thoughts, her own pain. The long and agonizing war she had fought for her daughter's heart and mind was now over. Through patience and stubbornness, she had spanned the chasm that once separated her from Trish, only to lose her this way. At times, in a dark and silent room, the pain was unbearable, as intolerable as contemplating the possibility that her killer might never be punished. That thought trod upon her sleep like an ogre and visited her every waking moment. Nothing short of biblical justice, an eye for an eye, would quiet the beast.

A chance to meet with the cops gave her new hope.

Detectives Ruet and McNabb were in uniform, so she assumed that the tall guy in cowboy boots and blue jeans was from the attorney general's office, a fact that was confirmed by the formal introductions.

"Mrs. Huish, I'd like for you to look at a few things and see if you recognize any of them," Lines said, opening a small box. "Don't touch anything, just look."

"Yes," Thera said without hesitation.

"What?"

"This pearl ring."

"Whose is it?"

"It's Trish's."

"How do you know?"

"I bought it for her in Malaysia."

Opening another box, Lines said, "Do you recognize anything here?"

"That's Trish's diamond . . . her wedding band. Where did you get it?"

"Are you sure?"

"Absolutely. I went with her to get it set. Where did you get these rings?"

"We'll tell you that in due time," Lines said. "Tell me about Dan Willoughby."

Thera wavered for an instant. These men were strangers to her and she felt uncomfortable in the austere surroundings of the detective's office. How much should she say? Was she being secretly tape recorded? Lines sensed her anxiety and tried to put her at ease.

"We just need to know as much as possible about the people who were close to Trish," he said.

Okay, he wants to know so I'll tell him. This is no time for diplomacy, Thera thought.

"I think Dan Willoughby was involved in the murder of my daughter," she said.

"In what way?"

"Well, I think they were having some marital problems and I know . . . I know that somewhere in this whole thing there is a Mexican woman involved. I think he's been having an affair with her. He says she is his Spanish teacher, but I think . . .''

"How do you know he's involved with her?" Lines asked.

"I don't know . . .''

"How deeply involved?"

Thera searched for the words that were eluding her.

"Just tell me what you're thinking, what you feel inside," Lines said, sounding less like a detective than an old friend of the family.

Finding the words and her courage once again, Thera straightened her back, looked the detective in the eye and said, "Mr. Lines, I don't know if I should say this or not, but I think Dan Willoughby murdered my daughter."

"That's what you should say if that's what you feel."

"It's just that I don't know it, but I feel it."

"We usually find in a situation like this that when people believe something so strongly, and they know what's going on, they are usually right," Lines said. For a moment, he seemed to be looking past her, or through her. "We'll find out."

Chapter Thirty-eight

Judy Richfield heard the buzz, but disregarded it. Dan Willoughby involved with another woman? Absurd. She knew him too well, had been the beneficiary of his kindness and generosity for too long, had seen too often the love and attention he gave her children as well as his own, to believe a nasty rumor that had not even merited a mention in the newspapers.

For all she knew, it was just dirt being dished up by his in-laws. Dan had confided in her that Thera Huish was trying to blame him for Trish's death, and while he was absolutely innocent, he feared that he might be arrested anyway, thanks to Thera's meddling.

He needed a contingency plan, someone to look after his children if he were jailed. He certainly did not want his mother-in-law to have custody of them. "She's against me and against the family," he said.

Taking her cue, Judy contacted some of Dan's neighbors, who were also members of the Houston Ward LDS Church, and arranged a meeting at the home of Richard and Helen Roberts. Duke Boggs and his wife would attend, as would

Frank and Rosa Bounds. And, of course, Judy Richfield and
Dan Willoughby.

Sipping light beverages, Willoughby's friends listened quietly as he explained his fear of being arrested, and he pleaded
for them to accept his children into their homes if that occurred.

In the Mormon tradition, they were willing, perhaps obligated, to render their services to a brother—but they would
not be led blindly into his corral. None believed he was capable
of harming his wife, or even that he was capable of straying
from his marriage, but they were entitled to ask a few questions.

*Dan, we've all heard about this woman. What is your rela-
tionship with her?*

"It is strictly professional," he said, shaking his head as if
in disbelief that anyone would think it was more than that.
"See, I had opened this branch in Mexico and she was doing
some work for me, translating stuff. I would take the papers
to her in the morning and pick them up in the evening."

Were you attracted to her, or she to you?

"Well, I didn't have feelings for her, but she was probably
attracted to me."

A fatal attraction?

"It could have been."

Could she have killed Trish?

"Yes."

*Did you see this woman in Rocky Point the weekend Trish
was killed?*

"No, of course not. I don't know anything about her being
down there."

Did you have anything to do with Trish's death?

"My God, no." The words came out like a wail and tears
clouded his eyes.

*We've heard rumors that this woman is in Mexico now. Do
you know where she is?*

"I feel like she is down there, but I haven't seen her."

How could she get there? Did she have any money?

"I guess I am guilty—of generosity. She wanted to go to

California to get a divorce, so I gave her three hundred and fifty dollars. She probably used that money to go to Mexico.''

His performance was passable and the meeting ended with assurances that the neighbors would do whatever they could when and if the time came. To guarantee that money would be available to care for the children, Dan gave Boggs a check for $5,000 to open a special trust account for that purpose.

For the next several days, Lines and Schwartz followed the copious paper trail Willoughby had strewn in the wake of his affair with Yesenia Patino. They obtained the M & I Thunderbird Bank's records of the account he used to pay Yesenia's living expenses and maintain his own lavish lifestyle. They talked with the florist, the photographer, the gold ring designer, the travel agent, the beach house broker at Rita's Mexican Vacations. From credit card records, they learned of every trip Willoughby and Patino had taken together, where they stayed, where they ate, how they played. It would be very difficult for Willoughby to stick with his insistence that Yesenia was no more than his Spanish tutor.

From neighbors and fellow church members, they received one picture of Willoughby, the one he had carefully fostered over the years. For all its flaunted overtness, his extramarital romance had gone undetected in those circles. There, the Willoughbys were happily married, an exemplary family.

Beyond that sequestered Gilbert haven, however, the converse face of Willoughby emerged with surprising ease and clarity. Tina Roush confirmed the affair and that Yesenia was pressuring Willoughby to buy her an engagement ring. Jack Mulkins confirmed that Willoughby had discussed ''getting rid'' of his wife, perhaps by taking her to Mexico, where ''you can get away with anything.'' Phil Cantrelli confirmed what Lines and Schwartz had suspected from the large checks Willoughby wrote frequently to several pharmacies in Mesa and Gilbert. ''Percodan was Dan's best friend,'' Cantrelli told them.

Cocaine, too. Dan liked cocaine and Cantrelli owned up to having sold him some on occasion. The legwork even led the investigators to a street prostitute that Willoughby frequented. She, too, attested to his fondness for coke. Pain killers, steroids, cocaine. What else could the guy have been into?

Maybe it was time to start jerking Willoughby's chain—or at least tugging it a little. Lines still was not prepared to grill him, or to ask questions with even vague accusatory overtones, but if this case was going to be a long waltz, it wouldn't hurt to see what kind of dancer Willoughby was.

On March 13, Willoughby arrived at the attorney general's office with his lawyer in tow—not Richard Fuller, who had handled civil matters for him and had helped Tony with his traffic tickets, but David Ochoa, a former Pinal County prosecutor who later served three years as a superior court judge before entering the practice of criminal law.

Lawyer and client signed in at the reception desks, were issued visitor passes and waited for Lines to come downstairs to escort them to his office, where Sergeant Ruet was waiting, along with the jewelry Thera had already identified as belonging to Trish.

"I just wanted to see if you could identify these rings," Lines said. One was a large diamond set in a gold band, the other a double pearl.

"I don't know," Willoughby said, speaking slowly and trying to maintain a facade of calm, at which he failed miserably. Until that moment, he had appeared confident, perhaps a little cocky, but the sight of the jewelry caused his face to flush and turn damp with perspiration. His hand trembled and then his whole body seemed to shake.

When he was questioned by the police in Rocky Point, Willoughby had told them that two of his wife's rings had been stolen. At their request, he drew a picture of the diamond, a drawing that was now in Lines's possession.

"You don't know if those were your wife's rings?"

"I can't be positive."

Lines thanked him for coming to his office and promised to be in touch, a pledge that accorded little comfort to Willoughby.

After the two men had departed, Lines put the rings back in a box.

"Kind of strange, wasn't it?" he mused to Ruet. "He didn't ask where we got these rings?"

The guy didn't dance well at all.

Within a week of Trish's murder, Willoughby had demanded an accounting of the business and insisted that he and Thera select a mediator to help them arrive at a fair settlement. Thera bristled.

"You will get an accounting, Danny, but I will do it in my own sweet time," she said. "This is my business."

"Oh, no," he said. "This is community property. What belonged to Trish now belongs to me."

"We put this business in a trust," Thera argued. "The trust says I own this business. Until this thing is solved and we find out who murdered Trish, I will do with you exactly like I did with Trish. Every month, I will pay the bills and whatever is left over, I will divide with you."

Although T&T Distributors was grossing about $40,000 a month, expenses consumed half of that, leaving about $14,000 to $16,000 to be divided. He demanded half the gross and they argued some more.

As the days passed, he become more insistent that Trish's half of the business was now his, and he wanted Thera to buy him out, using the one million dollars in proceeds from the two life insurance policies that Trish had taken out as a partner in T&T Distributors. It would be a humid day in Tonopah when she handed over a million dollars to the man she believed killed her daughter. Or so she thought.

On Wednesday, March 15, three weeks after Trish's death,

she received a letter from Lawrence Wright, another of Dan Willoughby's attorneys. It was a demand for one-half interest in T&T Distributors and Willoughby's share of the proceeds from the business-held life insurance on Trish Willoughby.

Val flew down from California on Saturday. Since his sister's death, he had been commuting to Phoenix frequently, in part to comfort his parents and in part to try to keep peace in the family. His mother was too emotional to deal with Dan in a calm manner, and Nick was not much better.

Thera handed him the attorney's letter as soon as he arrived. He read it quickly and left the house. When he reached the Willoughby residence, Dan was preparing to take Hayden and Thera to a tumbling class, so Val offered to go along. While the children went inside the gymnasium, the two men stayed outside. Val mentioned the letter from the lawyer.

"What are you trying to do?" he asked.

"I'm ready to get into a fight," Dan said. "Ready to file suit."

"You don't want to do that," Val said.

"If you don't pay me, I'm going to bring this family down," Dan threatened. "I'm going to tell all about when Trish and I were in California . . . about all the drugs she did . . . bring out all the mud."

"What good is that going to do?" Val said, on the brink of letting go of his temper.

"Just give me the money."

"You don't want to do it, Danny. You don't want to fight."

"Why not?"

"If you fight, you're going to take me on."

Val was speaking figuratively, but Dan took him literally. He stepped back as if to avoid a punch.

"If you sue my mother, it's me you're going to fight and I have deeper pockets than you, Dan," Val said.

"This is between me and your mom. It has nothing to do with you."

"It has everything to do with me. You sue my mother and I'll bury you."

Kay Lines considered the implications of Willoughby's threat. It could mean one of two things: Either he was innocent of killing his wife and was determined to claim what was rightfully his, or he was guilty and desperate, unable to walk away from the money even though reaching for it could imperil his life and liberty. Filing a lawsuit would subject him to sworn depositions and incriminating discovery. In his own mind, he had already resolved the question of Willoughby's guilt, so a lawsuit suggested that desperation, diluted with greed, was the operative motive. Good. As odious and brutal as a lawsuit would be for the Huishes, it would keep Dan Willoughby in town.

"As long as he's trying to get the money, we'll know where he is," he told Thera. "If he gets it, he'll be gone."

It was a factor she had already considered. Dan would get nothing from her.

Chapter Thirty-nine

Nick turned off of tree-lined Washington Street into the parking lot of the building that housed the attorney general's office, found a vacant space and made a dash for the front door.

Maybe, just maybe, things were starting to happen. Kay Lines had telephoned with another invitation, maddeningly cryptic and unilluminating, but glutted with promise. "We've got some new information," he said. "Would you like to come down to my office?"

Picking up his visitors ID badge from the receptionist, Nick hurried upstairs. The two men shook hands and, without warning, Lines embraced him in a bear hug.

Before Nick could decipher the gesture, Lines tossed a picture on the desk.

"Do you know that man?" he asked.

Nick leaned over the desk and studied the photograph on the Oregon driver's license. Alfredo Patino. The name meant nothing to him. "No," he replied.

Lines tossed another picture on the desk, this one a young woman with dark hair and skin.

"Do you know that girl?" he asked.

"Nope."

"Are you sure?"

"I'm sure."

"Neither one looks familiar?"

"Never seen them before."

"This girl is the girl we've been looking for. She's been seeing your brother-in-law for a year and a half. We found her fingerprints in the house in Rocky Point," Lines explained.

No surprise there. Nick had long been aware of Dan's eye for the ladies. He felt relief that the cops were making progress but wasn't sure what to make of the photographs. A young Mexican man and young Mexican woman. Did they kill his sister?

"See that girl?" Lines said.

"Uh-huh."

"See that guy?"

"Uh-huh."

"That girl used to be that guy."

For an instant, Nick stood transfixed over the images smiling up from the desk as the information soaked in—*Dan's been having an affair with a transsexual*—and then broke into laughter.

"You can't tell anyone, though," Lines said. After a brief pause, he amended the instruction. "Go ahead and tell your mother. This should give her some relief."

Nick couldn't wait. He raced through the late morning traffic straight to his mother's house.

"Mom," he said. "I gotta talk to you."

From his expression and the way the words jostled to escape his throat, Thera prepared for the worst. Nick explained that a woman's fingerprints had been found in the beach house, a woman with whom Dan had been having an affair. She tensed and glared at her son, impatient to hear more. There had to be more. Nick would not be wound this tightly over the discovery that Dan Willoughby had been unfaithful to Trish.

"This woman, they think, is part of the murder," Nick said. "There's something you need to know, Mom."

What? What? She wanted to scream. *Spit it out!*

"That woman used to be a man," he said as he began to snicker. "Danny's been having sex with her."

Her tension broken, Thera leaned back and joined her son's laughter.

"And Dan doesn't know she was a man?" she said.

"That's right, Mom, and Kay Lines doesn't want us to say anything to anybody . . . not Bob, not Val, not even Dad, not anybody."

"This is so wonderful," Thera sighed. The cops not only had a suspect and a fingerprint, they had information that would surely collapse Dan Willoughby's raging ego.

At midafternoon, Nick called Kay Lines at his office.

"I told Mom and she was ecstatic," he said.

"You know, Nick, I got to thinking . . . I'm glad you called because I wanted to find out what her reaction would be. I've got one more request."

"What's that?"

"Go ahead and tell your whole family, but just make sure it doesn't leak out to anybody else, especially the press."

"Agreed." This was too good to keep from the rest of the family.

"How would you feel about a meeting between you and Danny?" Lines asked.

"I guess . . . I guess I could meet with him," Nick said, hesitating a little.

"Can you get him in a situation where it's just the two of you?"

"Yeah, I suppose."

"I'd like you to take him to lunch or something. We'll rig you with a wire. Let's just see what he has to say."

* * *

Dan was agreeable. His relationship with the family had been strained, and a private talk with Nick would be a good opportunity to persuade the Huishes to call off the dogs. Little did he realize that he was dealing with the angriest dog of the pack.

When they first faced each other across the table at Bennigan's, a bar and grill on Southern Avenue in Mesa, Nick was stiff. The listening device Kay Lines had attached to his skin felt as heavy as a chain and he feared that something might reveal its presence to Dan.

As soon as the talk turned to Trish's murder, though, Nick's anger distracted him from the spy gear. Dan showed no grief— he had never shown any that was convincing to the Huishes— and now he was the salesman again, making his pitch for the biggest commission of his life, trying to convince Nick to stop prodding the cops, stop talking to reporters.

"We need to be careful, Nick," he said. "You guys are out there in the press and . . . everything's leading to me. I'm not guilty, Nick, and you know that."

Nick's eyes narrowed and he struggled to hold his tongue.

"If you guys keep on doing what you're doing, they're going to arrest me and, Nick, they're going to arrest the wrong man," Dan said.

Finally, Nick could hold back no longer. He wasn't here to argue with his brother-in-law, but to draw him out, allow him to say something on tape that was incriminating, or at least contradictory of his previous statements. But blaming the family for wanting to see justice done was the crown of insensitivity.

"Look, Dan, if that's the case why don't you get off your ass and do what we're doing?" he said. "Get involved with the case. If you're so innocent, get out there and start creating leads like we're doing."

"If you'll leave it alone, it will all go away. It will take care of itself," Dan said.

Nothing of value came from the meeting, just a tape of Willoughby protesting his innocence and sticking to his original story. As badly as Nick wanted to be the one to trip him up, he could offer nothing but his regrets to the investigators.

Lines already had the next move mapped out. From what he had learned about Dan Willoughby, he was convinced that Patino's background was the correct psychological pressure point to massage. Jack Mulkins had assured him that Willoughby knew nothing of Afredo's transformation into Yesenia. Phil Cantrelli had convinced him that Willoughby fancied himself the consummate ladies' man. One after another of Willoughby's old cohorts in the air freight business had described him as "Disco Dan" and recounted his ceaseless, almost compulsive, pursuit of every woman he met. Confronted with the fact that he had carried on a torrid affair with a transsexual, Willoughby might snap, might be driven by embarrassment or temper to do something foolish.

"I want you to set up a meeting between Dan and your family and let your mom and dad tell Dan about Yesenia," Lines said, "and I want you at the house with them when they tell him."

Believing Thera finally was willing to discuss a financial settlement, Dan arrived at the Huish residence promptly at six o'clock, and Nick escorted him into the family room. Dan sat down in a large, padded chair beside the sofa, where Thera and Sterling were seated. Nick sat in another chair facing him.

It was a cool night in early March, but Dan was sweating profusely. His shirt was soaked, and as fast as he could wipe it away, more perspiration formed on his face and neck, seeping out of his ears and dripping down the lobes onto his shirt.

"We want to talk to you about something very important," Thera said.

Dan's face twitched as the sweat dripped off his chin onto the carpet.

"We wanted to cover some issues wc felt needed to be cleared up," Thera continued. She rambled on about the business and her promise to split the profits with him until the investigation was cleared up—things he had heard before.

While the money had consumed him since Trish's death, he now showed little interest in the topic, if in fact he was even hearing what Thera was saying. He just sat quietly, mopping his face and losing the battle with the moisture.

After Thera had droned on aimlessly for fifteen minutes, she abruptly got his attention.

"The last thing we have to talk about is this woman you've been seeing while you were married to Trish," she said, as matter-of-factly as if mentioning a tax form.

Willoughby's head snapped back.

"Where is she?" Thera asked calmly and without rancor.

"Let me tell you about this woman," he said, jumping at the topic like a frog on hot sand. "I know that she is involved. If I could find her . . . I know she committed the murder . . . if I could find her . . ."

"Where is she, Danny?"

"I don't know, but I know she's the guilty one."

"Then why don't you find her?"

"Well, I would like to, but there's no need for me to get involved. You know the police are on my tail every day. If I went down to Mexico, where I think she is, they would probably arrest me, and I'd never see my family again. I can't leave the country. Besides, it would cost a lot of money."

"Danny, if you'll go to Mexico and find her, we'll pay for it," Thera said. "In fact, I'll cover it up so the police don't even know you're gone."

"They'll know if I left town."

"No, we'll help you get out of town." Thera could promise anything, knowing full well that he would accept nothing.

"What would I do with the children?" he asked, still searching for a reason not to participate in the search for Yesenia.

"I'll take care of them," Thera said.

Dan shifted in his chair, leaving wet spots where his arms had rested.

"What would you do if you found her?" Thera asked.

"I would bring her back here and make her go before the attorney general and admit she killed Trish," he said. "Thera, she had been pushing the idea of us getting married, but I was trying to break off the relationship."

"You gave her a ring, Danny."

"I know. I gave her that ring in friendship. I was trying to help her out." He was forever willing to plead guilty to generosity.

"Danny, what do you really know about Yesenia?" Thera asked.

"Just that she was my Spanish teacher. She's the one who pursued the relationship."

"I've got something to tell you, Danny," Thera said, pausing for effect. A glaze of stark terror crossed over his eyes. "I don't know how involved you got with her, but I think it was pretty involved . . . to the point that you were thinking of marrying her."

"No, no, no," he said, lowering his head until it hovered just above his knees.

"Do you know that Yesenia was once a man?"

He bolted upright.

"Her name used to be Alfredo, until she had a sex change operation a few years ago."

His face crimsoned and he raised his arms, as if in prayer, and said, "Well, I guess it's a wonderful thing for the *Enquirer* to talk about."

That was it, his entire reaction. With nothing more to say, Thera excused herself and went into the kitchen to prepare dinner. Dan stood up quickly. Silent and solemn, Nick and Sterling watched him cross the room and waited until the door had closed behind him before they exploded in laughter.

Chapter Forty

Even with the cops watching him, even with his in-laws resisting a financial settlement, things weren't looking too bad for Dan Willoughby. On March 20, he deposited the $150,000 check he had received from the policy he and Trish had purchased from Jim Parker of the IDS Life Insurance Company, and three days later—the one-month anniversary of his wife's murder—departed in a rented motor coach for a week-long trip to California with his children.

When he returned, he called Tony Patino and arranged a meeting the following day at La Parilla, a Mexican restaurant near Tony's home.

Sipping Tecate and lime, Willoughby plunged straight into his agenda.

"Any cops been around to see you?" he asked.

"Yeah, they come to my house and asked questions," Tony said.

"What kinds of questions?"

"About Rocky Point . . . about going there with Yesenia."

"What did you tell them?"

"You know, I told them . . . you know, the story Yesenia gave me."

Tony may have been lulled into believing that the cops were through with him. Detectives Ruet and Baty had visited him the day after Yesenia disappeared and he told them the story she wanted him to tell: They had gone to Rocky Point on Friday, partied on the beach all night and returned home on Saturday.

Ten days later, he was visited by Kay Lines, and again he recounted the tale of hanging out on the beach with four friends whose last names he didn't know.

The investigator appeared convinced. Now they would leave him alone. Yesenia was out of the country and there was no one to contradict him, no second party to slip up and betray the lie. Even if the police learned from the Customs Service that he and Yesenia had been detained at the border Saturday evening, that would not contradict the story. No reason to worry.

"Did they ask you if you had seen me in Rocky Point?"

"Yeah, they ask and I told them I didn't see you."

"Okay, just remember that. You didn't see me."

"What happened down there . . . the murder and all?"

"I feel sorry for what happened to my wife, Tony, but I didn't kill her. I wasn't even there when she was killed. I was with my kids."

He drained his glass, chased the beer with a bite of lime and said, "Do you know where Yesenia is?"

"I don't know. Why do you want to know where she is?"

"I just want to know that she's okay."

As they stood up to leave, Willoughby reminded him again, "You didn't see me in Rocky Point."

"I didn't see you. No problem."

What Tony didn't know was that at every border crossing, the U.S. Customs Service logs the tag numbers of vehicles entering and leaving the country, as well as the time of the crossing. From those records, the police had already learned the story was a fabrication—that they had gone to Mexico and returned the same day, the day of Trish's murder.

By early April, Lines and Schwartz, with help from the Gilbert detectives, had stitched together the rough fabric of a decent murder conspiracy case. Establishing motive and opportunity was easy enough. Willoughby's obsession with Patino and his wife's insurance policies were ample for him. Yesenia's calendar book revealed that she was not exactly a one-man woman and probably not obsessed with Willoughby, but the money alone could have been sufficient motive for her. As for opportunity, both were in Rocky Point the day of the murder and both were in the beach house—perhaps not at the same time, but both were there near the time of the murder.

Establishing jurisdiction did not seem to pose a problem. They could be indicted and tried in Arizona for conspiracy to commit murder if the investigators could prove that some elements of conceiving and planning the murder occurred in the state. Easy enough. The two trips the pair took to Rocky Point shortly before the murder, it could be argued, were necessary to perfect the plan. The engagement ring and engagement photographs strongly suggested that they had plans to marry soon—and there was no evidence that Willoughby planned to divorce his wife. To the contrary, he had told several people—Phil Cantrelli and Jack Mulkins, among others—that he could not divorce his wife because she "has too much on me," and he had talked openly about "getting rid" of Trish.

A conspiracy conviction might put Willoughby and Patino away for less than twenty years, and no one in the attorney general's office wanted to settle for that. To prosecute them for murder would be a little trickier. They would have to prove that an actual element of the murder, not just the planning of it, occurred in Arizona. In that regard, a couple of things occurred to Lines. First, Trish apparently was somehow rendered unconscious and her head wrapped in the towel before the first blow was struck—a fact made apparent by the absence of blood spatters in the beach house bedroom and the absence of defensive wounds on her arms and hands. Maybe she was drugged before she was beaten and stabbed to death, and if the drugs were acquired in Arizona, they would be an element of the murder. Secondly, the murder weapon. If it had been purchased or manufactured in Arizona, that would be sufficient to establish jurisdiction. That was a major snag. Only the three knives were found in the beach house, but the other weapon, the bludgeoning instrument, was still missing and in all probability would never be located.

Without the murder weapon and without Yesenia Patino to interrogate, some large questions were going unanswered. What exactly was the weapon and who had used it on Trish? Had someone besides the Willoughby family and Yesenia Patino been in the beach house? Could Yesenia have acted alone? Lines could not prove that Willoughby knew she was in Rocky Point that day. He had no evidence that they had actually seen each other that day.

For two months, Lines had been pacing the investigation, trying to avoid the kind of rash move or juicy disclosure that might send witnesses or suspects into hiding. Fortunately, Willoughby showed no signs of preparing to run, not without the million dollars from Trish's life insurance policies. No, Willoughby was still being himself. While he groused to the neighbors about financial distress, he seemed to be living pretty well. He even signed up with a dating service—Together of Phoenix—and paid with a check for $2,195. On the membership profile form, he listed his preference in women: Hispanic.

By the end of April, however, the investigators had learned as much as they felt they could learn about their suspects by scouring the streets and neighborhoods of the valley. The hunt for Yesenia had stalled out, so the most obvious course now was a direct one, straight to the heart of Dan Willoughby.

"I think it's time to pick up Tony Patino," Lines told Ruet. "Why don't you arrest him for conspiracy to commit murder?"

"You got it," Ruet said. He had begun to feel anxious about the investigation and welcomed the chance to step up the tempo. Tony was arrested at his home the next day.

Lines let him stew in jail for a few days before stopping by to question him. Faced with such a serious charge, Tony caved in and agreed to a deal, although one might not have been necessary. He had lied for his sister, sure, but he didn't even know why. He knew nothing about a murder that Saturday in Rocky Point, did not learn of it until his brother showed him the newspaper two days later. He was just there because Willoughby had called in a marker. Still, he had lied and Kay Lines knew it, and Tony did not want to be sucked deeper into the mire.

With his court-appointed lawyer present, with the investigator's tape recorder running, and with assurances that he would not be prosecuted, Tony told the whole story of repaying a favor to Dan by driving Yesenia to Rocky Point, of his and Yesenia's meeting with Dan on the beach, of Yesenia dropping him off in town and disappearing for nearly half an hour in his truck, of Dan and Yesenia asking him to lie if the police questioned him.

"It would be best if you didn't discuss this with anyone else," Lines told him when the interview ended.

Tony had no intentions of talking to anyone, especially not to Dan Willoughby.

Lines drove back to his office downtown, sat down at his computer and, surrounded by mounds of notes and transcripts and investigative reports, began typing up an affidavit of authenticity—an official request for a search warrant.

> *Your Affiant, Kay W. Lines, a peace officer in the state of Arizona, being duly sworn, upon oath, deposes and says:*

> *That the following facts establish probable cause for believing that extraditable offenses have been committed*

by Dan Willoughby and Yesenia Gonzales Patino aka
Victoria Yvonne Mulkins aka Alfredo Gonzales Patino
aka Victoria Yvonne McDonald.

Enclosed are several hundred pages of documents and
reports which comprise the evidence supporting these
facts. The investigation of these offenses continues to
accumulate additional evidence and facts.

For the next twenty-nine double-spaced pages, Lines laid
out the entire case and specified the items he believed would
be produced by a search of Willoughby's residence and that
of his neighbor, Duke Boggs, items that "may tend to prove
evidence of a conspiracy." Of all the neighbors, Boggs had
remained closest to Willoughby. He had opened a trust account
at a Bank of America branch in Mesa with money Willoughby
had given him, and he had also rented a safety deposit box at
that same location. He allowed Willoughby to place and receive
telephone calls from his house. He had permitted Willoughby
to store some boxes in his garage.

Among such things as financial records, photographs, calen-
dars and appointment books, Trish's will, correspondence
between Willoughby and Patino "showing any furtherance of
the conspiracy and any showing of the current whereabouts
of Yesenia Patino," Lines believed the search would yield
"prescription and other drugs."

The affiant intends to obtain a court order for exhuma-
tion of the victim's remains in order to check for residues
of any drugs. However, due to the multiplicity of possible
drugs that might have been used, it would prove helpful
to toxicologists to have knowledge of which drugs were
most accessible to Dan Willoughby and through him to
the victim.

Chapter Forty-one

Most of the neighbors all came to the garage sale, as did their children. The Willoughby family needed money and Dan spread the word that disposing of personal items was the only way he could raise funds to meet their living expenses.

Believing their father's tales of financial gloom, the Willoughby children placed some of their own treasured possessions on the block. Looking through the items that were offered, one neighborhood boy asked Hayden, "Why are you selling your G.I. Joe?"

"Because we don't have any money to eat," Hayden replied. "Grandma is not giving us any money."

Rather than downplay the probability that he was a suspect in his wife's murder, Willoughby had begun to use it as a kind of public relations ploy in the looming war with his in-laws. In the neighborhood and church, he presented himself as a victim of Thera's persecution. Because of her agitation, he moaned, he was being hounded by the police. Because of her, he could be arrested and wrongly accused. Because of her, he had no access to Trish's money. Unable to find decent work,

he was cleaning toilets at a health club to hold the family
together.

To his children, he portrayed their grandmother as a witch—
Elvira, the mistress of the dark—and suggested to them that
she had arranged their mother's death out of greed. Their mother
was insured through her business for one million dollars, he
told them, and their grandma was keeping it from them. He
also did not tell them that Thera had been splitting the monthly
profits of T&T Distributors with him and would continue to
do so.

Thera was aware of Dan's efforts to poison her relationship
with the children, but she was powerless to deflect his arrows.
As the days passed, as Dan's financial demands intensified, she
saw less and less of her grandchildren, and those infrequent
occasions were strained. Her grandchildren clearly were hostile
and resentful of her.

During one of their confrontations over the money, Thera
told Dan point blank that she felt he had something to do with
Trish's murder, and he stormed out of her office, calling her
"crazy," telling her she needed psychological help, and vowing
that she would never see his children again.

By early May, virtually all communications between her and
the children had ceased.

While not especially optimistic that Dan had had a change
of heart, she called him anyway. Mother's Day was approaching
and the Huishes were planning a special luncheon at the Rus-
tler's Roost in a resort complex at South Mountain Park. Nick
and Cara would be there, as would Cara's parents. Could the
children join them?

Inexplicably, Dan consented, but with a caveat—he would
come along. His presence would certainly give the occasion a
grim ambience, but she could accept that. It was obvious that
he did not want to give the Huish family an opportunity to
influence his children, and she could accept that, too.

For the most part, the gathering was civil enough. Dan and
Thera did not feign affection for each other, but neither did

they rattle their swords. The restaurant laid out a lavish buffet and provided live music. The children seemed to be enjoying themselves, and Thera began to relax, something she had not done in Dan's presence for many months.

She and Nick noticed it at about the same time. They finished their meal and were preparing to leave, but Dan was acting weird again. First, he squirmed in his chair and glanced over his shoulder, as if he were being stalked. His eyes roamed the crowded restaurant room and he stood up, paced back and forth for a moment and then approached a table across the room.

Marsha, too, had been watching her father. Now he was shaking hands with a man seated at the other table, slapping him on the back, shifting his weight from foot to foot as they talked.

Marsha stood up and said, "Uncle Nick, that's the doctor who tried to save Mom's life."

Willoughby left the table of Leigh and Harold Lowry and proceeded to the front door. As the rest of the Huish family followed him outside, Nick detoured to the doctor's table.

"I hate to bother you after what you just experienced," Nick said. The doctor appeared to be thoroughly ruffled and the look on his face was enough to silence Nick momentarily. "But I just want to let you know how much I appreciate you trying to save my sister's life."

"I tried everything I could," Lowry said.

"I hope Dan Willoughby didn't spoil your lunch."

"It was a little spooky . . . to think the man standing next to me was possibly the murderer."

"Not possibly the murderer," Nick said. "He is the murderer."

"What are you doing with him?"

"Just trying to see the kids."

"I commend you for that," Lowry said, "but I was shocked to see him here."

* * *

After two and a half months of trying to pry the one million dollars out of Thera's grip, Willoughby made good on his threat of legal action. On May 6, he filed a twelve-page lawsuit aimed not only at Sterling and Thera, but also at T&T Distributors, Transamerica Occidental Life Insurance Co., Matol Botanical International, Synergy Group and Emerging, Inc.—the entities that were the source or repository of Thera and Trish's business income.

He was the sole beneficiary of Trish's will, Dan argued in the complaint, and therefore he was entitled to her half of the business:

> Prior to the death of Patricia Willoughby, Thera Huish and Patricia Willoughby entered into a buyout agreement concerning the interest of each in T&T. The buyout was funded by separate $250,000 life insurance policies, one on the life of Patricia Willoughby and one on the life of Thera Huish, purchased from Beneficial Life, and separate $750,000 life insurance policies, one on the life of Patricia Willoughby and one on the life of Thera Huish, purchased from Transamerica. The beneficiary in the policies on the life of Patricia Willoughby was Thera Huish. The terms of the buyout agreement required the beneficiary of the policies to use the proceeds of the policy to purchase the interest of the deceased partner from the estate of the deceased partner.

On the surface, the lawsuit appeared to unleash a complex tangle of legal issues. Was Trish's interest in T&T community property, or, being a gift from her mother, was it an excluded asset? Was the trust into which T&T was placed a valid entity or a mechanism for evading the community property statutes? Beneficial Life had already paid Thera $250,000 on the policy it issued; Transamerica had not yet settled. Although she was the beneficiary of the policies, could she avoid using the proceeds to pay Dan for Trish's half of the business?

Under normal circumstances, her position would have been tenuous. Community property laws are not easily short-circuited with semantics and legal hedging, but the manner in which the insurance policies were written, the way in which T&T was started initially, the corporation that was formed to receive its monies and the subsequent assignment of it to a trust created some legal fences that Dan would have to tear down. He might have a legal entitlement to everything he demanded, but he would have to fight for it, and Thera had made certain that the bout would go a long fifteen rounds.

She called Val and told him the matter was now in court.

"Don't you worry about it," he said. "He may be sorry he picked this fight."

Kay Lines walked into the kitchen and saw Dan Willoughby erasing something from his appointment book. He confiscated the folio and told Patrick McNabb, "Take him out to the garage and keep him out of the way."

While Willoughby sat on a stool, watched by another Gilbert cop, Lines and McNabb went through the house. Across the street, Joe Ruet and another officer searched the residence of Duke Boggs, who had until that day extended cautious loyalty to his old friend. No more. He told the police that he had allowed Willoughby to store boxes in his garage, but later, suspecting that some might have contained illegal steroids or other drugs, he had requested that Willoughby remove them. All that remained in his custody were receipts of the joint trust account at Bank of America, checkbooks in Willoughby's name, a safety deposit box key and file folders with documents pertaining to the care and custody of the Willoughby children.

From Willoughby's residence, the investigators scooped up five dozen items: address books, business cards, tax returns, the appointment book, videocassettes, audiotapes, photos, jewelry receipts, prescription drug bottles and a suitcase containing a stained purse.

There was nothing to indicate Yesenia's whereabouts and nothing that appeared to incriminate Willoughby beyond the evidence they already had, but it would take a couple of days to make a full assessment.

On June 7, Thera and Sterling Huish filed an "answer and counterclaim" to Dan's lawsuit. If he wanted to play hardball, they would throw him the fast stuff. After a lengthy denial of his claims against T&T Distributors and proceeds from the insurance policies, they accused him, for the first time on the public record, of causing the death of their daughter, and they did it in a manner calculated to inflict maximum humiliation

> It is alleged on information and belief that Dan did enter into agreements with certain parties, the names of whom are unknown at the present time, the purpose of which was to intentionally cause the death of Trish.
>
> As a consequence of the agreements, Dan did himself, in concert with others, or through the instrumentality of others, intentionally, negligently, unlawfully, evilly and/ or maliciously kill or cause the death of Trish.
>
> It is alleged in the alternative that Dan knew, or should have known, of the danger and threats to Trish's life. It is alleged on information and belief that Dan had entered into an extramarital affair with one Valerie Doe, an unmarried man. It is alleged on information and belief that Valerie Doe participated in or did cause the murder of Trish . . .

Valerie Doe, an unmarried man. If the press interest in the case had begun to wane, that was a log certain to refire the furnace.

Chapter Forty-two

Because of the emotional toll it can exact from the family, exhumation was not a measure Lines and Schwartz approached with relish, especially not in this case. Trish Willoughby was at rest, and the ground where she lay had been duly consecrated in the Mormon way. For the deeply devout Huishes, a decision to disturb it would be agonizing, Lines knew. But it had to be done, and the quicker the better. If the family objected, the process could be prolonged, and with the murder already three months into history, speed was essential.

The two investigators met in Lines's office and went over, once again, the report of Dr. Jose Garcia Ramirez, the Puerto Penasco medical examiner who had performed an autopsy on Trish the day after the murder.

"Not much more than a sheet lift," Lines muttered, scanning the document, which had been translated from Spanish.

Since he first read it three months ago, the autopsy report had troubled him. The doctor concluded that death was caused by multiple wounds inflicted by three separate sharp objects and he explained the absence of defensive wounds by noting that "the findings indicate that she was probably first punched with a fist in the epigastrium, rendering her defenseless and face up."

This case had far too many implications to proceed any further on such flimsy testimony. First, no toxicology tests had been conducted, so it was impossible to know if Trish had been rendered defenseless by drugs rather than by a fist to her abdomen. Second, only an exterior examination had been conducted on the head and face, making it difficult to precisely define the types of weapons used. In all, it was inadequate for the kind of case that would have to be built to cinch a conviction, and Lines dreaded what lay ahead.

"I'll prepare the affidavit," Schwartz said.

Lines nodded and said, "I'll call the family."

Thera's chest tightened when Lines told her what needed to be done. *When,* she wondered, *will this finally be over? When will Trish finally be at rest?*

"It's important to our investigation, Thera," he said in the same empathic voice that had endeared him to her months before. "We wouldn't do it if it wasn't. If she was drugged before she was killed, that could make our case."

There was a short pause, then Thera said, "Kay, you do whatever you have to do." The resolution in her voice was as hard as quartz, but Lines felt the pain it concealed.

"I want you to know something," he said. "I'll make sure that everything is done to the satisfaction of church doctrine. She'll be put back just as she was. Everything will be the same."

Debbie Schwartz quickly typed a two page affidavit to accompany the motion for the exhumation and autopsy. It briefly recounted the known circumstances of Trish's murder and noted that:

"The autopsy performed in Mexico did not include a toxico-logical examination for drugs, a possible explanation for why

there was no evidence of a struggle or defensive wounds. Additional evidence gathered in a conspiracy to commit investigation includes information that Dan Willoughby, the victim's husband and a suspected conspirator, possessed and used barbiturates, depressants and opioids.''

She turned the document over to the lawyers, and the motion, bearing the signature of Attorney General Grant Woods, was filed in Superior Court on May 24. Permission was granted the same day. At the attorney general's request, the motion and the judge's order were sealed to help protect the investigation. No one wanted to spook Willoughby into fleeing the country. The order was delivered to the Bunker Family Mortuaries and arrangements were quickly made for the grave to be opened on June 3.

Schwartz and Lines began their day earlier than usual, rising before sunrise and driving through the cool morning air toward the outskirts of Mesa. Once the sun had cleared the horizon, the day would be as torrid as a potter's kiln. Best to get this over with early.

A few minutes before seven o'clock, they rendezvoused at section K, lot 46, space 12, of Mountain View Memorial Gardens. Randy Bunker, who had received the court order a few days earlier, was also there, as were the workers, with their backhoe and shovels.

Lines took photographs prior to the work beginning, and Schwartz kept detailed notes of every step of the procedure. The backhoe took its first bite of the earth at seven fifteen, she noted, and at four minutes past eight the lid to the concrete vault was hoisted out of the ground, followed by the casket.

Lines continued to photograph each movement. At eight fourteen, the casket was loaded into the van for the eleven-minute drive back to town. In an unusual step, the body was not taken directly to the medical examiner's office in downtown

Phoenix, but, at Lines's request, went instead to the Bunker Family Mortuaries in Mesa. The detective was intent upon keeping his word to the victim's mother. He would not entrust to the doctors downtown the responsibility for returning Trish Willoughby inviolable to the grave.

While Randy Bunker carefully removed Trish's wig and clothing, Schwartz telephoned the office of Dr. Heinz Karnitschnig, Chief Medical Examiner for Maricopa County, and informed him that the body would arrive in forty-five minutes.

At the ME's office, they were met by Roberta Stegan, an identification technologist, who would fingerprint the corpse to ensure that no error in identification had been made. It was nine thirty and the detectives were eager to get started. Soon, Dr. Karnitschnig came to the small foyer. His manner was terse and formal as he informed them that the autopsy could not begin until eleven o'clock. He was especially cool toward Lines.

After he had gone, Lines smiled at Schwartz and said, "I may not be able to go in there with you."

She, too, smiled and shook her head. Her partner was a good detective, but political tact was not always his strong suit.

Karnitschnig had been a medical examiner about as long as Lines had been a lawman and their paths had crossed many times, and not always pleasantly.

Though he had the easy, forbearing exterior of a horse whisperer, Lines was plodding and driven when it came to assembling evidence in a criminal case. He was disdainful of incompetence and impatient with imprecision. Over the years, he had formed the opinion that the Maricopa County medical examiner's office was downright shoddy. Perhaps the office was understaffed and overworked, but his perceived shortcoming of the agency gnawed at him nonetheless.

Detectives sometimes had difficulty wringing from the medical examiners a definitive cause of death. He felt the agency was especially lax about postmortem examinations of suspected suicide victims. Lines believed that too often murders were going uninvestigated because of that policy.

In one case, a teenager was found beside a road in Chandler with a bullet wound to the head and a .22-caliber pistol at his side. Two young officers, neither with experience in homicide cases, looked at the head wound, then at the gun, and ruled it a suicide. The young man was buried and the case was forgotten.

Two weeks later, the victim's friends walked into the Chandler police station and volunteered the real account of their friend's death. Two carloads of teenagers, they said, were engaged in a running gun battle that night and the dead youth, a passenger in their car, was shot in the head. Panicked, the driver stopped and pushed his slain passenger out of the car and sped away.

An autopsy soon after the shooting, Lines was convinced, would certainly have revealed that the death wound was not self-inflicted, and the murder investigation could have begun two weeks earlier.

Over the years, Lines developed a catalog of grievances against the ME, and he decided that before leaving the sheriff's staff he would use the only resource at his disposal to address them. He wrote a memo, the bureaucratic weapon of choice, itemizing twenty-three specific acts (including an incident in which a member of the ME's staff stole an autopsy photograph of a nude seven-year-old girl and gave it to a friend, a known child molester) which suggested a need for serious reform of the office.

As often happens with the internal communications of a public agency, that one found its way into the hands of a newspaper reporter—and into large headlines. In the uproar that followed, the county attorney expressed his outrage and urged the Maricopa County Board of Supervisors to fire Karnitschnig. The *ME* did not lose his job, but it was natural that the incident left him with an uncharitable disposition toward the deputy who had disparaged him and the work of his office.

So the detective and the doctor met now on the doctor's turf, and the encounter was mannerly, but hardly genial. Shortly after eleven, Karnitschnig came to escort the waiting parties into the autopsy room. Stegan and Schwartz went first and as Lines walked toward the door, the doctor turned to him and said, "I don't remember inviting you in here, Mr. Lines."

Medical examiners can be an imperious lot and they are masters of their domains, so Lines judiciously acquiesced. He especially did not want to antagonize the doctor at this time, not with so much possibly riding on the quality of this examination. He wanted a clean and reliable autopsy—a flawless one—that could not be discredited before a jury. In the beginning, Lines had not even wanted to take this case, but now it consumed him. He wanted Willoughby, and Karnitschnig could deliver him.

Maybe.

While Schwartz continued to fill her notebook, Stegan photographed the body prior to autopsy, giving several frames of film to close-ups of the hands and forearms. Then Karnitschnig began his examination, also inspecting the hands and arms first and declaring "nothing noteworthy."

As the camera followed his movements, the doctor described each procedure and finding. He noted the injuries to the body—paddle marks left on the chest by medical rescue attempts, the incision from the Mexican autopsy, the embalming incisions. With a small knifelike instrument, he scraped the wax off the scalp to reveal the head wounds, and measured each one.

He then peeled back the skin from the front of the skull and described a massive fracture, probably the cause of death, resulting from "heavy blow or blows with a blunt instrument such as a crowbar or tire iron."

There followed a gruesome recitation of the wreckage to this frail human.

"Over the left frontal region, an obliquely oriented wound measuring one and one-quarter inch in length . . . over the left parietal region, an obliquely oriented wound measuring three-quarters of an inch . . . over the mid-frontal region, a transversely oriented wound measuring one inch . . . over the right frontoparietal region, an obliquely oriented wound measuring one inch in length . . . over the right parietal region, a transversely oriented wound measuring one inch . . . over the right parietal region, one-quarter of an inch posterior to number five, a transversely oriented wound measuring one inch . . . over the right posterior parietal region, a transversely oriented wound measuring one and one-half inches . . . over the right temporoparietal region, an obliquely oriented wound, measuring one and one-quarter inches . . . over the right temporal region, an obliquely oriented wound measuring one-quarter of an inch . . .''

Schwartz wrote quickly as he spoke and his words were staggering. Nine separate wounds—nine distinct blows, any one of which might have killed Trish Willoughby. Somebody didn't just want her dead, somebody took great pleasure in killing her.

Nothing like a crowbar or tire iron had been found at the murder scene, she remembered, and Willoughby, by all accounts, was not carrying either when he came out of the house and met Marsha at the door. The wounds described by the medical examiner might even indicate a different instrument. They were short and deep, like indentions that might have been caused by a large ball peen hammer. But no hammer had been found at the scene either.

''The floor of the right anterior fossa is shattered into multiple fragments and sharp bone fragments are present in the right orbit,'' the doctor continued. ''The floor of the right middle fossa shows an oblique linear fracture.''

It was becoming obvious that, contrary to the Mexican autopsy, the knife driven into the victim's brain was not what killed her. It was little more than an afterthought, perhaps the act of a psychopath who whistled while he worked.

Next Karnitschnig removed the brain, and blood samples were taken from the skull—a location where the embalming would not have tainted the blood as much as it would have in the body organs. He worked quickly, removing the organs, removing samples and cross sections of each. Stegan then took prints from the fingers of the left hand, and the body was released back to the mortuary.

All day, Thera Huish had been on edge, pacing the floor, busying herself with household chores but unable to concentrate on any of them. She and Sterling had hardly spoken, and silence filled their home like stale gas until the phone rang a little after three o'clock.

"Trish is back in the ground," Lines said.

Thera thanked him, hung up the phone and slumped onto the sofa, every muscle suddenly as flaccid as worn leather. Sleep would come a little easier tonight.

Not so for the detectives. They would have to wait out the results of the toxicology tests.

Chapter Forty-three

So outrageous were they, Superior Court Judge Alfred Rogers's words were difficult for Thera to absorb.

"Mrs. Huish is not to receive any draws, salary, bonus or dividends of the business entities," he decreed.

That was it. The assets of T&T Distributors were frozen. Just by filing the lawsuit, Dan had virtually shut down her business, without which she and Sterling had no income, except for his military retirement pay, and that was insufficient, by far, to cover their expenses.

Willoughby's lawyers had urged Rogers to place T&T Distributors into receivership, but the judge deemed the court order sufficient, for now, to protect the interests of Willoughby and his children. Without the court's approval, Thera could touch nothing—a fact she did not fully comprehend in the beginning.

"Nick, what am I going to do?" she asked her son. "I've got twenty thousand dollars in bills to pay to keep this business running."

"Write a check," he said. "What are they going to do if you're paying the bills?"

It seemed reasonable. Going over the debts with her assistant, Janie Clepp, they selected the most pressing and wrote checks totaling six thousand dollars.

The next day, she received a call from Greg Miles, the attorney she had hired to handle the lawsuit.

"We've got a meeting with Judge Rogers," he told her. He did not sound happy.

Nick drove her to the courthouse, but he was not permitted to accompany her into the judge's chambers. Both were still in the dark about the purpose of this meeting.

"Mrs. Huish," the judge said, snuffing a cigarette into an ashtray and immediately lighting another, "you have violated a court order."

"What court order?" Thera asked. "What have I done."

"You took money from your account."

"I had to pay my bills. They were going to cut off my phone, my credit cards, everything."

"You spent six thousand dollars . . . money that was not yours."

"I only paid bills."

"Mrs. Huish, listen to me," the judge said. "You be in my courtroom tomorrow with a cashier's check for six thousand dollars or bring your toothbrush, because I'm going to throw your ass in jail."

Willoughby and his lawyer, Doug Tobler, exchanged smug smiles.

Trembling, Thera left the room with her lawyer. When he heard what had happened, Nick blew up. "This settles it," he said. "I'm calling Val and we're going to do this thing right. You're not going through this again."

Her own anger abated quicker than her son's, but even upon calmer reflection, something about this episode disturbed her nearly as much as the judge's threat.

How did Willoughby or his lawyer or the judge know so

quickly—within twelve or fifteen hours—that she had written six thousand dollars worth of checks?

She found out a few days later.

Kay Lines and Debbie Schwartz stopped by her office to share some of what they had learned from the items taken in the search of Willoughby's house.

"You've got a problem with your civil suit," Lines said.

"What's that?"

"Somebody is feeding him information from the inside."

"Who?"

"Your secretary."

Thera's heart sank. Not Janie Clepp. Janie had worked for her for two years and had become like a family member. Her sons loved Janie almost like a sister. Janie would house-sit when Thera and Sterling were out of town. And she sat in on family meetings when Tricia's murder or Dan's lawsuit was discussed.

"What makes you think that?" she asked.

"For some reason, Dan was taping most of his telephone conversations lately," Lines said. "She is on a lot of those tapes."

"I knew she went to his house pretty regularly," said Thera, still incredulous. "She said she was looking in on the children. She was always so good with Trish's kids. I appreciated her interest in them."

"We thought you should know that her interest in Dan may go beyond his children," Lines said.

"Thanks. I will handle that problem." She was curious about the investigation and switched to that subject. "Any word on Yesenia?"

"Nothing," Lines said. "But we're looking. She'll surface somewhere, sooner or later."

"What about the autopsy?"

"Well, it confirmed that the beating rather than the stabbing was the probable cause of death. She was hit nine times pretty hard with something pretty heavy. We don't know what.''

"Could they determine if Trish had been drugged?"

The disappointment was apparent in his face. "The toxicology reports said there was no presence of drugs."

"So Dan's off the hook again, I guess."

"For a while. That's all the more reason we've got to find Yesenia Patino. I know this lawsuit is unpleasant, but it wouldn't hurt to drag it out as long as you can. It'll give us more time to find her."

The next day, she fired Janie Clepp.

Nick and Val talked it over and decided that the family needed a more coherent strategy. Walls seemed to be going up everywhere, and so far they weren't being very successful at scaling them.

They had utter faith in Kay Lines and Debbie Schwartz, but the investigators were limited in their ability to scour Mexico, where Yesenia apparently was residing. They were limited by the enthusiasm, or lack of it, the Mexican authorities had for the chase, and they were limited by manpower and resources and by the dearth of Yesenia sightings. An organization called Silent Witness, which rewards and protects the identities of citizens who provide information about crime, had offered a one thousand dollar reward for information leading to her arrest, and the Huishes upped it to six thousand with their own money, but no one came forward.

The lawsuit also was not going well. The judge's position, logically, was that the family had only alleged, not proved, that Dan was a party to Trish's death, and until he was charged and convicted he had full standing as an innocent citizen and was entitled to all the legal protections that implies. They seemed to lose on every front, and the endless hearings and depositions sapped Thera's energy and her spirit. She was heavily reliant on her sons now. At first, Nick had accompanied her to each legal proceeding, but Dan's lawyers soon had him barred from attendance because of his confrontational attitude. With her money tied up by the court, Val was paying the monstrous legal bills—$20,000 to $30,000 a month. Bob watched glumly as the cost, emotional and financial, of fighting Dan Willoughby became crippling. Inevitably, disagreements began to develop within the family.

"Just give him the money, Mom," Bob told his mother. "It's not worth what it's doing to you."

Val countered, "Don't you even think about giving him a cent."

An objective analysis of their situation, therefore, led to a dismal conclusion: Not only might their brother-in-law get away with murder, but he could pocket a million dollars for his crime.

The two brothers agreed that Nick would focus on the investigation, generate any leads that he could, do whatever was possible to aid in the search for Yesenia Patino. Val would watch over the lawsuit and obtain his mother's power of attorney so he could attend conferences and depositions and occasionally act in her behalf. Their mother could relax a bit.

He went to the village where she was born and plodded through muddy streets in a hard rain and turned up nothing. In the border towns of Juarez and Agua Prieta and Nogales, he prowled the bordello districts and distributed flyers bearing her picture. Nothing. In Caborca and Hermosillo and Guaymas, he scouted the tourist haunts where American men sought the company of young Mexican women. Nothing.

Everywhere he went, he called on the local police chief and prosecutor. He left photographs of Yesenia and his business card. All seemed eager to assist in any way they could. Lines soon learned, however, that the ingrained corruption that held nearly all things hostage in Mexico mitigated the local officials' value to him.

The turnover was maddening. It seemed that as soon as he established a relationship with an attorney general, the scoundrel was indicted for drug trafficking. A police chief who was particularly cooperative was busted by the *federales* after drugs and a large amount of cash—American dollars—were found in his office. Others, those who were honest and hardworking, were simply lost to the times, saddled with rickety equipment—or none at all—and antiquated methods. In one small town, he paid a courtesy call on the police chief before beginning his search for Yesenia. The chief was not in, but his secretary directed Lines to the street where he could be found. When Lines arrived, the chief and several of his officers were in a raging gun battle with a felon.

The governor's plane was always available to him, as was an interpreter or anyone else he needed for his trips to Mexico, but as summer came and went, a sense of sheer futility settled upon him. *She could disappear too easily in Mexico. Maybe she isn't even here. She could be in California or Oregon or Europe, anywhere. She could have changed her appearance a little and gone back to living as a man. No, Yesenia would survive better as a woman. Men liked her and gladly shared their coins with her.* Lines believed that sooner or later she would be found turning tricks in some coastal resort, but which resort and on which coast? Including the Baja, Mexico probably had five thousand miles of shoreline, or close to it, he guessed. He couldn't travel it all.

No longer involved in the civil suit, Nick immersed himself in the criminal side of the family's quest. Not the investigation—he had exhausted the tips and leads he could supply the detectives—but the cause of keeping the case public and alive and the search for Yesenia Patino.

He leaked a few tidbits to the press—the item about Dan Willoughby paying more than two thousand dollars to a dating service within a few weeks of Trish's death eroded his brother-in-law's standing in the neighborhood and the Houston Ward church—and he persuaded his family to cooperate with a reporter for *New Times,* an alternative weekly in Phoenix, a paper with a reputation for delving deeply into a story and pulling few punches.

He made up a flyer, written in Spanish and bearing a photograph of Yesenia, pleading for information. A sympathetic printer reproduced thousands of copies at cost and Nick persuaded banks and supermarkets and other businesses throughout the valley to display them in their windows and lobbies. When that failed, the printer made blowups of the flyer, which Nick arranged to have mounted on the sides and rears of city buses.

To have not seen the photograph, anyone in the Valley of the Sun would have to have been comatose. It was as ubiquitous as sand, but it generated no leads.

Once again, the investigation was lodged on high center, and the civil case was going no better. It appeared that the judge would soon place the business in receivership and appoint a guardian to represent the interest of the Willoughby children. Without Yesenia and the testimony she could provide, Dan could walk free and rich.

"Mom, we're going on national television," Nick said late in November.

Thera was dubious. Eight months had passed since Trish's murder and neither ABC nor CBS nor NBC nor CNN had come calling. Why would anyone care now about an old story?

"What are you talking about?" she asked.

"I've contacted *Hard Copy, Inside Edition* and *America's Most Wanted.* We'll deal with the one who calls first."

From her expression, Nick could tell she had reservations.

"I know, you think it's tabloid journalism and all that, but let me tell you something. Everybody sneers at the tabloids, but millions of people read them. Same with the tabloid TV shows. They have huge audiences. This may be the best shot we've got."

She studied her son's face. Resolving Trish's murder had

been an all-consuming passion for him, and he had never been willing to acknowledge that the cause could be lost. Even when he was weary, the fire had burned in his belly and he had done all she could have asked of him.

"Okay," she said. "We'll do it."

Chapter Forty-four

Parked outside a Revco Drug Store in a Gilbert strip mall, Sgt. Joe Ruet watched as Dan Willoughby came through the door and walked toward his car.

Reaching for his keys, Willoughby suddenly spotted the detective, stared at him for a moment and then gave him the finger.

Ruet smiled and waved. He was getting used to Willoughby's belligerence.

Despite being part of a large and sprawling metropolitan matrix, Gilbert is a small town, small in the way the residents live and interact with each other. Ruet's children attended school with the Willoughby children, and so the hunter and the hunted were necessarily drawn from time to time into the same settings. They had an icy encounter at a high school football game, and sometimes their paths crossed at the grocery store. Each successive time, Willoughby was more confident, more defiant, more contentious. Why not? He was still on the streets and was about to come into an awful lot of money. The cops apparently were costing him little sleep these days.

Ruet's gut ached to put the cuffs on him, but his heart ached as much for the Willoughby children. His own daughter came home a few times and described how Marsha had become distraught at school and had to be taken home. He could only wonder how the younger children were coping. As well as their father, he hoped.

Ruet watched him drive away. *Enjoy yourself while you can,* he thought. *It ain't over yet.*

Even to the judge, it was a baffling display of arrogance, if not outright stupidity. Willoughby, whose lawyers had prosecuted his lawsuit with singular aggression and tenacity, was now grasping for some legal thread that would exclude his participation in the process.

Thera's lawyers were entitled to take a pretrial deposition from him, just as his lawyers had deposed her. They were entitled to ask questions he did not like—questions that concerned actions he may have taken to provoke and profit from his wife's death—and he was obliged to answer them. If he were innocent of murder, no harm would come of answering. If he were guilty, he could simply lie. Perjury in a civil case was small stuff compared to a capital murder charge. By refusing to answer questions, he could only jeopardize the civil suit and intensify the criminal suspicion.

"Did you ever suggest to Trish and Thera that they need to increase or obtain additional life insurance?" Greg Miles asked.

"Upon advice of my attorney, I stand on my Fifth Amendment right not to answer," Willoughby said.

"You thought before Trish's death that there was a buy-sell agreement between Trish and Thera, didn't you?"

"Upon the advice of my attorney, I stand on my Fifth Amendment right not to answer."

"You frequently encouraged Trish and Thera to get a buy-sell agreement prior to her death, didn't you?"

"Upon the advice of my attorney, I stand on my Fifth Amendment right not to answer."

"Why did you feel it was important that they have a buy-sell agreement in place prior to her death?"

"Upon the advice of my attorney, I stand on my Fifth Amendment right not to answer."

"As of February of 1991, did you believe there was a buy-sell agreement between Trish and Thera?"

"Upon the advice of my attorney, I stand on my Fifth Amendment right not to answer."

Miles moved to more personal areas, and it was clear where the questions were leading—straight to Dan Willoughby's motives, his state of mind in the months preceding Trish's death, his feelings toward his wife, his knowledge of her murder. Those issues were central to the Huish's counterclaim and wrongful death assertions. A civil jury could find Willoughby responsible for his wife's death and thereby deny his claim to her estate. That decision could be based on a *preponderance of evidence* standard, rather than the more rigid *beyond a reasonable doubt* standard applied in criminal cases. Willoughby was out of wiggle room and knew it. He had dealt himself a bad hand but would have to play it.

"How did it feel to go from being a district manager to being unemployed?"

"Upon the advice of my attorney, I stand on my Fifth Amendment right not to answer."

"Isn't it true that you looked for work after leaving A.E.I. but couldn't find any?"

"Upon the advice of my attorney, I stand on my Fifth Amendment right not to answer."

"Wasn't your wife disillusioned with you because of your spending habits and your affair with Yesenia Patino?"

"Upon the advice of my attorney, I stand on my Fifth Amendment right not to answer."

"Didn't your wife cut off your credit cards?"

"Upon the advice of my attorney, I stand on my Fifth Amendment right not to answer."

"Were you taking cocaine? Crack? Heroin?"

"Upon the advice of my attorney, I stand on my Fifth Amendment right not to answer."

Miles asked the judge to compel Willoughby to testify, and Rogers, his own patience expended, was ready to grant the motion. Witnesses have been allowed to invoke their constitutional right against self-incrimination in civil cases, but not under these circumstances, not when the witness instigated the litigation.

"Mr. Willoughby," the judge said, "you cannot continue to take the Fifth Amendment in a suit you yourself brought. You will either have to testify or drop the suit."

He gave Willoughby thirty days to comply or, "I will dismiss the suit."

Doug Tobler went immediately to the State Court of Criminal Appeals, but the higher court refused to hear the appeal. Willoughby would have to answer the questions.

It was a setback, perhaps the only setback he had suffered since his wife's death, but far more important to the Huish family and the attorney general's investigators was the setback in the time schedule of the civil proceedings. By balking at the lawyer's questions, Dan Willoughby had given them an extra thirty days to track down Yesenia Patino.

Another Christmas was approaching, but the season brought little joy to the Huish household. Judge Rogers had put T&T Distributors into receivership and appointed a guardian to represent the Willoughby children, and therefore the lawsuit was knotted with even more attorneys and hearings. Legal expenses were so overwhelming that Matol Botanical International had volunteered to advance Thera money against future commissions.

America's Most Wanted had not responded to Nick's plea. *Inside Edition* had called and, after discussing the story with him, opted out. Then on Friday, November 29, he received a call from a producer at *Hard Copy*. She listened for half an hour as he explained the murder, the lawsuit, Yesenia's disappearance, everything that he could pack into a brief conversation.

"We'd like to come to your house Monday and do the story," she said.

"Anything you want," Nick said.

Cameras and sound gear filled the living room of Thera and Sterling's home and for most of two days their story was soaked up by videotape.

When the show's producers contacted Willoughby to request an interview, he declined, but quickly arranged to hold a press conference the next morning at the office of his defense attorney, David Ochoa.

Citing the advice of his lawyer, he had consistently declined to give interviews about the murder and the investigation. Many reporters had tried, but his most expansive public remarks had been made to Deborah Laake, who had written about the case for *New Times*. "I am not involved in this murder in any way, shape or form," he told her. "This does not even involve the death of my wife anymore. This is all greed. I want to get the vengeful, evil mother-in-law who is taking money away from my children. She makes $40,000 a month and she does not give a penny to the children she says she loves so much. I want so badly to tell the true story, to tell how it really is."

Now he was going to talk, and in his lawyer's office. *Hard Copy* would air its segment on Tuesday night, December 3, and he would beat them to the punch, making the noon and evening news and taking the edge off their report.

Expecting an opportunity to quiz Dan Willoughby at last, local reporters packed into Ochoa's office on Tuesday morning.

Nick and Sterling went too.

"You can't come in," Ochoa's secretary told them.

"Why not?" Nick asked, goading her. "I thought this was a press conference, a public event."

"It is a press conference . . . for the press," she insisted. "You'll have to leave."

Fine, Nick thought, *but we won't go far.*

With the cameras humming and the microphones on, Willoughby met the press. He tried to appear sorrowful and wounded, but there was a steely tint to his voice as he began to read from a two-page prepared statement that railed against the "cloud of suspicion" the attorney general's office had placed over him.

"They have, if not said, at least implied that I am a suspect," he said. "It will be a relief to me when the final chapter is written on what can be described as a living nightmare. With respect to what has been written about my wife's murder, it would be inappropriate for me to comment in detail. It came as a shock to myself and my children to discover that my wife had been brutally beaten."

Yes, he knew Yesenia Patino, in fact his entire family knew her, but "none of us knew, however, that in years past she had undergone a sex change." He made a personal plea for Yesenia to contact the authorities and clear his name. "At this time, I have no idea of Miss Patino's whereabouts," he said. "I am confident that when she is located, that whatever she has to say will exonerate me of any wrongdoing regarding the death of my wife."

The prepared statement concluded, he refused to answer questions and left his lawyer's office, leaving the press knowing nothing more than it had known before.

Nick and Sterling were waiting outside where the reporters could easily find them. With a cluster of lenses aimed at him, Nick showed uncharacteristic restraint. He did not directly accuse his brother-in-law of murder, just hinted strongly at it.

"Why has it taken him ten months to come forward and say something?" he asked. "He's claimed he's innocent but he has chastised anyone with anything to say about this case."

Asked if he thought his brother-in-law murdered his sister, he replied, "I don't know who murdered her or why."

He didn't need to say more. *Hard Copy,* he hoped, would

say it for him. Flush with adrenaline, he and his father left
Phoenix and made their way through light traffic back to Mesa.
It had been a stimulating day and it promised to be an interesting
night of television.

Chapter Forty-five

Watching *Hard Copy* the previous evening, Kay Lines had felt no great rush of optimism that the national publicity would have much impact on his investigation. Images of the tormented parents and the enraged younger brother were powerful, and the scene of Dan Willoughby walking back into his house after refusing to speak to the show's producers was revealing. But the photographs of Yesenia were dated by a year or more. Wherever she was, surely she did not look the same now. The appeal for viewers to contact Silent Witness was a gesture of greater faith than Lines could find in his own skeptical soul. For weeks, her photographs had been splashed across the valley and had produced not a single lead. He had made more than twenty trips to Mexico, leaving reams of her likeness behind, and had heard from no one. Why should the outcome be any different this time?

A few hours after the program aired, he received a call from Steve Mitchell, the assistant AG assigned to prosecute the case. Hanging up the phone, Lines told his wife, "Looks like I'm going back to Mexico."

Silent Witness had received two tips, one from the East Coast and one from the West Coast, identical in substance. *That woman you're looking for . . . she's in Mazatlan, working at a joint called Joe's Oyster Bar. It's right on the beach.*

The next morning, Lines and Schwartz met with Mitchell and a few other AG staffers to determine what to do with the information. Lines and Mitchell, it was decided, would go to Mazatlan. Martin Marquez, the DPS liaison with Mexico, would accompany them as an interpreter. Schwartz would keep Willoughby under surveillance—close surveillance. If he got wind that they were onto Yesenia, he might run, so no one outside the AG's office, not even the Huishes, would be told what was going on. Might he not run anyway if he spotted detectives on his tail around the clock? Probably not, they figured. After ten months, he must be accustomed to being followed, and in recent weeks, his deportment had suggested supreme confidence that the cops would never bungle their way onto Yesenia. Besides, he was too close to getting the money to bolt now.

"Stay close anyway," Schwartz was told.

Mazatlan was no slumberous coastal village. Nearly six hundred miles down the coast from Rocky Point, where the Rio Presidio deposits its waters into the Pacific, it was a busy tourist port with a permanent population of 150,000, and tens of thousands more who washed in and out like the tides, coming and going by airplane and cruise ship, filling the streets and hotels and shops and beachside bars.

Lines suspected his task would not be as simple as walking into Joe's Oyster Bar, flashing a badge and walking out with Yesenia. His hunch was correct.

When they arrived, they hooked up with two local cops assigned to help them with the search and, if it were successful, the arrest. A murder warrant was out for her in Mexico, but Lines had no authority to arrest her there.

Mitchell drove the rented Volkswagen bus, Lines rode in the

front passenger seat and Marquez sat in back with the two Mexican cops. They made a stop at Joe's. It was too early in the day for Yesenia to be there. The real money was to be made at night.

Proceeding to their hotel, Lines looked to his right, and a dark-haired woman on the crowded sidewalk caught his attention.

"Make a U-turn," he said.

Mitchell turned the bus around and brought it to a stop. Lines got out and walked toward the woman, whose back was to him. She was walking slowly, window-shopping as she went, and he only wanted to get a look at her face.

Before he could reach her, the two Mexican cops shot by him, grabbed the woman by the arms and shouted, "Policia, policia."

To that mantra, the woman replied, "American citizen, American citizen."

Her husband, who had been standing nearby, showed the cops her passport, and Lines informed them that she was not the target of their search.

"Well, they're certainly eager," he said to Mitchell, as the two cops climbed back into the van.

For two days after the *Hard Copy* broadcast, the Huishes had heard nothing. Nick had called Silent Witness, but the organization, because of its confidentiality rules and upon the advice of the attorney general's office, would reveal nothing.

Kay Lines had not called all week, which Thera thought was unusual. He was concerned about her family and often called to offer encouragement or just to inquire about their well-being. If the *Hard Copy* episode had been a bust, she would have heard from him, if for no reason other than to console her.

She phoned his office and got no answer, so she phoned again and asked for Debbie Schwartz.

"Debbie, where's Kay?" she asked.

"He's out of town."

"Where?"

"Well . . . he's gone," Schwartz stammered. She disliked withholding information from the family, but it was necessary, and not just to prevent leaks that might find their way to Willoughby. There was no certainty that Patino would be found in Mazatlan, and she did not want to inflate the family hopes, only to have the bubble burst in disappointment.

"They've got a lead on Yesenia, haven't they?" Thera said.

"Oh, we've had lots of leads," Schwartz said. "We're following up on all of them."

"Debbie, my family and I are fasting until we find out something. I know you have to be careful what you say, but please let us know something when you can."

"Just stop worrying. If anything breaks, you'll be the first to know."

Their first day in Mazatlan had produced nothing. They had hung around Joe's until late in the evening, but Yesenia was a no-show. The next day, they continued to roam the streets in the hopes of chancing upon her. Fat chance. She probably spent most of the day sleeping.

On Friday night, December 6, they went back to Joe's about nine o'clock. The two Mexican officers stood outside the bar and the three Americans went inside, found a table and waited. They had not asked many questions about Yesenia, lest she learn of their presence and skip out on them again. Tonight, though, Lines was impatient. He asked a waitress if Yesenia Patino was working.

"She'll probably be in later," she said. At least he knew she was still around and that was enough to counter the fatigue he was starting to feel.

After two hours of waiting, though, he was bored. If you're not a drinker and you're too long in the tooth to be tempted by the young women who populate such a place, Joe's Oyster

Bar hasn't much to offer. At eleven o'clock he was almost ready to call it a night. He wandered outside, where the two Mexican cops were smoking cigarettes. They appeared as bored as he.

Back inside, he returned to the table. Mitchell and Marquez had gone to the bar for more beer, so he sat alone for a moment, studying the faces in the room.

Suddenly, as though she had ridden in on an ocean breeze, a young woman in a white blouse appeared at the bar. Her hair was shorter than when he last saw her, but Lines instantly recognized Yesenia Patino.

He stood up slowly and made his way to the other end of the bar, where Mitchell was waiting for his beer.

"She's here," he whispered, before stepping outside where the two cops were stationed.

He led one of them to the door, pointed out the woman and watched as they approached Yesenia. One spoke to her briefly and then led her outside, handcuffed her and put her in the backseat of the bus.

Lines got in the front seat and turned to face her. She showed no recognition. She was smiling, as though this were some kind of joke.

"Do you know Dan Willoughby?" he asked.

She leaned back and the sparkle went out of her eyes. Things were beginning to click. She wasn't smiling anymore.

At the police station, Lines questioned her for more than an hour, but she stuck with the story she had first given him at the Hilton Hotel in Phoenix the night before she disappeared. Her only relationship to Dan Willoughby was teaching him Spanish. She knew nothing about the murder of his wife.

"I think Dan Willoughby killed his wife," Lines said, "and he's trying to implicate you ... put it all on you. I don't think you were responsible, but that's what he's doing."

Yesenia didn't budge.

"You know you're going to be charged with murder in Sonora," he said. "You'll be taken to Hermosillo tomorrow.

You could go to prison for a long time while Dan goes free. If you helped me, maybe I could help you."

"Well, I think Danny had something to do with it," she said, loosening up just a little. "He was going to hire someone to do it."

She turned out to be an easy squeeze.

"That's what I think, too," Lines said. He would let her think about it. A night in jail should loosen her up a little more.

Debbie Schwartz had done as she was told. With officers from the Gilbert Police Department aiding her, she had attached herself to Dan Willoughby and stayed close enough to hit him with a nerf ball. That week, she, Joe Ruet and Patrick McNabb became his entourage, his personal motorcade. They tucked him into bed at night and escorted him to work in the mornings and saw him home in the evenings.

He was not, of course, oblivious to the tail he had acquired.

"This is crazy," John Sellers told her on the phone on Saturday morning. "Somebody is going to get killed."

Sellers was a retired Phoenix detective. Now a private investigator, he had been hired by David Ochoa to help build a defense in the event Dan Willoughby was charged with murder. Ochoa had asked him to see if he could get the AG off Willoughby's coattails

"We're just doing our job," Schwartz said.

"Why don't we have a meeting, see if we can work something out."

No harm in that, Schwartz thought. Willoughby wasn't going to leave her sight anyway, why not sit face to face with him? Knowing that Yesenia was in custody, she assumed it would only be a short time before her partner had the statement he needed to authorize Willoughby's arrest, and this would all be over. She agreed to meet Willoughby and Sellers on Monday morning at the Roadway Inn on Van Buren Avenue, the main drag between Phoenix and Tempe.

Kay Lines was bone-tired, but the exhilaration of finally having Yesenia Patino in custody made sleep difficult. He played over and over in his mind the scenario he would follow the next day. Yesenia was not a hard cookie, not hard enough to do hard time in a Mexican prison—or an Arizona prison, for that matter—if she could deal her way out of it.

Though he had slept only a few hours, he awoke on Saturday morning alert and eager. He, Mitchell and Marquez, along with a Mexican officer, would escort Yesenia to Hermosillo, where she would be officially charged with murdering Trish Willoughby, and he would have a chance to interrogate her further. He was certain that he would know before sundown what happened that night in the beach house in Rocky Point.

Arriving at the Mazatlan police headquarters, he discovered that it would be easier than he thought. After they had checked Yesenia out of jail and were leading her to the VW, she said to him, "Mr. Lines, I think I want to be on your team."

The waiting was wearing on everyone's nerves. On Sunday morning, Thera called Schwartz to try once more to find out what was happening.

"Go eat," Schwartz told her.

"Not 'til you tell me something," Thera pleaded.

"I'm telling you to go eat."

She called Nick and recounted the conversation.

"Well, let's go to lunch," he said.

Cara had heard only his end of the conversation, but she anticipated good news.

"I think it's over," Nick said. "I think something has happened . . . they got her."

* * *

Schwartz and her surveillance team followed Willoughby from his house to the Roadway Inn. She was mildly apprehensive as she parked her car and entered the restaurant just behind her suspect. Once seated, though, she relaxed. Through the window, she could see the police officers circling the parking lot.

Willoughby's proposal sounded reasonable. Whenever he left his house or his workplace, he would tell her where he was going and she could follow, but the others would back off. Only one surveillance car would park at the trucking company where he worked.

"You'll know where I am every minute," Willoughby promised, his teeth flashing through a cocksure grin.

"Okay," she said. "It's a deal."

They finished their coffee and Willoughby picked up the check. Schwartz followed him outside and fell in behind him as he pulled onto the street. On the radio, she told the other cars to back off.

She was still on the radio when Willoughby turned onto an Interstate 143 entrance ramp near University Drive, hit his brakes and screeched to a stop. Schwartz could not brake fast enough and rear-ended his Jag just hard enough to break a taillight.

After inspecting the damage, Willoughby smiled at her and said, "Look, I can forget about this."

Schwartz was flustered, but not so distracted that she did not detect the leer in his voice. *Does this guy ever quit playing the game?*

"No, whenever a state car is involved in an accident, a report has to be filed. Let's go to your office and fill out the accident form."

On the way to the trucking company, she regained her composure and could think of only one thing: *Why am I doing this? I'm probably going to be arresting him in a few minutes.*

Chapter Forty-six

Two months before the murder, Dan Willoughby described exactly how they would do it.

"I don't want to be involved," she protested.

"You are involved," he said. "You are as involved in this as I am."

"I don't want to be the one to kill her," she said.

"You don't have to. I want the satisfaction of killing her. You are going to make it look like a robbery."

He showed her the weapon he had made—a mace, the kind of device used in medieval combat to bush the heavy armor worn by knights. It was a metal ball, about the size of a shot put, perhaps eight or ten pounds, attached to an eighteen-inch length of nylon rope. It wasn't his first choice. He had planned to shoot her, equipping a pistol with a silencer he would acquire in Mexico. Silencers were illegal in Mexico and hard to acquire, so the mace would have to do.

Three weeks before the murder, they went to Rocky Point, checked into the Hotel Del Mar, made love on the cliffs overlooking the Sea of Cortez and cased the beach house in Las

Conchas. They stopped at the CEDO museum to check on its operating hours.

The museum would be the pretense to get his children out of the house. He would herd them into the van, go back inside, disable his wife with a blow to the abdomen, wrap her head in a towel to prevent blood spatters and be back in the van in a matter of minutes.

Yesenia would wait until they were gone, enter through the back door, which he would leave unlocked. She would remove Trish's rings, take the money from her purse and scatter the rest of the contents around the bedroom. It had to look like a robbery. He would have an alibi and no one would know that she had even been in Rocky Point.

They went back the week before the murder to walk through the plan one last time.

"Wear gloves," he told her, and gave her a length of nylon cord, just in case.

On the day of the murder, she and Tony arrived in Rocky Point and met Dan at Manny's Place on the beach. He hugged and kissed her and whispered, "Don't be nervous." They drank Corona beer and talked about nothing important in Tony's presence. When her brother went to the restroom, Dan leaned closer to her and said, "Remember, this has got to be done. Don't be nervous, it's for our own good."

She dropped Tony at the plaza across from the police station and drove his truck out to Las Conchas. She parked half a block away, facing the beach house, and saw Hayden and Thera playing outside. Dan and Marsha came outside and they all got in the van. Dan went back inside and Yesenia knew what he was doing. He was killing his wife. Several minutes later, she saw Marsha get out of the van and start back into the house, but Dan came out just as she reached the door. They got back into the van and drove away.

Yesenia knew they would be gone for at least two hours. She had told Dan to give her time to get out of Mexico before the murder was discovered. She pulled up to the rear of the house and went in through the door Dan had left unlocked.

Hearing strange noises coming from the bedroom, she called out Trish's name twice. At the bedroom door, she heard Trish gasping and choking, so she went into the kitchen, picked up three table knives and returned to the bedroom. She sat beside Trish on the bed and tried to stab her in the head, but the towel blunted the blow and she dropped the bent knife to the floor.

Lifting the towel up to the hairline, she tried again and this time the knife slid easily into Trish's brain. Still, the victim would not stop breathing, would not stop gasping and moaning. Yesenia took the nylon cord from her pocket and tried to silence Trish by pressing it against her neck, but Trish would not die.

Afraid to stay any longer, she removed the rings from Trish's fingers and took four hundred dollars from her purse. She scattered papers and personal items around the bedroom, and, before leaving, made one last trip to the kitchen, where she drained the last few swallows of Coke from a plastic two-liter bottle.

She drove back to the plaza, picked up Tony and left town. Along the way, she discarded the black beret Dan had told her to wear. It was then that she remembered she had forgotten to wear gloves.

Kay Lines turned off his tape recorder. He had spent Sunday afternoon and most of Monday morning taking Patino's statement, and it filled in all the gaps in his case against Willoughby. Her version of what happened inside the beach house was compatible with all the other evidence he had gathered, and at long last it gave him a murder weapon, one that Willoughby had made in Arizona. It might never be found—Dan told Yesenia he had dropped it in a dumpster—but the instrument she described fit perfectly the head wounds described in the autopsy.

Steve Mitchell called his boss, the attorney general, and filled him in.

"We'll pick him up," Grant Woods said.

* * *

Having broken their fast on Sunday, Sterling and Thera and Nick and Cara stayed by their phones all afternoon and evening, jumping at every incoming call. None was the one they wanted. They had notified Val and Bob, who were at their homes in California, of possible developments, and Thera wanted desperately to have something to report before bedtime. Nothing.

Just after ten o'clock Monday morning, Thera's phone rang. It was Grant Woods. "I would like to have you and your family at my office at one-thirty this afternoon," he said.

"Of course," Thera said, her heart pounding so loudly she was certain he could hear it. "Has something happened?"

"We can discuss that when you get here."

No one in the family felt like eating lunch. Thera and Sterling paced through the house like caged felines, checking the clock every few minutes. There was no stillness at Nick's house, either. He showered, dressed, called his brothers in California and drove to his parents' house to kill the rest of the time with them.

"This has got to be it," he said.

"That would be so wonderful," Thera said.

"He wouldn't ask us to come downtown just to tell us they had a tip that didn't check out . . . would he?"

Debbie Schwartz was instructed to sit on Willoughby as long as he was at his trucking company office and to pick him up when he left. No one could be certain how he would react. If he were armed and decided to resist, someone could get hurt. Best to nab him where there would be few bystanders.

Just after one o'clock, he came out of his office, got in the Jag and headed in the direction of Gilbert.

"Stay close," Schwartz told the surveillance team. "He's probably going to his house. We'll grab him there."

Joe Ruet, trailing her, accelerated and moved closer. He had waited a long time for this day. The motorcade entered the Superstition Freeway, crawled along at the speed limit, and exited on Gilbert Road. They snaked past the Houston Ward LDS Church and turned on to Encinas Avenue a couple of blocks from Willoughby's house.

Duke Boggs was sitting on a brick ledge in front of his house. Something was up and he wanted to watch it. A few minutes earlier he had seen Gilbert police officers arrive at the Willoughby house and conceal themselves in the foliage on both sides of the garage. He felt no pity for his old friend. His loyalty had stretched well beyond the necessary limits of Mormon brotherhood. Willoughby had used him, had stored drugs in his garage, had lied to him about his marriage, his affair, in fact, about his whole life. From the newspapers and neighborhood scuttlebutt, he now knew the depths of Dan Willoughby's deceit.

He watched the Jag purr to a stop in front of the garage. Debbie Schwartz stopped behind him and another police car passed and angled in front of the Jag. Three uniformed cops emerged from beside the garage.

Willoughby smiled and winked at Schwartz. She read him his Miranda rights while Ruet patted him down, placed him in handcuffs and escorted him to the squad car. Willoughby said nothing on the short drive to the jail, but he wasn't sweating either. *Cocky bastard,* Ruet thought.

At the police station, the handcuffs were removed and Willoughby was prepared to be mugged and printed.

"What do I charge him with?" Ruet asked Schwartz. He expected her to say *conspiracy to commit murder.*

"Book him for murder," she said.

Grant Woods greeted the Huishes with warm handshakes and invited them to sit down.

"I want to thank you for coming and I want to thank you

for all the help you have provided in this investigation,'' he began. ''You know, things don't always turn out like you expect . . .''

Nick closed his yes. *Here we go again. They almost had her but they missed her.*

''. . . but I just want to tell you . . .'' He paused—a blatant theatrical beat—and glanced at his watch. ''. . . that as of about twenty minutes ago, Dan Willoughby was arrested and charged with the murder of your daughter.''

For an instant, the family was immobilized by the news. Nick wanted to whoop and cry at the same time. He jumped to his feet, shook the attorney general's hand again and hugged his parents. Thera fought back tears. She felt a dizzying lightness; the stone finally had been rolled up the mountain and planted at the summit.

''Thank you so much, Mr. Woods,'' she sighed.

''Thank yourselves,'' he said. ''If it hadn't been for the efforts of your family, this case might not have been solved.''

On Tuesday morning, the Huishes drove back downtown, this time to the Maricopa County Courthouse. Reporters were swarming around when they took their seats in the courtroom of Superior Court Judge Ronald Reinstein.

Their son-in-law, handcuffed and clad in blue jail pajamas, was brought in through a side door, accompanied by his civil lawyer, Doug Tobler, because David Ochoa was out of town on other business. Dan stood before the bench, never once looking in their direction.

It was a swift ritual. The charges were read—murder and conspiracy to commit murder—and a bond of $2.5 million was set for the latter. For the murder charge, the judge denied bond. He would not be on the streets anytime soon. Thera and Sterling lifted clenched fists in a victory gesture.

In the corridor, reporters thrust microphones and tape

recorders at them, but did not receive comments of joy or victory.

"My heart dies for my little grandchildren," Thera told them. "They've lost their mother and probably will lose their father now."

Chapter Forty-seven

By no means was the state's case a slam dunk. With no physical evidence to connect Dan Willoughby to the murder, it was largely circumstantial and largely dependent on the testimony of two women.

Steve Mitchell could summon enough witnesses for a three-week trial. They could unmask the defendant, reveal the scheming, manipulative, philandering, immoral con man behind the righteous facade he maintained with painstaking care. They could provide motive and give insight into a mind capable of evil, and they could map the path to murder, but they could not prove murder.

Yesenia Patino's story was the core of the case. Only she had seen the murder weapon and only she, of those who would speak to the jury, was in the beach house that Saturday and participated in the crime. But there were problems with Yesenia. Of all the witnesses, her credibility was the most suspect, the easiest to demolish. Why would the jury believe her? Mitchell's own witnesses would deem her to be a habitual, chronic, pathological liar, and she herself would have to acknowledge a string of false statements to the investigators. Willoughby's lawyers might well lead the jury into reasonable doubt about anything she said. She would go into the Maricopa County courtroom a convicted murderer, serving forty years in Caborca, Sonora, for her part in the crime, her testimony given in exchange for the attorney general's help in shortening her sentence.

Marsha Willoughby's testimony was only slightly less imperative. Only she could place her father in the beach house alone with her mother for the time it would take to deliver nine blows with a homemade mace, and only she could tell the jury he locked the door behind him when he returned to get his passport. She had given several estimates of how long he was in the house and they were essentially consistent. Several minutes. Quite a while. Ten minutes. Fifteen minutes. Long enough to beat his wife to death.

At the time she gave those estimates, however, her father was not under indictment. She had no way of knowing that anything she said could send him to death row. Would she deviate from those statements at the trial? Her loyalty to her father was as unequivocal as her enmity for her grandmother.

Her father, as well as the prosecutors, was aware of the pivotal nature of her testimony. Mitchell was in possession of a sheaf of letters Willoughby had written to Marsha during the five months he was in jail awaiting trial. They were replete with disparaging references to Thera, reinforcements of the version of events that would best serve his defense, and promises of money and cars, perhaps even her own business.

In one missive, Willoughby wrote, "You know I wasn't in the house more than a minute or two and tucking in my shirt is something I always do ... I am optimistic that with your positive testimony about the love Mom and I had for each other and the fact that you know I had nothing to do with her death will help immensely at the trial."

In another, he wrote, "The two big issues that would involve you would be the amount of time I spent when I went back into the house. You have stated two minutes, which is as accurate as

I could best recall. Also, the door was left open when I went back into the house and was not closed or locked as they are trying to say. The only other issue would be the domestic relationship Mom and I enjoyed. I loved Mom with all my heart and remember her in my daily prayers.''

Continuing to target the points Willoughby wanted his daughter to remember, he wrote in another missive, ''I'm positive the door was open. However, when I was leaving the bathroom, the door could have closed momentarily.'' He reminded her that ''if the door closed it would automatically be locked.'' He was positive he locked the door when he left because he could remember turning the doorknob and it would not move. ''This part is so very important because the AG is trying to say I killed Mom before I left the house. Honey, you know I couldn't have been in the house more than two minutes! I'm not trying to confuse you, honey—HONEST.'' Willoughby then corrected her statement that he'd never found his passport, telling her it had been on the dresser with some paperwork. He'd stuck it in his back pocket and they'd left. ''You have to remember some of these critical time elements or they are going to try to execute me. . . . In fact, you may want to destroy this letter after you've read it thoroughly because the police can subpoena any letters I write. Keep it in your head.''

Mitchell would not know until she got on the stand just how much Marsha had been influenced by her father's tutoring.

From David Ochoa's vantage point, the state's case appeared less than a lock, but his own was far worse. After conducting a mock trial with ''jurors'' recruited by an expert he had retained, he realized there were issues that could not be overcome. It would be impossible to make his client a sympathetic figure to the jury. He could not rebut the sleaziness that would be trotted into the courtroom and he could not refute the critical circumstantial elements or the paper trail that attested to them. Tony Patino's testimony would be damning, and he could not cross-examine him too vigorously lest Tony reveal something the state did not know—that Willoughby had offered him $5,000 to lie about seeing him in Rocky Point on February 23. He could assail Yesenia's credibility, but without putting his client on the stand to contradict her, he could offer no alternative version to her story. He certainly was not going to put Willoughby on the witness stand.

His strategic options were limited.

Mitchell outlined the case in his opening statement to the jury on the afternoon of April 22, 1992, and it took less than thirty minutes to summarize the state's case. Then it was Ochoa's turn to rise and face the panel.

"Yes, the evidence will show that my client committed adultery. Yes, the evidence will show that my client engaged in conduct that you're going to classify as immoral and sleazy. And before all the evidence is in, you're probably going to say that my client rates a minus one or something like that. But you must bear in mind that . . . he is sitting here on a much more serious charge . . . murder.

"The state's case is entirely a circumstantial case. There will not be one piece of scientific evidence that connects my client to that homicide. What the evidence will show is that my client engaged in immoral behavior, that he committed adultery, that he humiliated his wife in the conduct that he engaged in and that he brought disrespect to himself."

After summarizing Willoughby's affair with Yesenia Patino, Willoughby's career wreckage and his wife's prosperous business, Ochoa introduced what would be the heart of his defense: A conspiracy by Willoughby and Patino, not to murder Trish but to blackmail her. By cutting off his credit cards, Trish had rendered her unemployed husband unable to support his mistress in the style to which she was accustomed, Ochoa said.

"He devised a plan that instead of him paying directly to Yesenia, he was going to get his wife to do it. He was going to use Yesenia, because Yesenia, when you see her, even though she is a man, or was a man, she is a very foxy little girl and she knows her way around men. I think that is why Trish was intimidated by her. She, Yesenia, was going to say, 'You either pay me some money or I'm going to take your husband away.' "

The confrontation would take place at the beach house in Rocky Point, while Dan and children were away, he said.

"But like all plans, something went wrong, and it's unfortunate. And only Yesenia knows what happened inside that house. I'm not even sure that when she went in that back door she had murder on her mind, but before she were to walk out of that back door, a murderer she would be."

That was it. Yesenia acted alone. The strongest point in favor of that hypothesis was the missing murder weapon. Willoughby did not have it when he came out of the house and met Marsha at the door, and it was not in the house when the police arrived that evening. Since Yesenia was in the house alone and left without being seen, she had ample opportunity to dispose of whatever she used to beat Trish to death.

It was a reach, but it was all he had, and he had no evidence to support it.

Thera watched her granddaughter walk confidently across the courtroom and take her seat at the witness stand. Marsha stared briefly at her father and then turned to face Steve Mitchell.

Her answers to the preliminary questions were brisk, and she showed no sign of being intimidated by her surroundings or the procedures. Only a few minutes into her testimony, she began to reveal a pattern of evasiveness that would infuriate the prosecutor.

"When was the last day you saw your mother alive?" Mitchell asked.

"The 28th of February, 1991 . . . the day she died," Marsha replied.

"If I told you it was February 23, would you argue with that?" Mitchell asked.

"Yes."

Judge Howe interrupted, suggesting that Marsha had misunderstood the question, so Mitchell rephrased it: "If I told you that it was actually February 23, would you agree with that statement?"

"No," Marsha answered.

"She did hear you," the judge said, surprised by her insistence.

Her willingness to argue about the date of her mother's murder was the first indication that Marsha would be trouble for the prosecution. Thera's heart sank. Dan Willoughby, she feared, had won this skirmish.

"Would you say that your parents' relationship was a bad one?" Mitchell asked.

"No," Marsha said.

"Would you say it was a good one?"

"Yes."

Mitchell would have a hard time with this young woman.

"Have you ever told someone that you thought your dad might divorce your mother . . . ?"

"Not that I recall."

". . . and soon marry another woman?"

"No, I don't recall that."

"Might you have?"

"I don't recall."

"Do you know who Heather Rogers is?"

"She's my neighbor."

"A friend of yours?"

"Yes."

"Just after your mother's death, did you not tell her that before the murder you expected that your father might divorce your mom and marry another woman?"

"I don't recall."

"So you might have?"

"I could have."

Did she recall telling another neighbor that after she had argued with her mother, her father said to her, "What shall we do with the witch? Do you think we should have her killed?"

"No, I don't."

"Do you deny having told her that?"

"I don't remember."

"So you might have?"

"I could have."

Although her recalcitrance was not entirely unforeseen, it did not bode well for the critical part of her testimony that was yet to come. Soon after the murder, she had told Kay Lines that her father arranged the trip to the museum, and although she did not want to go, he insisted that she come along. Now she told a different story.

"Did you tell your dad you didn't want to go?" Mitchell said.

"Yes, I did."

"What was his response?" Mitchell asked.

"He said I didn't have to go if I didn't want to," she said.

That statement alone could gouge a large hole in Mitchell's case. If Willoughby was going to commit murder in the house, he had to be certain that all of the children were elsewhere. If he had given Marsha the option of staying behind, it would be difficult for the jury to believe that Willoughby had carefully planned to murder his wife while his children waited in the van. And, if he went back into the house to kill his wife, the jury would have to believe that he was inside long enough to do it.

"How long did he remain in that house?" Mitchell asked. Her answer would be the closer, the last pitch of the ninth inning.

"Just a couple of minutes," Marsha said.

The prosecutor took a deep breath. Kay Lines turned his head slowly to see the jury's reaction. Sitting on a hard, wooden bench just a few feet away, Thera Huish slumped, lowered her head and glanced sideways at her husband. Sterling never looked away from his granddaughter.

"Did it seem like a long time?" Mitchell asked.

"No."

"Did it seem more like five or ten minutes?"

"No."

"Do you recall having previously told me at your deposition that he was in there about five minutes?"

"Yes."

"That's what you told me, isn't it?"

"As I recall."

Mitchell moved on, getting her to acknowledge that she eventually got out of the van and went back to the house.

"The door was closed, wasn't it?"

"Yes."

"Was the door locked?"

"Not that I recall."

"It could have been?"

"Yes."

"Do you believe that it was?"

"No."

"Why do you say that?"

"My dad was coming out and I was going in."

"But you never went in, did you?"

"No."

"Did you try the door?"

"Started to."

"Did it open when you tried it?"

"We both had hold of the handle at the same time."

Mitchell had never heard this story before. Neither had Kay Lines or the Huish family.

"He was on the inside and you were on the outside?" Mitchell asked.

"Yes."

"So it was just a pure coincidence that you both had your hands on the door at the same time?"

"Yes."

"What did you say to your father at the door?"

"I just told him I was getting a Granola bar."

"Did he tell you not to go in there?"

"No, he didn't."

Mitchell asked if she remembered telling her uncles, on the return trip from Puerto Penasco, that the door was locked.

"No, I don't."

"Do you deny having told them that?"

"I don't remember," Marsha said.

Did she recall telling her grandmother, on the Monday following the murder, that the door was locked.

"No, I don't."

"Do you deny having told her that the door was locked?"

"No, I don't."

Mitchell read from the statement Marsha had given Kay Lines in which she had volunteered the statement, "I remember the door being locked."

"Do you recall having told him that?"

"No, I don't."

"Do you deny it?"

"No, I don't."

Her dodging was artful and impenetrable. She denied remembering making previous statements without denying she made them. If the jury was going to hear incriminating words about her father, it would have to hear them from Steve Mitchell, not her. He could read from her previous statements and depositions all day, but the jury would not hear those words in her voice.

Willoughby was impassive except for an occasional faint smile when his daughter looked at him.

Mitchell needed to make the jury understand what it was witnessing, a daughter tutored in her testimony by a father to whom she was devoted. But it had to be done carefully, lest the jury perceive him as a bully. He couldn't bear the full measure of his frustration as he might with an older witness.

He could only contrast, again and again, Marsha's testimony with the contradictory documentation he had accumulated.

"Has your father asked you to lie about the door being locked?" Mitchell asked.

"No."

"Has he told you what to say with regard to the door being locked?"

"No."

"Has he told you what to say with regard to how long he was in the house alone?"

"No."

Mitchell produced Willoughby's letters, entered them into evidence and proceeded to read segments of them. Marsha readily agreed that her father had written the passages Mitchell cited. Then the prosecutor abruptly switched to a different subject, leaving the jury to draw its own conclusions as to the extent the letters had influenced his daughter's testimony.

Chapter Forty-eight

On April 30, 1992, the day Yesenia was to testify, Judge Joseph Howe's courtroom filled up early with the usual complement of reporters and an unusual contingent of spectators curious about the transsexual with whom Dan Willoughby had been obsessed. When every seat was taken, the curious continued to file in, lining the walls across the back and down the sides of the courtroom, and the room buzzed with anticipation as thick as taco sauce.

No one that day seemed more tense than Judge Howe. He was not pleased with the large crowd and quickly ordered all of those not seated to leave the courtroom. Then when the jury was brought in, Howe launched into a rambling diatribe on a matter that had no bearing on the case of *Arizona* vs. *Willoughby*.

"There's been considerable publicity about this King trial," he said, referring to the acquittal of two white California police officers who had been accused of beating a black man, Rodney King, in a videotaped arrest that was in the national news for months. "And the press . . . is doing whatever it can, I think to inflame passion and so forth. There have been no voices, as far as I can tell, that are suggesting that the jury was sane and normal and actually deliberated as it should have.''

A few spectators glanced at each other, the same question written on every face. *What is this about?*

''I want to make sure that you separate in your minds this trial from that one. We have done everything we can to make sure that you do not become public property,'' Howe continued.

The jurors stared blankly at the judge.

''It remains your job to decide this case on the evidence that is presented in this courtroom,'' Howe said. ''The outrage that is being fanned goes against a jury over there and goes against police over there. And do you all understand that this trial cannot be a vehicle for expressing any of that? In other words, if you're upset about what happened over there, one remedy is not, for instance, to convict Mr. Willoughby to make up for it or show the cops you don't like them by acquitting him. Is there anyone that's going to have problems with that? We're not going to solve their problem over there by anything we do in this trial. So keep your minds, please, on this case . . .

''Mr. Mitchell, your next witness, please.''

Mitchell rose from his chair, still digesting the judicial lecture, and uttered the only words appropriate under the circumstances: ''Thank you, judge. The state calls Yesenia Gonzalez Patino.''

Dan Willoughby's head was the only one that didn't turn toward the rear door to see the small woman in a short gray skirt and gray and white blouse being ushered in by a bailiff. Her hair was short and fiery orange—*she looks like Ronald McDonald,* Kay Lines had thought when he and Debbie Schwartz picked her up in Nogales the day before—and a heavy layer of powder and makeup covered her face. In prison she did not have access to the hormones and other treatments that helped her maintain certain feminine qualities, so a masculine coarseness had returned to her skin, along with a hint of facial hair.

She walked slowly to the witness stand, flinching visibly as she passed close to Willoughby. They had not seen each other since that night more than a year before when he bailed her out of jail and told her to disappear. His appearance had changed almost as starkly as hers. His hair was whiter and his face was shallow and pale. Gone was the suntan and dashing mustache and the bulk he had maintained with steroids and weight lifting. His blue suit hung as loosely as a hand-me-down from a bigger brother.

He registered no emotion, not even a flicker of recognition, as she sat down and glanced nervously in his direction.

"Are you okay?" Mitchell asked.

"Yes."

"A little afraid?"

"Yes."

After a brief discussion of her sex change operation and the various aliases she had used, Yesenia related how she had met Willoughby, how, with their involvement barely a month old, he took her to his house, introduced her to his children and told her, "I would like for you to be my wife and the mother of my kids." She described the flowers and the love notes he sent her and the annulment he helped her obtain from Abel Ramon so they could be married.

"Did he talk about when he was going to marry you?" Mitchell asked.

"We had a lot of problems with that because he wanted me to be one way and I didn't want to be, you know, Miss Patino. I wanted to be Yesenia, wild, not dressed the way he wanted me to dress. I wasn't ready yet," she said. "He wanted me to be a lady and not be just like any, you know, like girls of the street or something."

"Did you love Dan Willoughby?"

"No, I didn't love him."

"Why did you stay with him?"

"Well, he was paying for my rent, my clothing, my food. That's why."

Willoughby shifted his weight in his chair and rested his
ace against one hand. If he had believed that his fixation on
his woman was mutual, he was now discovering a humiliating
ruth, one that the Huish family would savor: Disco Dan, the
adies' man, had nothing this babe wanted except an open
heckbook.

"You considered marrying him, didn't you?"

"Yes, but if I would have married him, I would have left
im. That's what my plan was. I would have married him but
nowing that Abel was going to be out of prison soon, I would
ave left him and gone with Abel."

Watching Dan glare at the witness, Thera Huish realized that
he was deriving some pleasure from this public emasculation
f her daughter's killer.

Ochoa got his chance at the witness just before mid-afternoon,
ut he was not likely to undo the damage Yesenia had inflicted.
Ier performance had been deft and her story devastating. It
vas compatible with the voluminous evidence Lines and
chwartz had accumulated, and as she became more comfort-
ble on the stand, her credibility became more solid. It was
nlikely that Ochoa could elicit from her a different scenario
han the one she had laid out, and therefore his best strategy
vas to attempt to discredit her in broad terms, to show the jury
 liar, a manipulator, a sex deviant who betrayed her lovers as
asily as she beguiled them.

He read from previous statements she had given to him and
he attorney general's investigators and questioned her about
he inconsistencies, forcing her to admit that she had lied many
imes.

He dwelled on her promiscuity and suggested Willoughby
vas a victim of her seduction.

"After Danny would take you home, you would go out with
ther men, is that right?"

"At times."

"Do you remember talking to me on February 4 in Caborca?"

"Yes, I do."

"At the time, I asked you how many men you went to bed with after you ran off to Mexico, after Trish's death, and before you got arrested."

Mitchell stood to object to the question, but Ochoa continued: "Did you not say thousands of men?"

Yesenia grinned. "If you can't take a joke, Mr. Ochoa, then I don't know what to say. But I did say that."

"It doesn't take men long to fall in love with you, does it?"

"No."

"In fact, one of the men you met while you were in Mexico was a doctor, wasn't he?"

"Yes . . . from Tacoma, Washington."

"He proposed marriage to you, didn't he?"

"They all did."

Not once did he bring up the blackmail conspiracy. Given the testimony from the other state witnesses, people to whom Willoughby had flaunted the affair, people to whom he spoke of getting rid of his wife, it was a hollow argument.

After Mitchell had presented the last of his case and the state rested, Ochoa also rested without calling a single witness.

At ten o'clock on the morning of May 19, the bailiff informed the judge that the jury, which had deliberated for five and a half hours, had reached a verdict. Court was reconvened and the spectators packed back into the room. The Huish family sat together, all but Marsha. She sat across the aisle with her boyfriend.

Willoughby stood before the judge and showed no emotion as the verdict was read. Guilty on all counts.

Thera Huish trembled as she stood and embraced her husband and sons.

"Oh, my God," Marsha gasped. Thera saw tears streaming

down her face and she wanted to embrace her, too, but when Marsha looked at her, it was with eyes of pure loathing.

"You bitch," she shouted at Thera. She ran from the court-room and fainted in the hallway.

Judge Howe had the option of sending Willoughby to prison for life or ordering that he be put to death by lethal injection. Before imposing sentence, he ordered a psychological examination and held a hearing to allow the prosecutors and the defense to call witnesses and argue for one or the other.

Thera and Val appeared, but did not lobby for or against a sentence of death. Marsha came and said only, "The judge knows how I feel, that's all I have to say."

Ochoa found a generous sampling of his client's former neighbors and church friends who were still ready to testify to his goodness. Judy Richfield, especially, would not accept the guilty verdict, let alone the death penalty. Nothing from the trial, nothing from the press, nothing from the rumor mill, had convinced her that Dan Willoughby was evil.

The procedure dragged into autumn as Howe awaited the psychological profile being prepared by Dr. Thomas Nelson, a consulting psychologist for the Correctional Health Services. He described a man who had invented himself, or invented a shield, a persona to blot out public view of his real self.

"Judging from his own description of himself, Mr. Willoughby emerges as an individual without flaws: He never fought (except to stand up for others); he was honest, and he did not abuse alcohol or use other drugs, even on an experimental basis. All of his motives were altruistic. When I confronted him with the information from criminal justice records, he allowed that he did make some mistakes. As Dr. David Biegen and I were walking to the parking lot after this interview, I remarked to him that 'No one is as righteous as Mr. Willoughby believes he is.' Dr. Biegen agreed."

Not as righteous as he believes or as important as he wanted others to believe. Kay Lines had checked with police agencies on the West Coast and could find nothing to indicate that

Willoughby had worked undercover to nail Jimmy the Weasel or that he had ever had any involvement whatsoever with the Mafia. It was part of the construction of his own mythology.

On October 26, Willoughby was brought back into court. His tan had long since faded and his face appeared bloated and puffy. Standing before the judge, his hands clasped in front of him, he did not plead for leniency, but continued to argue his innocence.

"God knows that I had nothing to do with this. I did not conspire nor commit murder whatsoever. I am not a hard, callous man. I am not a heinous criminal. I love my wife more than my life. I pray to her every day. We had not come to the end of the relationship. It had just begun."

Once again, he was guilty of goodness.

"I helped the wrong person," he said tearfully, without mentioning Yesenia's name, "and got involved not in murder conspiracy, but in something I'm ashamed of."

When he had finished, Howe sentenced him to die.

Chapter Forty-nine

Her son-in-law went to death row at the state prison in Florence, sixty miles southeast of Phoenix, but she still was not rid of him. His civil lawsuit remained in the court, tangled now by his lawyers, her lawyers and lawyers for the children. But with her wrongful death claim now established, the squabbling was mostly over attorney's fees. The money would be divided among the children and their grandmother, and in Thera's mind, that was akin to putting it all in one pocket.

Val had custody of the two younger children. Marsha had moved to California and was living on her own. There was enough in Trish's estate to provide for all of them.

When the settlement finally was reached, it gave Thera her daughter's half of their business and $500,000 from the two life insurance policies. The children were to receive $70,000 each and a share in a $100,000 health care trust fund. The lawyers would be paid $100,000 and taxes would take $160,000.

Dan participated by telephone in the court hearing in which the settlement was approved. He asked that his remaining assets—the 1954 pickup and the family silver—be given to his children.

When the phone line went dead and the hearing was adjourned, Thera and Sterling went home to Mesa. She had a business to rebuild and wreckage to clear from her life.

Adjustment was hard for Hayden. Of the three children, he seemed closest to his father and adored him the most. Val sought psychological counseling for him, but months would pass before he could accept the separation from his father and the reason for it.

After one visit to the psychologist, he called Thera.

"I'm mad, grandma," he said.

"What about?"

"Nobody ever told me my dad killed my mom," he said. "Dad always told us you did it for the money."

"Hayden," she said, "I don't think you really believed that. I think you knew in your heart that wasn't true. Didn't you?"

Two and a half years passed before she saw Marsha again. The reunion took place when she answered the doorbell and found her granddaughter waiting.

"Can I come in?" Marsha asked.

"Of course," Thera said, pushing open the storm door.

Marsha handed her a Mother's Day card. Walking into the den, Thera opened it and read it after they were seated. There was a personal note, an apology.

"I'm so grateful that my mother had a mother like you," it said. "I want you to know how sorry I am for the way I've acted."

Thera looked at her through misty eyes.

"I want to come back to the family," Marsha said. "Is that possible?"

"Of course it is, sweetheart," Thera said. She hugged Marsha the way she had hugged her daughter after Trish rejoined the family. "You are a part of us."

MORE BONE-CHILLING STORIES
FROM PINNACLE TRUE CRIME